THE GERMAN REICHSBANK AND ECONOMIC GERMANY

A STUDY OF THE POLICIES OF THE REICHSBANK IN THEIR RELATION
TO THE ECONOMIC DEVELOPMENT OF GERMANY, WITH SPECIAL
REFERENCE TO THE PERIOD AFTER 1923

BY
SALOMON FLINK PH. D.
INSTRUCTOR OF ECONOMICS
IN THE
COLLEGE OF THE CITY OF NEW YORK

INTRODUCTION BY
HENRY PARKER WILLIS PH. D.
PROFESSOR OF BANKING
AT COLUMBIA UNIVERSITY, NEW YORK

GREENWOOD PRESS, PUBLISHERS
NEW YORK

TO
ELSIE AND FRANK SCHANKER
WHOSE NOBLE FRIENDSHIP HAS
EVER BEEN A SOURCE OF
INSPIRATION FOR ME

CONTENT.

Introduction.

PREFACE.

More than ten years have passed since the powers of the world signed the Treaty of Versailles and cast upon Germany the burden of paying for the devastation caused by the war. This burden still rests leavily upon the German nation, and has been the cause of a great upheaval in Germany's economic life.

The imposition of reparation payments of an amount of 132 billion marks (now reduced to about 36 billion marks by the Young Plan), together with the disorganization of German industry and trade caused by the war, resulted in a depreciation of the German currency hitherto unprecedented in monetary history.

It is the purpose of this volume to present a study of the causes, effects and solution of the problems created by this currency depreciation. In order to analyze such a development it is advisable that date when the German Reichsbank was created by the Bank Act of 1875.

A study of the policies of the Reichsbank offers many valuable suggestions to the theory of central banking and finance. The economic development of Germany since 1923 has compelled the banking authorities of that nation to resort to policies and measures novel in their nature and far-reaching in their effects. It is for this reason that the author has discussed this phase of the subject at so much length.

This work was begun upon the suggestion of Professor Henry Parker Willis, of Columbia University. The author wishes to acknowledge his deep indebtness to Professor Willis for his many helpful suggestions and inspiring assistance in the treatment of the problems discussed in the present volume. The author also wishes to acknowledge his indebtness to Doctor E. M. Burns of Columbia University who has read various chapters of the book and given helpful suggestions, and to Dr. E. R. Hollender, who has taken great pain to correct the English in various chapters, and to Mr. Soutor of Columbia University who has read the proof and given helpful advice. The author alone is responsible for the treatment of the subject and errors in opinion.

New York, December 1929.   S. Flink.

INTRODUCTION.

In the history of international finance and probably in that of central banking, the experience of Germany since the close of the World War will long stand as an example of social reconstruction and an illustration of the working of economic laws. It offers a peculiarly rich, indeed almost inexhaustible, field, for study and for the development of theories and inferences which serve to throw light both upon financial principle and monetary technique.

For this reason every inquiry in the field is likely to furnish a welcome addition to our stock of knowledge. The value of such investigations, moreover, is immensely greater when they are undertaken before the vast volume of fugitive material to be obtained from pamphlets, newspapers, personal interviews and impressions and other temporary sources of the same kind has become dispersed and largely lost. It has always been a serious handicap to financial writing that it has had to depend upon hearsay, tradition, and unwritten sources for so many of the data it employed.

Of late years there has been an encouraging change in this regard, and today it is much more nearly possible to obtain authentic data regarding the great financial events of the time than has ever been the case in the past. Still it remains true that there is much to be done and that the student who is willing to devote himself to contemporary studies is more than repaid for the difficulty of the investigation by the fresh value of his results. On the other hand, he furnishes to the world at large a service of such worth as will more than offset any disappointment that might otherwise be felt because of judgments that must be suspended or because of statements that can not as yet be fully completed or proven.

The author of this book has had a fruitful field of research and has assembled a mass of unusually valuable material with reference to the experience of Germany and its central bank during the past few years. He has reviewed with care the major outlines of German experience subsequent to the World War, and has thus placed at the disposal of American readers much that has not been accessible to them since it must be collected at considerable pains from scattered foreign sources. He has also offered to the financial community a constructive piece of work conservative in its tenor and well informed in its judgements with respect to recent financial developments.

The management of the Reichsbank itself during the years which Mr. Flink has surveyed, has been a problem in central banking more difficult perhaps than any of like sort that had been presented since the opening of the nineteenth century and the subsequent appearance of central banking as a special phase of banking policy and management. Perhaps it is not too positive a statement if we say that the handling of the bank's affairs during these crucial years has been marked by exceptional ability, vision and enterprise, and that these qualities as shown by Dr. Schacht, the head of the institution for the steady recovery of the German banking system from the evils and disasters into which it had been plunged during the three or four years just after the close of the war. In one sense this volume therefore is a study of the remarkable service of a great banker — probably the most distinguished mind of the world among practical central bankers in the period in question.

A final appraisal of the difficulties faced by the institution, its relation to other banks, and its dealings with central banks of foreign countries must be deferred until a more enlightened attitude in all countries results in making public many data which possess an important bearing upon the entire development of financial policy during the years in question. Meantime enough is known and, by reason of the necessary publicity involved in reparations policy enough statistical data have unavoidably been made public, to afford a sound basis for Mr. Flink's analyses. He gives to the American reader a clearcut and sufficiently inclusive survey of what has been to many a tangled and unintelligible sequence of events.

Naturally the striking feature of the Reichsbank experience during the years in question is found in its handling of foreign exchange and its treatment of the question of new capital and loan funds brought into Germany from abroad. The Reichsbank had the problem of providing for great transfers in the form of interest and installments on reparations, and at the same time of dealing satisfactionly with the counter-current furnished by the proceeds of bond sales and stock issues placed in other countries by German citizens. To keep the balance even and to maintain a stable rate of exchange, while at the same time holding in check the natural effort of other banks to profit from the situation in a way prejudicial to the general welfare, was a task of first magnitude.

It is this task which Mr. Flink in the present book has reviewed. In his eighth chapter relating to the "Effect of Foreign Loans Upon The Economic Readjustment Of Germany" he traces the consequences brought about, through the introduction of foreign capital, upon the domestic price level and upon the general structure of business. The movement of money rates in the Berlin market, as influenced by these conditions was sometimes under the control of the Reichsbank and at other times likely to get out of its sphere of influence. That the public did not fully understand what was being done or appreciate the magnitude of the issues involved was to be expected.

Yet on the whole the German people have shown great patience and commendable disposition to bear with their difficulties and to support the leaders who were endeavoring to find a path through the financial obstacles by which they were so closely surrounded. The progress of Germany in following this line of recovery as it was gradually marked out, and the leadership of the Reichsbank in guiding the nations steps occupy the bulk of Mr. Flink's final chapters. He brings the story practically to the date of the Paris conference, and in so doing supplies a valuable background upon which future writers may sketch the outcome of that conference and the development of the new bank of international settlements.

It is both as a survey of a crucial period in the history of Germany, an analysis of an unprecedented series of problems in central banking and a basis for the continued study of banking problems of post-war Germany, that Mr. Flink presents his work. In the opinion of the present writer it will serve a good purpose in all of these capacities.

H. Parker Willis.

CHAPTER I.

THE GERMAN BANK ACT OF 1875.

The history of the monetary situation in Germany prior to the foundation of the German Reichsbank clearly reflects the influence of the same political forces which were responsible for the tardy occurrence of the Industrial Revolution in Germany. More than in any other country, the idea of the State as a distinct and separate entity affected German ceonomic development. Tariff walls were erected between many of the independent States which constituted what is now the German Reich. Jealously guarded rights of autonomy and independence by the various small German states, together with rivalry between the northern and southern parts of Germany, created an almost unsurmountable obstacle to economic development and unity. As a result, it was not until the second half of the nineteenth century that the forces of modern capitalism came into play and transformed Germany from an agricultural nation into an Industrial country of the first rank.

As we have already noted, Germany was predominantly an agricultural country prior to 1850. As a result, there was no need for an elaborate financial system, for a farming population is apt to hoard its cash reserves. This is probably responsible for the fact that there were no banks in our modern sense, (i. e., highly elaborated institutions for the sole purpose of carrying on monetary transactions) in Germany until after 1850.

At the beginning of the nineteenth century there was only one institution which issued bank notes in Germany. This function was exercised by the Royal Deposit and Loan Bank in Berlin, which had been founded by Frederic the Great in 1765. These banknotes, however, had only a limited circulation. In 1806 this bank ceased to issue notes and merely issued negotiable certificates of deposit (Depotscheine) in which the bank acknowledged the receipt of a certain amount of money as a deposit. These receipts were issued only for amounts exceeding one hundred thaler (three hundred marks) and were redeemable by the bearer at the bank. By 1836, when the Royal Loan and Deposit Bank was liquidated, it had put into circulation deposit receipts for a total of 4,514,300 thaler.[1] In 1846, the Royal Bank was reorganized as the Bank of Prussia, which later became the German Reichsbank. It was during the fourth decade of the nineteenth century that three new banks of issue were founded, of which the Mortgage and Acceptance Bank of Bavaria (Bayrische Hypotheken and Wechselbank) and the Bank of Leipzig are still prominent today.

A fundamental change in this monetary situation was brought about by the revolution of 1848. A new spirit of free and unrestricted trade and business activity swept over Germany. The first signs of the industrial revolution in Germany became manifest, and it was during the following years that a great number of banks of issue were founded.

Banks of issue could be created only by special act of the legislature, or by special franchise granted by the sovereign of the state. The state of Prussia, having established the Bank of Prussia in 1846 with the right to issue notes up to an amount of 21 million thalers, deemed this institution sufficient for the promotion of its trade and industry and refused to grant any other banks the privilege of issuing notes. Many banks which had been refused this right of note issue succeeded in inducing small states neighboring Prussia to grant them those privileges which they had vainly sought in Prussia. Very frequently these small states granted these franchises not only because they expected a material promotion of industry and trade in their state but also because they derived substantial revenues from the bank of issue in the form of annual payments for the privilege to issue notes. As a result of this liberal attitude of the small states to grant these rights, many more banks of issue were founded than were actually needed. Of the 32 note issuing banks which existed at the time of the foundation of the Reichsbank, no less than 28 had been created after 1848.

---

1. One thaler represents a money unit of an equivalent of three marks.

This rapid increase in the number of banks of issue is also reflected in the tremendous increase of notes in circulation. While the total of notes during the early 1850's is estimated at about 120 million marks, by 1873 it had increased to 1352 millions of which about one third was not covered by gold.[2] So far as their reserve policy was concerned, most of the issuing banks had only about one third of their outstanding notes covered by a gold reserve. The cover for the remaining two thirds was greatly neglected by the small banks. Very frequently these institutions invested their funds in long term investments and thus violated the most fundamental principle of banking,[3] i. e. that the assets must conform to the liabilities. The liabilities of a bank of issue are of a short term nature, viz. its notes in circulation. The latter may be presented at any time for redemption in gold and the bank must be in a position to meet its obligation. In order to be able to redeem its notes on demand, it must endeavor to invest its funds in short term assets, such as bills of exchange, notes, etc.

Such short term investments afford a high degree of probability that the issuing institution will always be in a position to redeem its notes. Bills of exchange are the result of business transactions involving goods already produced and to be marketed, and the indorsement of these notes by the buyer and seller render their redemption at maturity very probable. Moreover, it may safely be assumed that no prudent business man purchases commodities for sale unless he feels warranted in doing so by the existing market conditions. One fundamental principle is thus fulfilled, i. e. the redemption of the bills within a short period. This fact has two results which are of great importance for the bank of issue. When the note matures the borrower must redeem it with banknotes, which he obtained from the sale of the goods which had originally started this process of borrowing. Thus, an amount of notes equal to the amount issued by the bank at the time of the discount flows back to the bank and is withdrawn from circulation. Simultaneously the liability of the bank dec-

---

2. Werner Sombart, Die deutsche Volkswirtschaft im neunzehnten Jahrhundert, p. 173.
3. Professor Lotz mentions a case in which the Bank of Meiningen had invested a large part of its funds in two factories. "Geschichte und Kritik des deutschen Bankgesetzes" p. 48 ff.

reases by the amount of repaid notes. The profit derived by the issuing institution is the interest paid by the borrower to the bank, while the latter does not pay any interest for the notes which it itself had issued. Because of the fact that the greater part of the notes in circulation tends to remain there for a long period without being presented at the bank for redemption the latter need keep a gold reserve for only part of its outstanding obligations on notes. Furthermore, in the case of short term investments the bank is always in a position to regulate its liabilities in such a way as to secure their liquidity. The returning notes enable the bank to decrease the total of its notes in circulation, thus increasing the proportion between reserves to liabilities. Such elasticity of note issue is of utmost importance in periods of fluctuating business activities.

During the period under discussion, most of the German banks of issue violated this fundamental principle of banking by investing very substantial parts of their funds in long term investments. Another common practice at that time was to issue large quantities of notes of small denominations, a practice which tended to increase the bank's outstanding obligations because these notes remained in circulation for a long time. In many cases small banks of issue paid commissions to agents in large industrial cities to put their notes in circulation. These methods naturally tended to arouse public opinion against the small institution, and the failure of some of these small banks to meet their obligations during the crisis of 1857 was the cause for a general movement to curtail their activities. The first state to adopt means against these abuses was Prussia. At the same time, the Bank of Prussia was given authority to issue notes without any fixed conditions.

Other states soon followed the example set by the State of Prussia, but this did not remedy the confusing monetary situation in Germany. Interstate trade was considerably handicapped by these limitations and regulations, and the large number of different types of bank notes in circulation aggravated the situation. When one considers the fact that at the time of the passage of the German Bank Act of 1875, there were no less than 140 different kinds of money in circulation, it is obvious that such a condition was a very serious obstacle in the way of economic development. It was therefore no coincidence that the great industrial development of Germany falls in the period after the foundation of the Reichsbank, which marks the beginning of a new monetary era in Germany.

But before discussing the German Reichsbank in detail, it is necessary to consider the development of the German Loan Banks which originated at that time, and which were to play a very important role in the monetary conditions of Germany during and after the Great War. It will be recalled that the erroneous investment policy of many small banks of issue had rendered their assets highly immobile. Very frequently, therefore, these banks were unable to grant credit in periods of great business activity, when the demand for credit was greatest. In order to avoid business crises, the various states and municipalities often resorted to the device of establishing so-called Loan Banks (Darlehnskassen). These institutions granted credit to businessmen, — who gave collateral in the form of merchandise or securities, — and issued notes up to the amount of credit granted. It must however be emphasized that the policy of these banks can be justified only when the banknotes were issued in case of emergency, in order to avoid a panic. Under normal business condition their issue of notes involves the same violation of the banking principle of liquidity as the above mentioned practice of many issuing banks to grant long term credit. Credit granted by a bank of issue against collateral of merchandise which is not easily sold becomes just as illiquid as credit in form of mortgages. The main criterion for the credit policy of a bank of issue is that the borrower avail himself of the credit for the purpose of financing short-term business transactions and not in order to finance the storage of goods.

It was obvious that the monetary situation in Germany demanded thorough reform through federal regulation. But prior to the foundation of the German Empire in 1871, the rivalry between the Northern part of Germany led by Prussia and the southern part headed by Bavaria had frustrated any efforts by economists and financiers to come to an agreement during the '60's. Immediately after the foundation of the Empire, however, the German Reichstag began to devote a considerable part of its work to this task. This activity on the part of the German government in monetary reform was the result of the farspread belief in

Germany that the government ought to have a substantial control of the issue of bank notes. For a long time the Reichstag seriously considered the creation of a bank controlled entirely by the government, without participation of private capital or interests. Unlike English economists, the German economists had always demanded a greater participation of the government in economic enterprises. Friedrich List was among the leaders in this demand for government control.

The above conditions together with the public demand for government participation, led to the creation of the Reichsbank by the Bank Act of March 14, 1875. Strictly speaking, however, the Bank was more a reorganization of the Bank of Prussia than a new institution. It had been deemed wise to take over the Bank of Prussia with its branches and experienced personel, instead of creating a new bank. The Bank of Prussia had repeatedly proved its ability to meet sudden demands for credit, especially in periods of crisis and war. The capital of the bank had partly been contributed by private individuals and partly by the State of Prussia, while the directorate was appointed by the Prussian Government. This combination of private and public capital had the advantages of uniting private initiative with state control and resulted in a broad national policy.

A transformation of the Bank of Prussia required the consent of the State of Prussia to such a transaction. Prior to 1875 the latter State had derived very substantial amounts either from the profits of the bank, which it shared as an owner of stock, or from the imposition of taxes for the privilege of note issue granted to the bank. As a result of the negotiations between the Reich and the State of Prussia, the latter renounced finally its rights as a shareholder and the right to impose a franchise tax upon the new Reichsbank for the privilege of note issue. As a compensation the State of Prussia received 24 million marks. Of this amount 9 millions represented its share in the capital and reserve funds of the Bank while 15 millions represented an outright payment for the loss of future franchise taxes from the Bank.

The capital of the new Reichsbank was then increased from 65,720,400 marks, which had been the capital of the Bank of Prussia, to 120 million marks. There had been a long and ardent discussion in the Reichstag whether the shares of the Bank should be owned by private individuals or by the federal government. It was pointed out, however, that an elimination of private interest from the Bank would correspondingly eliminate private initiative from its management. Moreover, if the Bank was owned by the federal government, the proposed tax levied upon an excess issue of uncovered notes would be without effect. It was therefore provided that the shares of the Reichsbank should be owned by private individuals while the management of the Reichsbank was exercised by a directorate appointed by the government.

The functions of the new Bank were to regulate the monetary circulation within the jurisdiction of the Empire, to facilitate settlements, and to utilize available capital.[4] The business which the Bank was authorized to carry on[5] was that of a central bank. The powers of the bank were as follows: To discount bills of exchange, the maturity of which did not exceed three months and signed by no less than two indorsers; to purchase and sell bonds of the Empire, of the federal states and of inland municipal corporations, which are due at their face value at the latest in three months; to grant collateral loans on portable pledges of a prescribed kind; to trade in certain absolutely safe German securities; to collect commercial bills; and to accept non-interest bearing money as deposits and transfer accounts (Giroverkehr).

One of the most interesting provisions of the Bank Act was its reserve requirements. The Bank Act distinguished between the so-called covered and the uncovered notes. So far as the former were concerned, the Reichsbank was required to maintain at all times a bullion and money reserve amounting to at least one third of its notes in circulation. This reserve included gold in bullion, Imperial notes, or foreign coin in the vaults of the Reichsbank. The remainder could be covered by discounted bills maturing no later than three months and protected by three or at least two solvent sureties.[6] The provision that the Reichsbank could discount bills secured by two indorsers and avail itself of these bills for its legal

---

4. Bank Act of 1875, Section VI, Article 12.
5. Ibid. Article 13.
6. Bank Act, article 9.

reserve was enacted in order to meet an urgent economic need. Commercial banking in Germany at that time was still in its infancy and in many cases, especially in the small towns, it was impossible for a borrower to obtain the third indorsement. In addition to these notes issued by the Reichsbank, one third of which were secured by bullion, the Reichsbank was authorized to issue notes which were secured only by bills of exchange.[7] In case the total of these notes exceeded the provided limit, the Reichsbank had to pay to the Imperial treasury a tax of five per cent of the excess issue.

This provision concerning the 'uncovered' notes represented the solution of the legislature for one of the most important problems of central banking. The German Reichstag had the choice of following either the principles laid down in Peel's Act of 1844, well known as the currency theory, or of adopting the banking theory represented by the policy of the Bank of France. The currency theory which is embodied in Peel's Act is based upon two assumptions. First, it holds that the main task of a central bank is to secure full convertibility for its notes in circulation. These notes must therefore be covered by a gold reserve of one hundred per cent. Secondly, the central bank should be in a position to vary its total of outstanding notes in accordance with the need of the business community without endangering the convertibility of the notes. Thus, the currency theory proposes that the central bank be authorized to issue an additional amount of notes which are secured by government bonds. This additional quantity of notes must be limited and in no case shall the central bank be allowed to exceed this limit, unless especially authorized by parliament. This theory assumes that the increase of uncovered notes in circulation correspondingly increases the price level and thus tends to stimulate larger imports and less exports. In consequence gold will have to be exported from the country with the higher price level in order to pay for the excess of imports over exports. By such a process the gold reserves of the central bank will decrease rapidly, its credit will have to be restricted and result in a general business panic. Such a crisis, the currency school assumes, can be avoided if the central bank would increase the rate

---

7. Ibid. article 17.

of discount instead of increasing the issue of uncovered banknotes, thus making it more expensive for the business man to borrow, and causing a diminuition in the demand for credit. In order to prevent an over-issue of uncovered notes, the central bank must be limited in its power to issue more than a specified amount.

The banking theory, on the contrary, assumes that the amount of notes in circulation is entirely determined by the demands of the market for additional money units, and, therefore, that any surplus quantity would automatically flow back to the issuing bank. In consequence, there is never an excess of notes in circulation, if they are issued only for current transactions; and the causes of an inflation of prices are to be found in commodity shortages and not in the fluctuating total of notes in circulation. The banking school, therefore, demands that it be left to the discretion of the central bank to issue as many notes as it sees fit without endangering the convertibility of the notes. Undoubtedly, this theory is based upon the clear distinction between an increased demand for purchasing power originating in greater productivity and larger market-demand, and an increased demand for notes caused by a disproportion between demand and supply in periods of overproduction. In case of economic expansion a rigid limitation of the quantity of uncovered notes which may be issued by the central bank will therefore prove to be a great harm to the economy as a whole. If one reviews the policy of the Bank of France which had adopted the banking theory as its policy, one must admit that before the world war the Bank had shown its ability to make the necessary distinction between economic need for increased note issue and a demand for more purchasing power caused by an unwarranted anticipation of future market demands. The Bank of France has usually regulated its discount rate with regard to economic need rather than to the mere proportion of its gold reserves to the total of notes in circulation.

The reserve provision of the Bank Act, respecting the issuance of banknotes secured by commercial paper only, represents therefore, an excellent combination of these two theories. It enabled the Reichsbank to increase its note issue in order to grant additional credit in periods of business expansion. Under modern economic conditions people do not keep their cash reserves in their homes but deposit them in banks, and draw upon their balances when necessary. There are, however, certain days when a large part of the population is accustomed to make payments and withdraws very substantial sums from their banks, i. e. at the end of the month, and before holidays. Under such circumstances it is of paramount importance for the central bank to be in a position to enlarge its note issue in order to relieve this temporary stress. The need is even greater where the increased demand for credit is caused by economic expansion, since such expansion carries with it a tendency to produce those values which will result in a strengthening of the central bank's reserves.

Under the Banking Act of 1875, the Reichsbank was authorized to issue not more than 250 million marks in unsecured notes, while the private note issuing banks were allotted a total of 135 million marks. The issuance of more than these specific amounts was not a criminal offense as in the case of the Bank of England, but merely resulted in the levy of a tax of five per cent of the excess issue by the Imperial treasury. The purpose of this tax was two-fold. First, it discouraged the circulation of an excessive amount of uncovered notes. Secondly, such a tax automatically forced the Reichsbank to increase its discount rate above five per cent, and thus resulted in a decreased demand for credit, and cause an inflow of gold from abroad.

The Bank Act further provided that if any of the note-issuing banks failed to exercise their authority to issue uncovered notes the amount allotted to such banks should automatically be added to the total which could be issued by the Reichsbank. This provision was employed as a lever to centralize the note-issuing power, and by the use of strict regulatory laws the Reichsbank practically compelled most of the other banks of issue to renounce their authority. Twelve banks of issue renounced their rights even before the Bank Act was put into effect, while fifteen others followed during the next twenty five years, so that in 1907 there were only four banks, beside the Reichsbank, which issued banknotes. These four, the Bank of Bavaria, the Bank of Saxony, the Bank of Wuertemberg, and the Bank of Baden still exist today.

The character of the Reichsbank as an institution owned by private individuals and managed by the government is reflected in the structure of its administration. The latter consisted of three bodies: the Bank Curatorium, the Directorate, and the Central Committee.

The Federal Council of Curators (Bankkuratorium)[8] represented the Empire. It will be recalled that the Bank Act provided for the supervision and direction of the Bank by the Empire. The Federal Council of Curators was composed of the Chancellor of the Empire, and four other members, one of whom was appointed by the Emperor and the remaining three by the Federal Council (Bundesrat). This curatorium possessed merely regulatory functions, however. It met quarterly and received the reports of all operations and business arrangements of the Bank. It took no active part in the actual administration of the Bank.

The 'direction by the Empire' as provided in the Act was exercised officially by the Chancellor of the Empire who was ex officio president of the Reichsbank.[9] He, or his representative, was to direct the entire administration of the Bank, both issuing orders for its business operations to the Imperial Board of Directors and also fixing the rules and working instructions which regulated the bank officials. Although this provision was intended to enable the chancellor to control the policy of the Reichsbank, the power was never exercised by the government, because the conservative policy followed by the bank never made government intervention necessary.

The actual management and administration of the Reichsbank, as viewed by the public, was in the hands of the Imperial Board of Directors.[10] The latter was composed of a president and eight members, who were in the civil service of the Federal Government and were appointed by the Emperor for life. The latter provision was deemed necessary in order to make the Board independent of any political interference which might be detrimental to the interest of the Bank. Furthermore, to avoid bureaucracy in the administration of the Bank, it was provided that the greater part of the salary of the directors should consist of a share in the earn-

---

8. Bank Act, sec. VI, Article 25.
9. Ibid. Article 26.
10. Bank Act, Sec. VI, Article 27.

ing of the Bank from its discount business. The Board of Directors exercised all functions of actual management, decided upon the discount and credit policy and only in certain minor matters, provided by the Bank Act, consulted the representatives of the shareholders.

The shareholders of the Reichsbank took only a very limited part in the administration of this institution. They were represented by the Central Committee[11] which was composed of fifteen members elected at the annual meeting of the shareholders. The main function of this Committee was to provide the directors of the Bank with the expert advice of men prominent in business, industry and commerce. They met at least once a month under the chairmanship of the President of the Reichsbank, and received the reports of the total business and the view of the Directorate concerning the state of business. Any proposals for measures which required their approval were stated before them. Their opinion was sought on the determination of the discount rate and the quantity of Bank funds which should be used for the purchase of securities. The Committee was also consulted concerning the amount which the institution could lend on collateral. From this Committee there were elected three deputies with advisory vote who exercised control and attended all meetings of the Board of Directors.

The double character of the Reichsbank as a semi-public and a semi-private institute is also reflected in the provisions concerning the business relations of the Bank with the Reich, and in the distribution of the profits. So far as the Reichsbank's relation to the government is concerned, the Bank Act provides that the Bank "must receive and make payments for the account of the Empire without compensation. It is authorized to undertake the same transactions for the federal states".[12] This clause is considerably extended in the Reichsbank Statute which reads "it is incumbent upon the Reichsbank to manage gratuitously the balance of the Empire's credit and to keep and render account of all payments received and made for the Empire."[13]

---

11. Ibid. Articles 30, 31, 32.
12. Bank Act, Section VI, Article 22.
13. Reichsbank Statute, Article 11.

With regard to the distribution of the earnings of the Bank,[14] it was provided that the shareholders have a preferential claim on an annual dividend of four and one half per cent on the nominal value of the shares. Of the remainder twenty per cent had to be paid first into the reserve fund of the bank. Of the then remaining surplus one half was to go to the shareholders and one half to the Reich, with the limitation that this proportion was to be taken as a basis until the total dividend of the shareholders reached eight per cent. If there was still a surplus the shareholders received one fourth of it and the Reich three fourths.

The Bank Act did not grant the notes issued by the Reichsbank or by the other private banks the character of legal tender.[15] They were convertible upon presentation to these banks of issue either into Imperial Treasury notes which were legal tender or into gold. However, the Bank Act prescribes the purchase of gold by the Reichsbank at a fixed rate of 1392 marks for one pound fine, the pound taken at 500 gramm 1000/000. By this provision the lower value of gold was definitely fixed at a rate of 1392 marks for one pound. The purpose of this clause was to facilitate the introduction of the gold standard which had been adopted by the Reichstag in 1873.[16]

The charter of the Reichsbank was to expire in 1891, at which time the Empire reserved to itself the right to dissolve the Reichsbank or to acquire its outstanding shares at their nominal value from the shareholders and to take over the Reichsbank in its own right. Either action, however, had to be preceded by a preliminary notice of one year before the charter expired.[17]

The question of the acquisition of the Reichsbank by the Empire was discussed by the Reichstag in 1889, when the bank applied for a new charter.[18] There was strong opposition to conversion of the Reichsbank into a State bank, and the danger of abuse of the bank for purposes of state finance finally resulted in

14. Bank Act, Sec. VI, Article 24.
15. Ibid. Article 2.
16. Bank Act, Article 14.
17. Coinage Act of July 9 th, 1873.
18. Novelle zum Bank-Gesetz vom 18. Februar 1889.

the prolongation of the charter for ten more years. The Reichstag, however, decided to change the clauses concerning the distribution of the earnings in favour of the Empire. It provided that the shareholders should first receive a dividend of three and one half per cent. Again twenty per cent of the remaining surplus were to be put into the reserve funds; of the remaining excess the shareholders were to be paid one half and the Reich one half as long as the total dividend of the shareholders did not exceed 6 per cent. In case their total reached six per cent, any remaining surplus was to be divided between the shareholders and the Reich in the proportion of one to three.

When the Reichsbank petitioned for a new charter ten years later, the Reichstag took the opportunity to change a few of the minor clauses in the Bank Act of 1876. The charter was prolonged for ten more years until 1911.[19] The distribution of the earnings remained unchanged. The capital of the Reichsbank was increased to 180 million marks. Furthermore the total tax-free contingent of uncovered notes was increased to 541 million marks, of which the share of the Reichsbank amounted to 450 millions. An important new provision was that, beginning from the first of January, 1901, the Reichsbank was legally prohibited from discounting bills below the official discount rate if the latter reached or exceeded four per cent. Simultaneously, the private banks of issue were forbidden to discount bills below the official Reichsbank rate if the latter reached or exceeded four per cent. The causes and effect of these two provisions concerning the fixing of the discount rate will be discussed in the next chapter.

In 1909[20] the charter of the Reichsbank was again prolonged by the Reichstag for ten more years. The Reichsbank notes were granted the character of legal tender. The total of tax-free uncovered notes which the Reichsbank could issue was increased to 500 million marks and could be increased at the end of any quarter to 750 millions. Another important provision was the authorization for the Reichsbank to use cheques as a part of the reserves. The Bank was also empowered to discount, purchase and sell

---

19. Novelle zum Bank-Gesetz vom 7. Juni 1899.
20. Novelle zum Bank-Gesetz von 1909.

cheques which bore three, and in no case less than two, accredited indorsers.

The above enumerated amendments to and changes in the Bank Act of 1875 were the outcome of an economic development that rendered necessary an adaptation of the Reichsbank's policy to the economic structure. In general, however, it may fairly be stated that the later provisions did not alter the relation of the Bank to the economy, as a whole. It remained throughout this period a pure central bank, performing social-economic functions and exercising an influence more or less equal to that exercised by other central banks. This function of the Reichsbank underwent fundamental changes during the Great War. The various legislative provisions which were passed after 1914 will therefore be analyzed in connection with the discussion of that period.

CHAPTER II.
THE REICHSBANK POLICY 1876 TO 1914.

The period from 1876 to 1914 saw a tremendous growth in German industry and commerce.[1] It was an epoch of continuous expansion, an era which witnessed the transition of Germany from an agricultural to an industrial state. The population increased from 42,500,000 in 1875 to 65 millions in 1910; 222 million tons of coal were produced in 1910 as compared with 47,8 million tons in 1876. During the same period the deposits in savings-banks rose from 1869 million marks in 1875 to 16,781 millions in 1910; the number of Joint Stock Companies increased from 2,143 in 1886 with a capital of 4,876 million marks to 5,340 Joint Stock Companies in 1911 with a total capital of over 16 billion marks. The total assets of Joint Stock Banks with a capital of more than one million marks increased from 1,961 million marks in 1883 to 16,649 millions in 1911. Coincident with this increase in industrial and commercial activity, the per centage of the population employed in agriculture decreased from 42.5 per cent in 1882 to 28.6 per cent in 1907, while the per centage of the population engaged in mining and industry rose from 35.5 per cent in 1882 to 42.8 per cent in 1907.[1]

[1] This growth naturally increased the responsibility of the Reichsbank. The demand for credit and additional money units placed a great strain upon the resources of the bank, and it was of paramount importance that existing credit facilities be used as intensively as possible. [1]

---

1. The above mentioned statistics have been compiled from the following sources: Statistche Jahrbuch of 1910 as to population and coal production; deposits in savings-banks from Werner Sombart "Der moderne Kapitalismus" v. iii part ii p. 209; the other figures are from the booklet "Germany's Economic Forces" published by the Dresdener Bank of Berlin in 1913.

In a modern industrial community a large part of the population are wage earners. Unlike a farming population they do not consume a part of their products in natura but exchange their labor for wages or salaries in form of money with which they then buy commodities for consumption. It is apparent that the quantity of cash needed under such a system increases with the number of people employed in industry, commerce and trade. This larger demand for money can be partially satisfied by increasing the velocity of circulation. In order to make this possible, it is necessary to elaborate and develop the various types of banking and credit institutions. This problem of elaboration and development of the financial system of Germany was precisely the problem which confronted the Reichsbank after it was organized.

┃ After the foundation of the German Empire in 1871, the Reichstag began the task of reforming the currency and coinage system of Germany. Because of various political obstacles, the currency reform was not accomplished until 1875, when the Bank Act was passed. The Reichstag, which had anticipated this delay, decided to reform the German coinage system first. As in many other European countries, the monetary unit was based on the silver standard. It was the aim of the federal government to abolish the silver standard and to introduce the gold standard.┃ This reform was completed by the Coinage Act of July 9th, 1873, which proclaimed the imperial gold standard and abolished all other standards existing in the various states. One of the tasks which faced the Reichsbank, therefore, was to replace silver coin with gold coin at the rate of one mark silver to one mark gold.┃ The process by which this conversion was accomplished was as follows: The Reichsbank accepted 1392 marks in silver coin in exchange for one pound of gold. This ratio remained fixed for both, larger and smaller quantities of siver marks. The Bank then debited the federal government with the amount of silver marks received in exchange for gold. These silver coins were then converted into bars, which were turned over to the Reichsbank for further sale. The Reichsbank then sold these silver bars, mostly in London, against gold and credited the Empire with the proceeds of these transactions. ┃ It was thus a continuous purchase of silver by the Reichsbank in Germany and acquisition of gold abroad for the silver bars. [1] This purchase of gold in the world market prevented the complete drainage of the bank's gold reserve, but it could not make up for the loss occasioned by the purchase of silver at a price the bank could not get abroad.[1] That this is true may be seen from the following figures: the total gold reserves of the Bank decreased from 346 million marks in 1876 to 164 millions in 1878, despite purchases of gold which amounted to more than 320 millions during the same period.[2] With this loss of gold there went a corresponding increase in the holdings of silver coins by the Bank, which amounted to 292 million marks in 1878 as compared with 100 millions in 1876.

In 1879 the Reichsbank ceased to sell the converted silver in foreign markets but kept the silver bars in its vaults. It continued, however, to convert the incoming silver coins into gold coins and thus maintained the gold standard in Germany. The cessation of the silver sales made it very difficult for the Reichsbank to maintain its policy of conversion. [1] The situation became still more critical during the following year because of the decreased world production of gold, and on account of the ever increasing purchases of this precious metal by the United States and Italy, both of which nations were about to introduce the gold standard. In 1881, the gold reserve of the Reichsbank had decreased to 207 million marks, which were only 28 per cent of the total of notes in circulation, and which compared with 350 million marks in silver coin.[3] [1]Only by increasing the discount rate, which attracted the precious metal from abroad, was the Bank able to maintain the gold standard[1] When increased world production of gold began in 1883 the Bank once more was able to enlarge its reserves without resorting to higher discount rates. The average annual reserve of gold rose from 276 million marks in 1885 to 584 millions in 1895.[4]

It will be recalled that the Reichsbank was not the sole institution in Germany that issued notes, although it was by far the most important in size and influence. There were a number of

---

2. United States National Monetary Commission ‚The Reichsbank' 1914 p. 228—229.
3. Helfferich, Geschichte der deutschen Geldreform pp. 383 ff.
4. Ibid. p. 470.

private banks of issue which had not surrendered their privilege of note issue, but had conformed with the very strict regulations of the Bank Act. These banks soon became very keen competitors of the Reichsbank. Since the latter was the central bank of issue in Germany, it held the commercial paper which it discounted until maturity. By its very nature the Reichsbank was not in a position to rediscount its paper with any other institution. It had to keep the bills simply because they were presented to it for discount when other banks had either not been able to discount them or desired to rediscount for the purpose of granting additional credit to their customers or of increasing their cash reserves. In addition to this position as the bank of last resort for credit, the Reichsbank as the central bank of issue, had the further task of adapting the quantity of notes put into circulation to the economic needs. It was for this reason that the Bank Act had authorized the banks of issue to put an additional amount of uncovered notes into circulation. Naturally, the total of these tax free notes as mentioned in the Bank Act was meant as a limit which should not be exceeded except in cases of emergency. It was the intention of the legislature to give the banks a certain range within which they could extend their issue in order to meet the increasing demand for credit which accompanies industrial expansion, and when business conditions warranted it, the bank withdrew some of its banknotes from circulation. The following table reflects clearly the great fluctuations in the total of uncovered notes issued by the Reichsbank.[5]

Year:	Average Difference Between Maximum and Minimum of Uncovered Notes in Circulation:		In Per Cent of the Average Total of Notes in Circulation:	
1876/1880	267,5 million marks		39,3 per cent	
1881/1885	302,4	„ „	41,0	„ „
1886/1890	566,6	„ „	62,0	„ „
1891/1895	619,4	„ „	61,5	„ „
1896/1900	692,7	„ „	62,1	„ „
1901/1905	961,7	„ „	76,4	„ „
1906/1910	1 010,9	„ „	66,7	„ „

5. Reichsbank, Die Reichsbank 1876—1900, p. 47.

On the other hand, the uncovered note contingent of the other private banks showed a difference of approximately only 20 million marks. The reason for this surprising fact is to be found in the attitude of these institutions toward the Reichsbank. The private banks considered the Reichsbank the central bank, and shifted their responsibility to it by taking advantage of their privilege to issue uncovered notes, but leaving it to the Bank to vary its uncovered note contingent. They also adopted the custom of rediscounting a part of their rediscounted commercial paper with the Reichsbank in order to increase their discount business. They sometimes went so far as to buy commercial paper in the market below the official rate of discount. Fearing that such a policy on the part of the private banks would result in its losing contact with the money market, the Reichsbank protested, and even went so far as to attempt to have the practice declared illegal. The Federal Council, however, refused to pass the necessary decree, and, as a result, the Reichsbank was forced to adopt the same policy. This was done in 1880, when the bank officials adopted a "private discount rate", i. e. preferential rate for bankers' acceptances. The private banks, however, were able to underbid the rate offered by the Reichsbank, and the latter finally came to an agreement with the other issuing institutions by which the latter undertook not to discount below the official rate if there was any danger of an immediate outflow of gold. This agreement prevented the depletion of the gold reserves of the legal limit. I Their policy of rediscounting with the Reichsbank in periods of money scarcity, and the fact that they issued the maximum of their tax-free note contingent, compelled the Reichsbank to adopt a very cautious credit policy. The following table shows the relative gold reserves kept by the Reichsbank and the private banks of issue:[6]

---

6. Helfferich, Die Entwicklung des deutschen Notenwesens, p. 307.

GOLD RESERVES OF THE REICHSBANK AND THE PRIVATE BANKS.

Year:	Gold reserves in per cent of the total of notes in circulation	
	Reichsbank:	Private Banks of Issue:
1876/80	75,2%	48,2%
1881/85	75,7%	43,3%
1886/90	85,2%	42,8%
1891/95	90,4%	45,2%
1896	82,3%	45,2%
1897	80,3%	44,9%

In 1901 this difficulty was cleared up by the passage of a statute which permitted a "private discount" only when the official rate was below four per cent. This applied equally to the Reichsbank and the private banks.[7]

The next problem which the Reichsbank had to face after its foundation was to bring about the utmost utilization of the existing means of payment. At that time, German banking was still in its infancy, and the whole burden of solving the problem rested upon the Bank. The bank management realized that its own capital was not large enough to enable the bank to maintain an effective control of the market and to establish a liberal credit policy. It was, therefore, of paramount importance for the Reichsbank to secure additional capital for its task. This need for outside capital was further aggravated by the withdrawal of the funds which had formerly been deposited with the Bank of Prussia by the State of Prussia. This withdrawal amounted to approximately 120 million marks.

In order to secure larger resources the Reichsbank established an elaborate transfer-account system (Giroverkehr) in its main office and in its 138 branches. The economic advantages of the transfer-system from the point of view of a central bank are obvious. Under modern economic conditions an increasingly large proportion of the population deposits its surplus capital with banks. They dispose of their claims upon the banks by drawing cheques

---

7. Novelle zum Bank-Gesetz von 1899.

or drafts against these deposits. There is, however, a tendency in a well established banking system for only a part of the actual deposits to be withdrawn in cash while the larger part is simply transferred on the books of the banks from the account of the drawer of a cheque to that of the drawee. The first apparent advantage of such a transfer account is that it prevents a constant withdrawal of cash.

But the transfer system involves a still more important advantage for banks and the community as a whole. Experience shows that, if the larger part of the population utilizes the existing bank facilities, only a part of the actual deposits need be kept in cash by the banks, while the remainder may be used for the granting of credit to businessmen. Banks are thus in a position to give credit to those who seek capital and are able to pay their debt within a reasonably short time. As a result, the banks are always in a position to avail themselves of the cash deposits by treating them as reserves and by granting more credit than the actual cash reserves would permit. With increasing use of banks by the population, there is a great probability that credit transactions will, for the most part involve merely a transfer of credits and debits on the books of the bank. It is this process of „creating" purchasing power which has made our modern banks such a powerful factor in our economic society.

It is apparent from this brief statement of the nature and importance of transfer accounts that the introduction of this system tended to strengthen the position of the Reichsbank in the German money market. The temptation to use this means of enlarging its credit facilities was great, in view of the fact that the Bank Act did not prescribe any special reserve for giro-accounts. It is, however, to the credit of the bank's management that it clearly recognized the fact that „from the banking standpoint, transfer accounts are similar to notes and, furthermore, that the security of the convertibility of the notes in circulation is determined by the ratio of reserves in cash to the total of daily callable liabilities (including transfer-accounts)."[8] The Reichsbank was always careful not to abuse this method of creating additional credit. In order

---

8. Reichsbank, Die Reichsbank 1876—1900, p. 51, 126.

to make the transfer-account attractive, (one must bear in mind that the Reichsbank was prohibited from accepting interest-bearing deposits), the Bank did not charge anything for transfer services, even between distant localities, but required a certain minimum balance which ranged from one thousand marks to several thousand marks, depending upon the amount of business done in the district where the branch was located. The great value of this system for the Reichsbank becomes obvious from the fact that of the 16 billion marks which were transferred by it in 1876, 10 billions were merely transferred on its books.[9] By 1910 the total of transfers had increased to 314,1 billions of which 276 billions or 87,9 per cent were transferred on the books of the bank.

The Reichsbank's most powerful weapon in regulating the circulation of banknotes and credit was its discount policy. By raising or lowering the rate of discount the bank was able to influence the whole credit structure of the nation. Banks do not wish to keep their funds idle but give as much credit as is constistent with the principle of liquidity. They maintain a cash reserve which will under normal circumstances suffice to meet the current demand for cash. In case the demand for cash increases, or if the banks notice a greater demand for credit, they discount a part of their commercial paper at the central bank, thus obtaining new funds. The credit policy of the smaller banks depends, therefore, upon that of the central bank which is the last resort of the community for credit. But a central bank, too, is limited in its capacity to grant credit. Like any ordinary bank it has to observe the law of liquidity, and must take into consideration the fact that it may be called upon to redeem its notes in cash. It must therefore maintain a certain ratio between its notes in circulation and the gold reserves in its vaults. If the ratio of the gold reserves is high and the international trade conditions of the particular country make it appear improbable that there will be a material drainage of gold in the near future, it will lower its discount rate. The smaller banks will accept this as an indication that the central bank intends to pursue a more liberal credit policy, and this attitude of the central bank will be reflected in the attitude of the other banks towards their

---

9. These figures have been compiled from „Die Reichsbank 1876—1910" pp. 111 ff., published by the Reichsbank, 1912.

customers, who will be able to obtain more credit at easier terms. It must, however, be borne in mind that the discount policy of a central bank must be based not only upon the internal credit situation, but also upon the international situation.

√ An increase in the discount rate serves two purposes: First, it decreases the domestic demand for credit by eliminating the marginal borrower. Secondly, it will attract funds from those foreign countries where the interest rate for short term money is lower. Conversely, a lowered discount rate stimulates borrowing from banks and finally from the central bank and, if sufficiently low, the low interest rate encourages the banks to send their funds to foreign markets, where the return is higher. There are, however, situations in which a mere increase in the discount rate does not prove sufficient to cause a diminution of credit. In such cases more severe steps must be adopted by the central bank.

The regulation and control of the monetary demand in Germany by the Reichsbank from 1875 to 1914 may be divided into three periods: from 1876 to 1890, from 1890 to 1907 and from 1907 to 1914.

When the Reichsbank began its activities as the German central bank, banking in that country was still in its infancy.[10] The following comparative statistics show how the Reichsbank dominated the money market during the earlier periods:

Bills discounted in Germany by: (in million marks)[11]

Year:	Reichsbank	Deutsche Bank	Disconte Gesellschaft	Dresdner	Darmstädter
1880:	376	37	37	4	7
1912:	1238	646	232	286	121

Acceptance Credit Granted by Nine Great Banks of Berlin:[12]

1860	8,2 million marks	1900	670,9 million marks
1870	18,9 „ „	1910	1140,2 „ „
1880	80,3 „ „	1913	1391,8 „ „

10. Professor's Riessers book 'The German Great Banks and their Concentration in Connection with the Economic Development of Germany' is undoubtedly the best book on this subject.

11. W. Sombart, Der moderne Kapitalismus v. iii, 1 p. 216.

12. Ibid. 210.

Deposits, Outstanding Acceptances, and Creditors of Eight Great Banks[13] in Berlin:

1880	328,1 million marks	1905	3670,4 million marks
1890	799.1 „ „	1910	5626,1 „ „
1895	1235,8 „ „	1914	6336,6 „ „

The foregoing data indicate clearly the important role which the Reichsbank played in the development of the German credit system without which Germany could never have been industrialized. It is but natural that in view of the absence of adequate banking facilities almost the total demand for credit directed itself against the Reichsbank. It will also be recalled that in order to facilitate the task of the Bank to provide credit for the small business man the Bank Act had permitted the Reichsbank to discount notes with only two indorsers and to use these bills as part of its legal reserves.

During the first few decades of its existence, the Reichsbank considered it as its most important task to grant all credit required as long as the discounted bills conformed to the legally set standard. The natural result was that the quantity of notes in circulation was determined rather by the demand for credit without any definite attempt on part of the Bank's management to influence the demand as such. Only when the ratio of the gold reserves approached the legal minimum did the institute exercise a pressure upon the demand for credit by suddenly raising its discount rate. It curtailed the total credit demand without giving the market a warning in the nature of restricted or differentiated discount of the offered papers. Such a policy of credit regulation solely on the basis of the gold reserves proved later of great potential danger as will be shown in due time.

The management of the Bank considered the business cycle as an inevitable economic fact. It did not endeavour to avail itself of the discount rate as a means to regulate the trend of business through anticipation of the periods of economic depression and expansion. In the light of economic theories of that time such a viewpoint is not surprising. Among German economists the theory

---

13. Ibid. 208.

was generally advanced that it was the primary task of a central bank to satisfy the demand for credit and not to attempt arbitrary regulation of the quantity of notes in circulation. Hellferich expressed but the opinion of most economists of that time when he wrote "the adaptation of the quantity of money in circulation to the fluctuations of the demand for means of payments is, as is generally recognized, the most important task of central banks; it is but the very justification of their existence".[14] The practical results of this policy are described by von Lumm who was then a member of the directorate when he asserted „that in times of money scarcity, surprisingly large quantities of commercial paper have been thrown into the portfolio of the Reichsbank which the latter could not prevent".[15]

The dangers of such a note policy did not become obvious until the panic of 1907 as will be shown later on. It must, however, be emphasized that during the first periods from 1876 to 1890, the Reichsbank through the policy above mentioned greatly stimulated the industrial development of Germany and controlled the monetary situation satisfactorily. Only when subjected to a severe economic crisis such as that of 1907 did the inefficiency of such an attitude under modern credit conditions become apparent.

The second era of the Reichsbank policy from 1890 to 1907 was a period in which occured a tremendous growth of the German credit banks, as a result of the great industrial expansion which took place in those years. It was during that time that the credit banks became the predominant factor in the German money market. When industry began to progress there were no special institutions to provide the long term funds. There were no investment banks or money brokers to supply the necessary funds and to float stock issues. It was but natural that the German credit banks were called upon to assume the function of investment houses and to provide the necessary long term funds. The credit banks readily responded to this call; and since that time they have come to govern the money and capital market in Germany.

---

14. Hellferich, Die Entwicklung des deutschen Notenwesens unter dem Bankgesetz, p. 315.
15. von Lumm, Die Stellung der Notenbanken in der Volkswirtschaft, p, 19.

It was also at the beginning of the '90 that the German Great Banks gained their dominant position in the German economy. Germany does not prohibit the establishment of branches by banks and thus these great banks were in a position to extend their influence over the whole country.

These credit banks provided the long term funds for the industry in two ways. They either floated the new stock or bond issues of the particular industry in the Bourse (German term for stock market) or granted so-called transition credit. In the latter case the credit banks used the funds which they controlled to grant credit to the enterprise in need of it in the form of short-term obligations. The instrument used in these transactions was a bill of exchange although there was a mutual understanding between the banks and the debtor that the bill would be prolonged at maturity and later on redeemed with the proceeds of a stock or bond issue. Thus the banks actually financed long term investments with short term credit. The stocks or bonds which were later issued by the debtor were marketed by the credit bank which had granted the short term credit. The banks usually offered these investments to their own customers, who frequently absorbed a large part of the issue. Undoubtedly, the credit banks thus contributed to the transformation of potential savings into long term investments. The readiness of the Reichsbank to rediscount such „finance bills", although it violated the fundamental principle of central banking, facilitated this method of financing by the credit banks.

With increasing industrialization of Germany, the credit banks correspondingly expanded their activities. It has been shown that modern banks are in a position to grant many times as much credit as they dispose of deposits in cash. The German banks were greatly favored in this policy by their ability to establish many branches and by the growing use of bank facilities by the public which is reflected in the increasing amount of deposits, as shown on page 24.[16] The German banking law does not set any definite reserve minimum for banks but leaves this matter to their own discretion. Thus, the ratio of reserves in cash to total liabilities of the

---

16. The very considerable growth of the German credit banks can also be seen from the other figures on page 24.

banks continuously decreased after 1890 as shown by the following data: C a s h - R e s e r v e s   o f   G e r m a n   C r e d i t   B a n k s   i n   P e r   C e n t   o f   T o t a l   L i a b i l i t i e s :[17] 1893 . . . 13,5 per cent; 1903 . . . 10 per cent; 1913 . . . 7,5 per cent. It was the policy of the banks to maintain only a cash reserve which was under normal conditions sufficient to meet the current demand of the community for cash. They depended entirely upon the Reichsbank in periods of money scarcity for additional funds.

The German „Great Banks" which numbered eight and represented about three quarters of the German private banking strength, always kept their reserves as low as possible, depending entirely upon the Reichsbank to furnish them with funds in periods of money scarcity. These great banking houses helped materially in financing German industry and exercised great influence in the capital and money market. The large resources which they controlled exceeded by far the amount of cash in the money market, and these institutions therefore held a dominating position in German financial affairs. Those banks also developed a system of interclearing by which they used the Reichsbank merely as an agent to transfer on its books the final balance between the various banks.

The Reichsbank became concerned over this policy of the banks which tended to put the Bank in the position of a „bankers' bank". Unwilling to lose its contact with trade and industry, which the Bank deeemed essential for its control of credit, it endeavoured

17. Werner Sombart, Der moderne Kapitalismus, v. iii, part. 1, p. 216. However, these figures give only the reserve ratios as published in the annual balance sheet, which from obvious reasons show a higher ratio than was actually maintained throughout the year. Alfred Lansburgh, a financial authority, stated in his book "Die Maßnahmen der Reichsbank zur Erhöhung der Liquidität der deutschen Kreditwirtschaft", on page 11, that many of the great banks at the end of the months, when normally large payments were due, did not dispose of more cash reserves than three per cent of their total liabilities.

The attitude of the banks in their reserve policy is also reflected in the testimony of Director Mommsen of the Mitteldeutsche Creditbank, one of the Great Banks before the Bank Enquete Committee in 1908: "For us (refers to the credit banks) cash reserves are not reserves at all; they are merely what we necessarily need to satisfy the momentary demand for money in cash." Bank-Enquete 1908—1909, Question VI, page 186.

to maintain a large portfolio of directly discounted bills through an improved transfer system, which offered its customers additional advantages. It succeeded in these efforts and continued to discount a fairly large amount of bills with only two indorsers. However, this policy placed an additional strain upon the note issue of the Reichsbank./ The maintenance of its large portfolio in connection with the seasonal and eruptive demand for credit by the banks caused very great fluctuations in the note issue of the Reichsbank. Especially at the end of the monthly and quarterly periods, the Bank was frequently forced to exceed substantially the tax free contingent of uncovered notes.

In view of these conditions it is not surprising to find that the large quantity of uncovered notes in circulation tended to decrease the gold reserves below the legally required minimum. Repeatedly the Bank was therefore forced to increase its discount rate in order to prevent burther drainage of its gold supply. In the late 90 it began to buy gold abroad at a premium in order to achieve the same results, camouflaging these premiums under the name of „interest-free advances". The following table[18] shows the reasons for the increase in the discount rate in the period from 1876 to 1900 while table 2 shows the foreign exchange quotations of pound sterling at the Bourse of Berlin from 1896 to 1910:

---

18. Die Reichsbank, Denkschrift 1876 to 1910, table 84, page 222.

TABLE I

Causes for Increase in Discount Rate During Period 1876 to 1910:

Year:	Discount increased .. times	Increased Rate Due to		
		Outflow of Gold or for its prevention	Larger Demand for Credit	Internal and External Demand for Gold
1876	3	—	1	2
1877	3	2	1	—
1878	1	1	—	—
1879	2	1	1	—
1880	2	2	—	—
1881	2	1	—	1
1882	2	1	—	—
1883	—	—	—	—
1884	—	—	—	-
1885	1	1	—	—
1886	3	—	1	2
1887	—	—	—	—
1888	2	1	1	—
1889	2	—	2	—
1890	2	—	—	2
1891	1	—	—	1
1892	1	—	—	1
1893	2	—	—	2
1894	—	—	—	—
1895	1	—	1	—
1896	2	—	1	1
1897	2	—	2	—
1898	4	1	3	—
1899	4	—	2	2
1900	—	—	—	—
1901	1	—	1	—
1902	1	—	1	—
1903	1	—	1	—
1904	1	—	1	—
1905	4	—	4	—

TABLE II[19]

Foreign Exchange Rate of Pound Sterling in Berlin.

Year:	Total of Days Quoted	Below Par	On Par Par	Above Par	On Or Below Gold Imp. Point	On Or Above Gold Export Point
1896	156	94	2	60	—	—
1897	517	150	5	2	—	—
1898	156	69	3	84	—	22
1899	156	34	7	115	—	19
1900	157	19	4	134	—	48
1901	155	70	18	67	—	—
1902	157	13	3	141	—	—
1903	157	66	6	85	—	21
1904	157	79	6	72	2	6
1905	156	24	8	124	—	—
1906	157	4	1	152	—	42
1907	156	—	—	156	—	77
1908	157	76	6	75	—	5
1909	308	32	13	260	—	40
1910	304	3	12	289	—	27

These figures clearly reflect the tendency of the uncovered notes to drive out gold.

These defects in the reserve policy of the credit banks, and the lack of an efficient pressure by the Reichsbank, became apparent during the international economic depression of 1907. This depression was caused by the economic disturbances in the United States which occurred during that year. Large quantities of American merchandise were brought into the European market and soon the continental market was also subjected to a severe crisis. American banks asked for credit from European banks and in consequence of the credits granted large amounts of gold were withdrawn from the European markets, while at the same time the economic depression on the Continent caused the banks to adopt a cautious credit policy. Germany was also drawn into this inter-

19. Ibid. pp. 210, 212.

national depression and the demand for credit at the banks increased continuously. Although the Reichsbank during the autumn of 1907 had disposed of almost all of its available capital, the tense conditions in the money and capital market did not show any signs of relief. In spite of a higher discount rate and an increased quantity of notes in circulation, there was no noticeable diminution in the demand for credit. At the end of December, 1907, 438 Joint Stock banks still had in their portfolios bills to an amount of 2,950 million marks, the larger part of which were eligible for rediscount at the Reichsbank.

In the course of a few weeks the discount rate had been raised by the Bank from 5,5 per cent to 7,5 per cent without causing any appreciable decrease in the demand for credit. At the same time the gold reserves of the Bank approached the legal minimum, and showed in December the unprecedentedly low level of 37,5 per cent of the total of notes in circulation. If one includes in the total of outstanding notes the amount of small notes which the Bank had been authorized in 1906 to issue, and which had been circulated during this period, the actual reserves were even less than 33 per cent.

However, the real amazing fact for the management of the Reichsbank and the German public was that the Bank of England had successfully overcome the international depression, although the English market had been the first to encounter the pressure. It was then that the fundamental difference between a positive and a passive discount policy was clearly demonstrated. Both institutions, the Reichsbank and the Bank of England had increased their discount rate at the same time to almost the same level, the English rate being always about one half of one per cent lower. The effect was, however, different in each country. In England, after the rate had been raised, the market directed its efforts toward a readjustment without increasing the demand for credit at the Bank of England. The English market knew very well, by tradition and experience, that the Bank of England would not hesitate to limit and even further to restrict credit if the demand should not decrease substantially. The market therefore endeavored to achieve a readjustment and succeeded without the aid of the Bank. At the same time, when the Reichsbank was forced to increase its rate to 7,5 per cent in December, 1907, the Bank of England lowered its rate to 6 per cent.

It became evident that a mere increase in the discount rate could not stand the test of a severe crisis and merely injured industry without affecting the demand for credit as a whole. The credit banks adapted their rates to those of the Reichsbank without altering their general credit policy. The Reichsbank had always discounted their bills if they conformed to the legally set standard and they did not think it necessary to alter their policy. The inadequate control of the Reichsbank over the private banks and the lack of sufficient reserves to meet any unusual demand were apparent. The public reaction to this failure of the Bank's management forced Koch, who was then President of the Reichsbank to resign, and Havenstein was appointed to his office, which he kept until his death in 1923.

Immediately ofter taking office, Havenstein endeavored to regain control over the money and capital market in Germany. As a result of its experience in 1907, the bank changed its foreign exchange policy. In order to increase its lending power in times of depression and in order to strengthen its position in the foreign exchange market, the Bank began to purchase considerable quantities of gold abroad. At the same time, it devoted special attention to the acquisition of foreign short term bills of exchange, which could easily be converted into gold if circumstances required. These foreign bills yielded interest and were therefore very attractive as a supplementary reserve to gold. The effect of this new reserve policy is reflected in the following figures, which show the increase in the purchase of gold and foreign bills of the Reichsbank as compared with the acquisitions prior to 1907:

Purchase of Gold and Devisen by Reichsbank from 1907 to 1911:[20]

Year:	Gold Bought:	Devisen Bought:
1906	27 million marks	292 million marks
1907	111,5 ,, ,,	268 ,, ,,
1908	298,9 ,, ,,	484 ,, ,,
1909	155,2 ,, ,,	589 ,, ,,
1910	164,7 ,, ,,	847 ,, ,,
1911		939 ,, ,,

20. Denkschrift, Die Reichsbank 1876—1910.

The Bank also changed its general credit policy. It refused to discount commercial paper which did not originate in commercial transactions, but which were in the nature of 'finance bills'. Although such a policy seems but natural in view of the legal provision in the Bank Act that the Bank should only discount commercial bills of exchange, the management under Koch had continuously discounted bills without any objection. In consequence of this measure the credit banks were forced to maintain a larger portfolio of bills and a higher cash reserve. Though these reforms do not appear to have been very material, they seemed at that time suficient to increase the liquidity of the credit banks. Furthermore, it must be borne in mind that it was practically impossible to introduce fundamental changes in the policy of the banks in a short period. The credit system of any country is too subtle to stand sudden changes without severe effects upon the whole economic structure.

The indifference which the German banks manifested toward any fundamental change in their reserve policy and their failure to strengthen their reserves for periods of great stress became apparent during the crisis of 1911. This depression was caused by the Marocco-affair, a political controversy between Germany and France and almost led to the outbreak of war; it showed clearly that the Reichsbank was the only credit institution prepared to meet unforeseen economic pressure. The credit banks were not able to meet the increased demand for cash during this period. They lacked the necessary funds for the purpose, having pursued the policy of maintaning only the indispensable minimum in cash reserves. The banks could avoid a severe bank crisis only by shifting the blow to the economic community as a whole. They called in most of the outstanding credits, especially at the Bourse, and refused to grant new credit to any appreciable degree. In the course of a few weeks eight large Banks of Berlin withdrew 300 million marks from the Bourse thus causing a very substantial decrease in stock and bond prices.[21] The Reichsbank, however, had prepared itself for this crisis, and was able to meet the unusual

---

21. Lansburgh, Die Maßnahmen der Reichsbank zur Erhöhung der Liquidität der deutschen Wirtschaft, p. 44.

demand for credit without increasing the discount rate above five per cent. The seriousness of the situation can be inferred from the fact that the federal ministry considered for a certain time a moratorium for all credit banks.

After the depression had been successfully overcome by the market with the aid of the Reichsbank, the President of the Reichsbank placed before the private banks the alternative of altering their reserve policy or of facing more rigorous measures on the part of the Reichsbank to enforce such a necessity. The Bankers' Association of Berlin (Stempelvereinigung) conformed to this demand by nominating a committee, which was to investigate this matter and submit recommendations as to the best way to adopt the new policy. However, the outbreak of the Great War interrupted these negotiations. It might not be amiss to enumerate briefly the reforms which were desired by the Reichsbank. First, the Bank objected to the large amount of capital funds directed by the banks to the Bourse in the nature of credit for speculation. Secondly the banks were requested to cease the granting of credit on margins as low as ten per cent of the nominal value of the stocks or bonds. Thirdly, the banks should diminish their total of acceptance credit outstanding. Finally, but most important the Reichsbank demanded an increase in the cash reserves of the banks up to fifteen per cent of their liabilities.

CHAPTER III.

THE GERMAN REICHSBANK 1914—1918.

Before the World War began, the Reichsbank's influence upon the open market was steadily decreasing.[1] This situation changed fundamentally with the commencement of the mobilization. State necessity imposed tasks upon the Reichsbank which, though not in accord with the principles of central banks, had by force of necessity, to be predominant in its policy. At the outset of the Great War, Germany was confronted by two great financial problems: the problem of public credit and that of private credit. So far as private credit was concerned, the problem was to secure the uninterrupted flow of credit for industry and commerce. In a modern economic system, no enterprise hoards money in cash for emergencies, but the cash-reserves are deposited in banks. Credit is the basic foundation of our organization. Without recourse to credit, industry and commerce would cease.[2] On the other hand, modern wars require such tremendous amounts of capital that recourse to credit is inevitable.[3]

---

1. It had gradually lost its direct contact with industry and commerce. The credit institutions in Germany had correspondingly put themselves in the position of intermediaries between the Reichsbank and those who wished to obtain credit. At the outbreak of the war, this struggle had not yet been finally decided.

2. In order to render possible an immediate transition of the productive powers of the country into the channels of war production and in order to provide the necessary means for industry and commerce, it was of paramount importance to secure the basis of a financial mobilization, i. e. the undisturbed flow of credit.

3. In this case the government faces the problem of how to obtain the necessary funds without affecting the productive power of the necessary funds without affecting the productive power of the nation. Or, to put it in other words the question arises of how to attract the entire savings of the community for war purposes, leaving at the same time untouched the capital employed in production.

So far as war finance is concerned, there are theoretically three ways in which a modern war can be financed. First, by flotation of long term obligations in foreign markets. This recourse Germany was prevented from taking, owing to the fact that the main money centers of Europe were situated in hostile countries. Secondly, the government can obtain the necessary funds by issuing long term loans in the domestic market and by increasing taxes.[4] But the lack of democracy in pre-war Germany, together with the firm belief of the government in a quick victory, and furthermore the official lack of confidence in the sufficient yield of taxes, caused the adoption of the third alternative.| In this case, the financing of the war costs in Germany was accomplished with the aid of short term loans in the form of discounted Treasury bills and their redemption with the receipts from the War Loan Bonds (Kriegsanleihen), which were to be issued annually in spring and autumn.|

The problem of private credit was of a different nature and was the result of Germany's development during the half century preceding the great war. During that period, industry and commerce were based entirely upon credit. Large amounts of capital had been invested in foreign countries. The yields of these investments were so considerable that the deficit of Germany's balance of trade, mainly due to large imports of food, which amounted in 1913 to approximately one billion marks, was not only compensated by the revenues from investments abroad, but these revenues even exceeded the balance of trade by one and a half billion marks in favour of Germany. The seizure of German capital in foreign countries at the outbreak of the war and the blockade to which she was exposed, naturally tended to have disturbing influences upon the German economy. The outbreak of a war is inevitably followed by economic disturbances in the domestic market. First, the importing and exporting industries are directly and primarily affected by the interruption of international relations. Likewise the credit institutions which under

---

4. This second policy was adopted by England where 20 per cent of the war expenditures were defrayed with the receipts of increased taxes, while in Germany only six per cent of the total war expenditures were covered by the revenues derived from higher taxation.

normal circumstances are in constant contact with international money and capital markets, and rely upon these markets for funds in times of money scarcity, are left entirely to themselves during a war. The same holds true to a greater extent of the central bank which is the last monetary reserve of a country. There is therefore a natural tendency among banks to become very restrained in their credit policy, and their reluctant credit policy causes disturbances all over the community.

It was for these reasons that in most belligerent countries general financial moratoriums were granted. The Bank of England increased its discount rate on July 31, 1914, from four per cent to eight per cent, and again increased this rate to ten per cent on the following day. The official attitude of the German government towards a general moratorium was uncertain. For a short time this uncertainty of the business world about the exact plans of the government in regard to the mobilization of private credit provoked a panic. Large amounts of deposits were withdrawn in the course of a few days while the demand for credit at the banks increased. The restrained credit policy of the banks accelerated the general fear of a moratorium and resulted in a panic at the Bourse. The great fall in security prices, ensuing from this panic, resulted in the closure of the Bourse on July 31, 1914, and made suddenly unmarketable the large supplies of securities and bonds in the possession of the public. It was only due to the fact that the outbreak of the war fell in a period of declining business with its accompanying liquidity in the money market, that a greater crisis was prevented. The very slight increase in the discount rate of the Reichsbank from five to six per cent contributed largely to the return of general confidence. The panic-like situation in the last week of July, 1914, is well reflected in the following figures showing the changes in the portfolio of the Reichsbank which occurred from July 24 th to July 31st, 1914:

Reichsbank Portfolio (in mills of marks) on:

	Notes outstanding:	Bill of Exchange:	Collateral Loans:
July 24th	1890,3	750,9	50,5
July 31st	2909,0	2081,0	212,2

Gold Reserves:	Gold Reserves in Per Cent of Notes in Circulation:
July 24th	1356,9	71,8 per cent
July 31st	1253,2	43,1 „ „

This substantial decrease in the reserve ratio caused the Reichsbank to suspend the conversion of its notes into gold on July 31st, 1914.

The prevailing situation required immediate relief. It was necessary first, to calm the business world about the possibility of obtaining credit in the future, and, secondly, to relieve the Reichsbank from the burden of private credit. Only by diverting the demand for credit by the public from the Imperial Bank to other institutions was it possible for the Reichsbank to concentrate its activities on the financial assistance of the government. On August 4, 1914, the German Parliament passed various laws, the purpose of which was to promote these policies.

The Reichsbank was empowered to discount Imperial Treasury debentures if due not later than three months and was authorized to use these Treasury notes as a part of its legal reserves. These notes, which bore only the signature of the Treasury, were thus rendered equal to commercial bills in respect to the Bank's reserves. This provision marks a fundamental change in the discount policy of the Reichsbank during the war and its effect upon the note issue cannot be overstressed. According to article 13 of the Bank Act of 1875, the Reichsbank had been empowered to discount treasury bills if due not later than three months and if at least one other indorser besides the treasury stood good for them. The new amendment to the Bank Act dispensed with the additional indorsement of another voucher besides the treasury. The Reich was therefore able to draw a debenture upon the treasury, that means upon itself, and could then discount this debenture at the Bank. In this way the German government was in a position to finance the war by discount of its treasury debentures in the same way as a businessman finances his transactions. The only justification for such a policy was the plan to convert these debts into long term obligations through the issue of War Loan Bonds which were to be floated twice annually in spring and autumn.

The official comment which accompanied the recommendation of this bill to the legislature reveals, however, a fallacy in the concept of the authorities as to the nature of these one-name bills. In the comment, the government points out that „debentures of the Reich which are due after three months are of the same nature as the former treasury bills, the only difference being one of a formal character, in so far as there was no other voucher for those debentures. In view of the liability of the Reich, however, the fact that these debentures are not in the form of a bill cannot be of any material importance. There is no justification for excluding these debentures from the legal reserves of the Reichsbank as long as they are due in a short time and thus conform to the requirements which the reserves for notes must fulfill from the standpoint of liquidity".[5] This concept of the nature of these debentures is partly eroneous. These notes were only short term papers de juro but not de facto. Actually the Reich had to take into account insufficient returns from the flotations of long term loans in which case these debentures would become illiquid assets in the portfolio. As a matter of fact, during the second half of the war the yield of the flotation of War Loan Bonds did not suffice to redeem the discounted treasury debentures, an increasing amount of which remained in the portfolio of the Reichsbank.

This provision concerning the discount of treasury debentures necessitated the adoption of other supplementary laws to the same end. It was apparent to the government that the discount of the these debentures might easily result in an issue of Reichsbank notes in excess of an amount covered by one third in gold. In consequence the provision of the Bank Act requiring the maintenance of a gold reserve of at least one third was suspended. This provision was but the mere legal sanction of what the Reichsbank had already actually done on July 31st, 1914 when it refused to redeem its notes in gold. Simultaneously, the other note issuing banks were granted the right to convert their notes into Reichsbank notes instead of

---

5. Gesetz betreffend Aenderung des Bank-Gesetzes vom 4. 8. 1914. The official comment is to be found in „Drucksachen des Reichstages, 12. Legislaturperiode, 2. Session 1914, page 111.

6. Gesetz über die Aenderung des Bankgesetzes vom 4. August 1914.

into gold.[7] Furthermore, the inefficiency tax on the excess issue of uncovered notes was removed.

In order to secure the undisturbed flow of credit for industry and trade without imposing this additional task upon the Reichsbank, the Reichstag passed a law providing the establishment of the German Loan Banks (Darlehnskassen).[8] It was the task of these banks to divert the demand for credit from the Reichsbank. These banks were authorized to grant credit against collateral which included: securities, merchandise stored within the Reich, and other tangible assets. Moreover, these institutions were empowered to issue notes up to the amount of credit granted. From a monetary standpoint such a „cover" lacked every character of a reserve for notes in circulation. Instead of being secured by commercial bills of exchange which are the result of exchange of goods in the market and which are redeemed with the proceeds of a further exchange of the goods for which the bill has been drawn, the notes issued by the Loan Banks were covered by assets which did not circulate in the market. These assets were therefore to be considered as illiquid brom the point of reserves.

By their very nature the notes issued by the Loan Banks tended to inflate prices. They gave the debtor who obtained them from the institution against collateral, claims upon the social output while this individual did not contribute to the total of goods in the market. In consequence there were then more claims in the market than was warranted by the preceding process of production, and prices tended to increase. Owing to circumstances which will be discussed later on in this chapter their inflating influence did not become effective until after the Great War.

The law creating these institutions, furthermore, granted the notes issued by them the same legal character as the Imperial notes, i. e. they could be used by the Reichsbank as a part of its legally required reserves. In other words the Reichsbank could now use these notes issued by the Loan Banks as the basis for issue of three times as many Reichsbanknotes. The inflating influence of such a note issuing policy is obvious.

---

7. Gesetz über die Reichskassenscheine und Banknoten vom 4. August 1914.

8. Darlehnskassengesetz vom 4. August 1914. Reichsgesetzblatt, S. 340.

These provisions altered materially the fundamental principles of central banking which were embodied in the Bank Act of 1875. The Reichsbank was no longer the German central bank with the duty 'to regulate the circulation of money within the Reich and to facilitate settlements of payments.' Instead it became now an institution entrusted with the task of providing financial assistance to the government in its war policy. One must, however, be very cautious not to regard such an action as extraordinary. The last Great War imposed such tremendous financial burdens upon all belligerent nations that none of them could resist the temptation to create artificial purchasing power through considerable loans from their respective central banks. It was an inevitable step if the various governments wished to obtain the necessary funds. Moreover, one should not forget that legally the Chancellor of the Empire was president of the Reichsbank, so that in this particular case, the institution would have had to carry out his instructions.

The financial mobilization plan of the government was now clear. No moratorium was decreed but the possibility was provided to obtain credit against securities from the Loan Banks or by discount of commercial bills at the Reichsbank. In a relatively short time, industry and commerce adapted themselves to these conditions. Industrial production was transformed from a peace to a war production and the German government became now the greatest consumer. In a short time the fear of a financial crisis had disappeared as is reflected in the following figures:[9] On July 23, the portfolio of the Imperial Bank contained bills of exchange dis counted to an amount of 750,9 million marks; this total increased to 1330 million in the week to July 31, and to 2979,9 millions during the two following weeks until August 15. After this period, a distinct decrease to 1198 millions on December 31, took place. This declining tendency continued throughout the war, and in 1918 the annual average of bills of exchange in the portfolio of the Reichsbank was as low as 218 million marks. The decrease in the portfolio of bills is largely due to the great liquidity of the money market which was caused by the financial policy of the government to make all payments in cash and also by activities of the Loan banks in granting credit.

---

9. Annual report of the Reichsbank, 1914.

The large amounts of money necessary for the military operations at the outbreak of the war were obtained by the government through discount of treasury notes. These discounts increased the note circulation from 1890,3 millions on July 23, to 5049,9 million marks on December 31, 1914. The payments in cash by the government resulted in a very liquid money market. So far as payments were made in treasury notes these were readily rediscounted at the Reichsbank. It was the aim of the government to stimulate industry by prompt payments. The exclusion of Germany from most sources of raw material intensified the efforts of industry to overcome these hindrances, and it is to the credit of Germany that she was capable of carrying on her production with only those commodites which she had at her disposal.

After 1916, a fresh impulse to the above mentioned intensification of industry and commerce was given by the so-called Hindenburg Program. Its aim was to induce industry to produce with the utmost intensity by appealing to economic selfishness. Every price demanded was to be paid promptly. This elimination of competition among the producers had a twofold result. First, the note circulation increased continuously, and secondly, as a result of this accelerated note issue prices increased.[10] This increase in the level of prices, which undoubtedly was caused by the continuous expansion of notes in circulation, was attributed by the financial leaders and even by the Reichsbank authorities to the influence of foreign speculation and to hoarding of money by the public. The fallacy of these assumptions will be shown in due time. Another reason for the increase of money in circulation is also to be found in the necessity felt by the German government to provide means of payment for the occupied territories in Belgium, Rumania, North France, Poland and certain parts of Russia. The Reichsbank endeavored, however, to restrict this growth in the note issue by the establishment of banks in the occupied territories, which were authorized to issue their own notes while an equivalent amount in Reichsbank notes had to be deposited at the Imperial Bank.[11]

---

10. The increase in the circulation of notes is shown in table in the appendix to part I.

11. The importance which the notes issued in Belgium during the war have come to assume in the recent conference of the Young Committee in

Originally, it had been the plan of the government to redeem the treasury notes with the receipts from the war loans. Though the war operations until October 1916 required the amount of 52 billion marks, the revenues from the war loans up to this period amounted to 46 billion marks. Thus, the total of credit outstanding from the Reichsbank was at that time seven billions, six of which represented discounted treasury notes, while one billion were discounted commercial bills. Notes in circulation were about 7200 million marks and the gold reserves of 2500 millions constituted approximately 35%. This favorable status changed entirely in the second half of the war. The policy of the government to pay every price demanded necessitated an increase in the discount of treasury notes. The costs of the military expenditures increased rapidly and the revenues from the war loans did not more than suffice to redeem the treasury notes.

From the commencement of the war, it had been the aim of the Reichsbank to accumulate as much gold as possible in its vaults. The Bank urged the citizens of Germany to help the Fatherland in its heroic efforts by turning over their gold. It was assisted in its campaign by the press, schools, and many social and political organizations. In every town, city and village, committees were constituted which urged deliveries of gold to the Reichsbank. The

---

Paris in connection with the Young Plan justifies a brief outline of the procedure adopted by the German government in floating these notes during the war. After the occupation of Belgium the difficulty arose as to how provide the necessary means of payment for theGerman troops, as well as for the populations. The printing plates of the Belgian Bank of Issue had been removed prior to the occupation by the German troops. Dr. Schacht the present president of the Reichsbank who was then advisor of the official military administrative body, proposed to the Belgian authorities the substitution of payments in cash instead of the required free deliveries of goods for the troops. The Belgian authorities then turned over obligations to an amount of 480 million francs which were deposited with the Société Générale de Belgique and the National Bank. The latter two institutions then issued emergency notes up to the amount of 480 million francs, for which the German troops then acquired goods from the population. Later on the Société Générale was authorized to issue additional notes against the deposit of Reichsbank notes at the Reichsbank. Up to the end of the war, a total of 1600 million marks had been deposited in this way, representing the compulsory contributions of the Belgian population to the German troops.

supply of gold in the vaults of the Reichsbank increased throughout the war and only at the end of the war did a slight decrease take place. —

Although this supply of gold proved to be of great importance to Germany after the war, the aim of the Reichsbank in accunulating so large a stock of gold was soon frustrated by the economic blockade. The economic blockade to which Germany was subjected soon after the outbreak of the hostilities rendered impossible the utilization of this supply of gold for purchases of commodities in neutral countries. So far as the gold was then used in increasing the reserve ratio of gold for the quantity of notes in circulation such a policy was from a monetary viewpoint without avail. Under the peculiar conditions prevailing in Germany during the war the gold reserve did not matter from the standpoint of prices. Prices are determined in the last analysis by supply and demand and it is immaterial whether the demand is represented by bank notes covered only to one per cent in gold. The criterion for the quantity of notes in circulation was the demand of the market for means of payment and the confidence in the value of the currency. Doubtless the greatly inflated German currency commanded the same confidence among the population as the convertible Reichsbank notes had before the war. However, the artificial purchasing power directed into the market through the discount of treasury debentures exercised its influence upon the value of the currency, i. e. it caused an increase in the general price level.

The inflating effect of the note issue of the Reichsbank in connection with the notes put into circulation by the Loan banks did not become obvious to its full extent on account of governmental regulation of prices throughout the war. At the beginning of the war the Reichstag had passed a law authorizing the government to regulate and fix the prices at which commodities could be sold and to determine the quantity of goods which could be bought by an individual within a certain period. These regulations related chiefly to food, raw material, heating and lighting materials. Such federal regulation was but natural in view of the economic blockade and the insufficient supply of food and raw material produced on German soil. Prior to the war, Germany had always been an importer of food and certain raw materials. An official regulation of prices and quantities consumed was, therefore, imperative. However, the actual regulation of prices affected the prices for commodities, rent and labor unequally. While rent remained almost unchanged, commodity prices increased slightly and wages rose far above their pre-war level. In consequence there was a larger demand for commodities without a corresponding increase in the supply. But as the quantity of goods which could be bought by an individual in a certain time-interval was limited, a large part of the population was forced to save more than they would have done under normal circumstances.

It will be recalled that the German government pursued the principle of paying for every delivery of goods for military purposes in cash or treasury notes which could be discounted at the Reichsbank. It would have been logical and natural to pay a part of the price in cash and the remainder in War Loan Bonds. In view of the general conditions in the domestic market of Germany it is very probable that such a method would not have met with serious objection on the part of businessmen. Instead of such advisable partial cash payments the producers obtained the whole amount in cash. It was therefore natural that their purchasing power directed itself to those goods which were not under official regulation, i. e. luxuries. In this way, competition tended to increase wages above the normal war level, and correspondingly increased the prices of all goods above the level which would have been otherwise established. Only the very rigid enforcement of the regulation of food prices and rent partially neutralized the inflating influence of the potential purchasing power in the market. The domestic price level cannot, therefore, be taken as a true index of the inflating effect of the note policy of the Reichsbank.

It was in a similar way that the German government in cooperation with the Reichsbank endeavored to influence the foreign exchange rate in the German market and abroad. If demand and supply are left to themselves in the market, the foreign exchange rate reflects the relative value of one currency in terms of another. A higher exchange rate for the German mark in the New York market, for instance, indicates a higher valuation of marks in terms of dollars in New York. The level from which the fluctuations of the foreign exchange rate are measured is the relative content of gold of the respective currencies. If both countries are on a gold standard the foreign exchange rate cannot fall below that rate where it becomes more favorable to import gold instead of selling bills of exchange. Conversely, the rate of exchange can not increase above that rate where it is more profitable for the debtor to export gold instead of buying a bill of exchange. These two limits are called the specie points. If, however, one or both of the countries involved have a paper standard the exchange rate reflects the relative purchasing power of the respective money units in their domestic markets.

As a result of the strong influence exercised by the German government during the War, in Germany, the foreign exchange rate lost its usefulness as an indication of relative purchasing power. By decree of January 20th, 1916, the sale and purchase of foreign exchange was prohibited. Only 26 banks under the leadership of the Reichsbank were authorized to buy and sell foreign exchanges in accordance with certain regulations concerning the cases in which individuals were permitted to acquire foreign currencies. These permits were granted almost exclusively to important exporting or importing industries. Moreover, the publication of foreign exchange rates in the press was forbidden. Simultaneously with these measures adopted to regulate the domestic quotations of foreign exchange rates, the Reichsbank endeavored to maintain the mark rate abroad as near to par as possible by buying marks against foreign currencies or gold. These interventions necessitated a continuous export of foreign exchange and gold, a process by which the Reichsbank lost about 450 million marks in foreign currencies or gold during the war.

These attempts of the Reichsbank to influence the exchange rate abroad were greatly facilitated by foreign speculation. Speculative purchases of marks tended to increase the value of the mark and partly neutralized the inflating effect of the increasing note issue. It was not until the last six months of the war that the foreign exchange rate of the mark decreased materially. A comparison of the price level in Germany with the foreign exchange rate, as shown in the following table shows clearly that prices in Germany increased much more and earlier than the foreign exchange value of the mark.

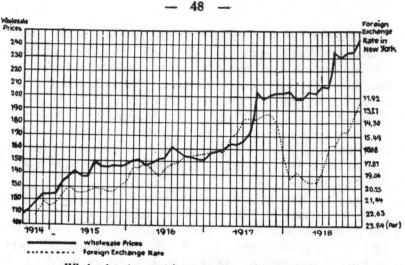

Wholesale prices and foreign exchange rate 1914/1918.

Another peculiar feature in the war-policy of the Reichsbank ought to be mentioned here. Throughout the war the Bank advocated and actively urged an increased use of the transfer and cheque system of the Reichsbank, credit institutions, and of the Post Office (which also maintained a transfer system). Obviously the aim of the Bank's management was to keep the total of notes in circulation as low as possible. Such a policy is easily understood in case of a gold standard where it results in a saving of notes in circulation and strengthens the reserves of the central bank, as has been shown in chapter one. The reason for this war policy seems, however, to have been the assumption of the Bank management that such deposits would occur if the money were held by the population.[12] It is true that bank deposits do not affect the price level as long as they are not withdrawn by the depositor in cash for the purpose of making purchases in the market. But the same holds true for bank notes. It is not the amount of money outstanding that affects the price level, but the quantity of money purchasing power circulating

12. In his book "Die Politik der Reichsbank und der Reichsschatzanweisungen", Alfred Lansburgh cites on page 22 an article written the vice-president of the Reichsbank and published in the "Bank Archiv" at the end of 1918. In this article the real causes for the increasing amount of notes issued and their inflating influence are said to be the hoarding of money by the population. The inflation is attributed almost exclusively to hoarding of money by the population and to speculation abroad.

in the market. If the owner of money in cash does not exercise his claims in the market upon a share of the social output he cannot affect the price level. On the other hand, if a depositor of a bank competes in the market by means of his claims upon the bank, his competition affects the price level in the same way as if he had offered cash. From the standpoint of price it does not matter whether the demand in the market is based upon bank deposits or upon banks notes. In either case there is purchasing power in the market and the effect upon the price level is the same.

In this connection, two other assumptions in the policy of the Reichsbank should be discussed at this point. It has always been argued by the bank that speculation abroad and hoarding of money by the German public were to a great extent responsible for the increased note issue and in consequence for the inflation.[13] The Reichsbank did not recognise that the issue of the larger quantity of money was caused by its discount of treasury debentures, which economically meant loans for consumptive purposes and which were to be considered as the sole cause of the inflation during the war. A critical analysis of the facts however reveals that the bank mistook cause and effect. First,as far as speculation is concerned:Speculation creates an increased demand for currency, in this instance German currency, and causes increased imports to Germany, because of the higher valuation of marks abroad. Thus, the quantity of goods in Germany increases while the total of money decreased, and hence prices fall. If the money, held by the speculators, is thrown into the market, the reverse process takes place. A careful study of the rates of exchange reveals the fact that speculation in marks always coincided with increasing confidence in Germany's future, i. e., with the belief that she would succeed in making favorable peace settlements. Naturally, the disturbance of these hopes by the actual developments of the war caused a depreciation in the rate of exchange.

So far as the influence of hoarding is concerned the fallacy is obvious. If people sell their goods in the markets and do not ex-

---

13. See cited article by the vice-president of the Reichsbank published in „Bank Archiv" in 1918.

change their revenues for other commodities, the demand in the market diminishes, while the quantity of goods remains unaltered. Here, too, the result is a fall in prices. The actual increase in prices during the war was due to the artificial purchasing power which the government obtained by discounting its treasury debentures. In this case the purchasing power of the government was not the outcome of any productivity. This purchasing power competed in the market, and, having no economic background, it tended to increase prices. If the people who sold their products to the government and hoarded their receipts no longer competed in the market, the economic result was the same as if they had given their products to the government without receiving payment. Only when these people wanted to purchase commodities in the market did their demand tend to increase prices. But due to the official regulation of prices the latter did not inflate in proportion to the excessive note issue.

TREASURY DEBENTURES AND BILLS HELD BY REICHSBANK:[14]

	Treasury Bills:	Commercial Bills:
July 31, 1914	0,3 billion	2,1 billions
December 31, 1914	2,7 „	1,2 „
December 31, 1915	5,2 „	0,6 „
December 31, 1916	8,9 „	0,7 „
December 31, 1917	14,2 „	0,4 „
December 31, 1918	21,8 „	0,3 „

Since December 1914 the discount rate had been five per cent and it became the policy of the Reichsbank to maintain this discount rate throughout the war. The reason for the maintenance of this relatively low rate was twofold. First, it was necessitated by economic conditions. It must be recalled that at the outbreak of the war the granting of a general moratorium had been seriously considered. An increased discount rate would undoubtedly have

---

14. A. Lansburgh, Die Politik der Schatzanweisungen etc.

increased the rate of interest in the market, too, and would also have caused many bankruptcies. The political reason, which was the deciding factor, was the aim of making possible the marketing of the war loan bonds. A low discount rate was a political necessity and therefore maintained by the Reichsbank. The preponderance of political considerations in the policy of the Reichsbank over economic needs is also noticeable in the postwar period, as will be shown in the next chapter.

CHAPTER IV.

THE REICHSBANK 1919—1923.

The years which followed the end of the war saw the complete breakdown of Germany's economic system. On November 11, 1918 the armistice agreement was signed. In it Germany promised to deliver to the Allies in the course of the next months the following: the entire German war fleet and all arms; 5,000 locomotives and 150,000 rail-road cars in good condition;[1] 5,000 trucks; and all the gold seized during the war in Rumania and Russia. But the economic blockade, was not lifted by the Allies but continued until two weeks after the Treaty of Versailles was signed. The deliveries of the locomotives and of the railroad cars practically paralyzed German transportation facilities. Domestic disturbances of a political and social character increased economic difficulties. On November 9, 1918 the German Monarchy was overthrown and the German Republic formed. The new government saw itself confronted with political and economic obstacles which for the next four years threatened the very existence of the nation.

Communistic insurrections, which began in Berlin on December 7, 1918 continued during the next months and spread all over Germany. Strikes and lockouts in Berlin and various other parts of the country were the result of the economic hardship which followed the loss of the Great War. Industry was greatly affected by the rail-road strikes which prevented regular transportation service and consequently contributed to the general panic. Though the government succeeded within a few months in overcoming most

---

1. These figures gain importance if one visualizes that before the Great War Germany had a total of 29 000 locomotives, 65,961 rail-road cars, and 667,148 freight cars. (Statistisches Jahrbuch für 1915.)

of the political obstacles, their after effects could not be removed in such a short time. Great social tasks were also imposed upon the government by increasing unemployment, caused by the return of the German army and the annexation of German territory.

These difficulties increased the financial burden of the government which faced the problem of raising adequate revenue for larger expenditures. Originally, the financial authorities of Germany had planned to convert the treasury debentures which amounted to 33 billion marks in August 1918 into a funded debt through the flotation of long term obligations in the German market. This project, however, was not carried out because of the additional financial burden which it would have imposed upon the federal budget. Such a conversion of the outstanding debentures would have resulted in larger payments of interest caused by the prevailing market conditions.

In the budget estimate of the federal government the payments of interest represented the greater part of the total expenditures. Of 17,5 billion marks for 1919, ten billion marks were for the payment of interest on the national debt. This amount was estimated upon the assumption that the public debt would increase to 200 million marks in the course of the fiscal year, as a result of larger expenditures for social tasks and for the immediate relief of certain conditions brought about by the war. A conversion of the debt, however, would have increased the total of government expenditures for the payment of interest considerably. The War Loan Bonds which yielded five per cent interest rated in the market between 75 and 80 per cent of their nominal value. A new issue of these Bonds would therefore, have been marketable only with an interest rate of about 6,5 per cent. On the other hand, the great liquidity of the money market rendered it possible to discount the treasury debentures in the market at a rate of from 4,5 to $4^5/_8$ per cent, amounting to a saving of two per cent interest. Although the government discounted its debentures regularly at the Reichsbank at a rate of five per cent it received a part of this interest payment in the form of taxes as its share in the profits of the bank. Later the federal government went so far as to accept War Loan Bonds as payment for taxes. In order to cover the ensuing deficit in the revenues, the government discounted additional debentures at the Reichsbank. Thus the funded debt was gradually converted into a floating debt. As a result of this financial policy, the total of War

Loan Bonds which amounted to 103 billion marks in the autumn of 1918 decreased to 55 billions in the summer of 1923.[2]

As we have seen, the signing of the Armistice did not bring about an immediate discontinuance of the economic blockade. The great scarcity of food was the most vital problem of Germany and its pressure can best be visualized from the fact that in February 1919 the quantity of potatoes which could be sold to a person was legally limited to five pounds per head per week. The importation of food was, therefore, the most pressing task of the government. Over a billion marks in gold had to be exported in the course of half a year for this purpose. As a result the gold stock of the Reichsbank decreased from 2,253,712,000 marks on January 31, 1919 to 1109,348,000 marks on July 31, 1919.[3]

On June 28, 1919 the Treaty of Versailles was signed and two weeks later the economic blockade was removed. But the annexation of German provinces by the Allies reduced the productive power of Germany as well as her taxable resources. The total of reparation payments to be made by Germany to the allies was not yet finally fixed. She was merely informed that the total damages and losses had been estimated at 185,822,3 million marks or about 42,5 billion dollars, and that the Reparation Commission would determine the ultimate amount. Its decision should be announced to Germany not later than May 1, 1921. But until then Germany was obliged to make certain deliveries and payments in advance which would be deducted from the final amount. This uncertainty about its future obligation made it almost impossible for Germany to obtain any foreign loans.

The German government, facing the problem of providing the necessary funds for the provisional payment of reparations, resorted to its former policy of discounting treasury debentures with the Reichsbank. The continuance of this policy of discounting its own debentures without providing at the same time adequate revenues was undoubtly the main cause of the depreciation of the German currency. On the other hand, attention must be called to the excessively high reparation payments which practically pompelled the

---

2. These figures are estimated by the „Wirtschaftskurve" 1923, Heft 3.
3. Annual report of the Reichsbank 1919.

German government to pursue the above policy. Both, the financial policy of the German government during the war and the excessive reparation payments are in the last analysis responsible for the breakdown of Germany's monetary system. Various other factors have more or less hurried the process but the two factors above mentioned are the main causes.

The uninterrupted discount of debentures hurried the process of inflation. The Reich discounted a certain amount of its debentures at the Reichsbank, obtaining an equivalent amount of bank notes or claims upon the Reichsbank. It then competed in a market where prices were already in a process of inflation as a result of purchasing stored during the Great War, which was now exercised in the market. In addition to this purchasing power the government then competed with the credit obtained from the Bank which was in its very nature artificial and tended to inflate prices.

From the point of view of central banking theory these debentures of the Reich were highly illiquid and credit based upon them tended to increase prices. It becomes evident, therefore, that the funds obtained by the government from the Reichsbank had a highly inflating effect upon the general price level. In turn this increase of prices rendered the amount obtained by the government insufficient to meet anticipated expenditures. In order to defray these expenditures the Reich was forced to discount an additional quantity of debentures at the Reichsbank. The result was a further increase in prices, again causing larger discounts at the Reichsbank. In this way the vicious circle of the German currency depreciation repeated itself continously.

The financial policy of the government, with its inflating effect seriously affected the general business conditions of the country. After the end of the Great War, German industry and trade lacked capital for the necessary reorganization of their enterprises from war production to peacetime production. This shortage of funds is natural in view of the great expansion which occured during the war, and which had continuously been stimulated by the government. In addition to this demand for funds the currency inflation was the cause for a continuous loss of circulating and fixed capital for industry and commerce.

It will be recalled that during the Great War, the German government had exercised a very rigid control over the price level. Special federal and communal bureaus had prescribed the rate of profit and various prices which could legally be charged by producers, wholesalers and retailers. Such a regulative policy is necessary in times of war, in view of the economic blockade to which Germany was then subjected and of the necessity to provide an equal distribution of the limited supply of raw material and foodstuffs. This necessity no longer existed after the summer of 1919, when Germany had again entered international trade relations. Nevertheless, the German government continued its policy of regulating the general price level in the same way as it had done during the war. It went even further by including a larger number of goods than had been regulated during the war.

This policy of price regulation was partly necessitated by social considerations. During a currency depreciation wages always increase more slowly than prices for commodities. As an inevitable result, there occurs a constant loss of purchasing power of the working class. It was therefore a primary task of the Reich to prevent a discrepancy between wages and standard of living which at that time tended to lower the latter to the minimum of existence. In pursuing this policy of price regulation the German government during the later part of the inflation adhered too strictly to its principle of „mark equals mark". The exaggerated execution of this principle led gradually to an impoverishment of the middle-class in Germany. Businessmen and industrialists were forced to sell their goods at prices far below their cost of replacement. The passage of „usury laws" (Wuchergesetze) prohibited the computation of prices on the basis of the foreign exchange quotation of the mark, thus rendering impossible the constant adjustment of prices to the intrinsic value of the mark. These special laws also prohibited the addition of profit to the cost of aquisition above a certain prescribed limit which was inadequate to compensate for the loss of purchasing power of the currency. As a result, the money which the seller received in exchange for his goods represented less than was necessary to repurchase the same quantity of commodities. This process of continuous loss caused the small business man in Germany to dissipate almost all of his capital during the process of currency depreciation.

The decision of the Reichsgericht (the highest court of Germany) had also very grave effects upon the saving class, especially upon the owners of mortgages and bonds. It forced these creditors to accept depreciated marks as a payment for their claims, and thus impoverished the entire German savings-class. On account of this depreciation of mortgages and the resulting negligible interest payments thereon, the government regulated the rent charges for apartments and business enterprises far below the rate which would have conformed to the actual depreciation of the currency. As a result business man and industrialists were able to sell their goods at prices which included a negligible part for rent as compared with the part which rent represented in pre-war prices.

The continuous loss of purchasing power by the monetary unit forced the business man to increase his demand for credit or capital funds in order to acquire a stock of commodities equal to that which he had been compelled to sell at prices below the cost of re-acquisition. These funds were then obtained either by an issue of bonds or stocks in the capital market, or in form of credit from the banks. The continuous depreciation of the mark enabled the debtor to redeem his debts at maturity with a fraction of that purchasing power which he had obtained at the time when the debt was contracted. This process is best illustrated by the following example. An industrialist A, who had produced goods at a price of one million marks was forced by the existing usury laws to sell these commodities at a price of about ten per cent above his own cost of production. Let us now assume the buyer paid at delivery. The producer received his money then under the most favorable conditions about two weeks after the goods had been produced. During that period, however, the mark had depreciated by about 20 per cent or in the last two years of the inflation by much more. It is obvious that the producer was unable to acquire raw material sufficient to reproduce a quantity of goods equal to the amount he had sold. He had lost a very substantial part of his capital. In order to attain his original stock, he either floated bonds in the market or asked for credit at his bank. He then was able to reproduce as much as he had sold and to redeem the incurred debt at maturity with a fraction of what he had bought with that money when he had obtained the credit. In this way the industrialist had shifted his loss either to the bank or to the buyer of the bond.

The question may justly be asked whether the banks were entirely unaware of the real nature of the inflation and of the losses which they incurred by granting loans at interest rates ranging between six and ten per cent per annum, which naturally did not compensate for the loss of purchasing power of the monetary unit. Surprising as it may seem, the banks actually did not recognize clearly the course of the inflation and deceived themselves about the real nature of the situation. Otherwise it is impossible to explain the fact that the banks lost during this process of inflation approximately 15 billion marks, a substantial part of which represented their own capital.[4] The balance sheets of the German Great Banks which were computed in 1924 on the basis of the gold-mark, which in its foreign exchange value equals one pre-war mark, show a reduction of their capital from 1500 million marks in 1913 to 452 million marks in December 31, 1924.[5] This reduction in their capital indicates the direct losses incurred by these banks owing to their credit policy.

Many outside factors contributed to this self-deception of the German credit institutions and enabled them to provide the necessary funds for the business world. The first increase in the demand for credit after the revolution was met by the banks from the very substantial cash reserves which they had accumulated during the war. An additional supply of funds was provided by the

---

4. In his book 'Die Bankpolitik der Inflationszeit und die Milliardenwerte der Banken' Dr. Richard Hauser estimates the total loss of the German credit banks during the inflation at 15 billion marks; the loss of the Deutsche Bank amounted to 1.5 billion marks including (continued on next page) own capital and deposits. These figures refer to gold-mark, i. e. a rate of 4.20 mark for one dollar, so that the total loss amounted to ab out 3.345 billion dollars. Dr. Hauser, who was at that time director at the Deutsche Bank, mentions the case of this bank, where the board of directors refused to follow his (Hauser's) advice to contract loans only on the basis of a moving index in the same way as the business world.

5. Die Wirtschaftskurve 1924.

receipts from purchases of securities, real estate, and commodities by foreigners who were attracted by the relatively low level of prices in Germany. The large majority of the population which did not recognize the nature of the inflation, continued to deposit their money with the banks and enabled the latter to grant the required loans to the business world.

For a short period from the autumn of 1920 to June 1921, the mark retained its foreign exchange quotation at a rate of about 60 marks for one dollar. The relative stability throughout this period was partly caused by intervention on part of the Reichsbank, which successfully kept the demand for foreign exchange so low as to prevent a further increase, and partly by foreign speculation in marks which favorably affected the rate of exchange abroad. It is interesting to note that during this period indications of a slight business depression occurred as a result of the stable value of the mark after a long period of depreciation. Prices declined slightly and the demand for „inflation credit", which had been so strong in the preceding months, decreased. There were no serious business disturbances, however, and the economy was in a rather liquid state.

This situation changed fundamentally after the London Ultimatum of May 21st, 1921, which informed the German government that the total of reparation payments had been fixed by the Reparation Commission at 132 billion marks. Finding it impossible to make the necessary payments out of its tax revenues, the government once more resorted to its policy of discounting treasury debentures. As a result the mark depreciated continuously in the course of the next year. Again the demand for „inflation credit" increased, which was this time met by the banks with the receipts from foreign investments in German securities and other tangible assets. The artificially maintained low level of prices in Germany rendered it profitable for the foreigner to invest funds in Germany. It must be mentioned, however, that although no reliable statistics are available the assumption seems justified that very substantial amounts of German currency were hoarded during this period by foreign speculators. Furthermore, the low prices of stocks in the Bourse attracted very large funds from abroad, thus uncreasing the liquidity of the money market.

About the middle of 1922, the last stage of the inflation commenced. The effort of the Reich to obtain a loan abroad had failed. Gradually the monetary unit almost lost its function as a means of payment and its foreign exchange value diminished to such a small fraction of its pre-war value that it is almost impossible to express it in figures. Reference has already been made to the causes of this development. It was the vicious circle of: reparation payments — discount of treasury debentures — instability of the federal budget — increased prices — renewed discount of treasury debentures etc. Throughout these years the Reichsbank had continued to discount the treasury debentures although this inevitably resulted in an inflated price level.

Before discussing further the monetary development in Germany reference must be made here to the renewal of the Reichsbank charter in 1920. At that time the question arose whether the federal government should take over the Reichsbank in its own right. Realizing that the aquisition of the institution by the Reich would have entirely undermined the credit of the Bank, the Reichstag agreed upon the prolongation of the charter for ten more years. The economic and political situation rendered various changes in the provisions of the Bank Act inevitable, and the act was ammended by the legislature. As far as the organization is concerned the main administration remained in the hands of the Chancellor of the Reich. The Bank Curatorium which until 1919 was composed of four members, was increased to six, thus making possible the representation of the ministers of the Republic and of the States. Furthermore, the Central Committee, which until then consisted of only fifteen members was increased to eighteen members. The three additional representatives were to be appointed by the labor unions, the savings banks, and the co-operative societes, each of these groups electing one delegate. So far as business operations were concerned the Bank was authorized to buy and to sell foreign bills of exchange in the market. This provision was necessary to enable the Reichsbank to centralize and to distribute foreign bills for the export trade. The General Assembly of the shareholders agreed upon these provisions and on December 22, 1919 the Bank charter was renewed an the above mentioned amendents enacted into law.

The continuous acceleration of Reichsbank notes in circulation rendered it impossible to maintain the legally prescribed cover of one third, even with the aid of the Loan Bank notes.† Owing to the payments on reparation and to the importation of food, the gold reserves of the Reichsbank decreased continuously. The Reichstag passed, therefore, on May 8, 1921 a law relieving the Reichsbank of the necessity of maintaining a legal reserve of one third for its outstanding notes. This provision was limited to three years.¦

By its very nature such a provision left the issue of notes entirely to the discretion of the Bank. The latter was authorized to issue as many notes as it saw fit. In view of the policy of the Reich to discount continuously its debentures at the Reichsbank the mark lost its monetary functions as a measure of value. It functioned merely as legal tender deriving its value solely from the authority of the State which sanctioned the cancellation of debts by payments with paper marks. As long as the public still had a belief in future stabilization of the currency, the depreciation was a slow one and mainly caused by the balance of payment. But the instant this confidence was lost, a panic was inevitable.

The peculiar attitude of the Reichsbank towards this development is worthy of a brief discussion. It was not until 1921 that the management of the Bank referred to the increased note issue as a cause of the inflation.[6] Until then, it had attributed the depreciation of the currency to the exportation of gold to meet the reparation payments, and to speculation abroad. But even after recognizing that the continuously increasing amount of money in circulation was the cause rather than the effect of the inflation, the Bank considered this development as inevitable. In its report for 1922, it describes the situation as follows:[7] „This interrelation between the creation of purchasing power, depreciation of currency and increase of prices and wages will repeat itself continuously, and always in more and more grotesque forms, as the burdensome reparation-payments

---

6. Lansburgh, „Die Politik der Schatzanweisungen etc." p. 36.

7. Page 5, „Diese Wechselwirkung zwischen Geldschöpfung, Valutaverschlechterung und Steigen des Preis- und Lohnniveaus wird sich solange wiederholen, und zwar unter immer grotesekeren Formen, wie der übermäßige Umfang der Reparationslasten eine Deckung der Reichsfinanzen und eine Besserung unserer Zahlungsbilanz verhindert."

prevent sufficient revenues for the budget, and, moreover, an improvement in the balance of payment." This theory that inflation was inevitable is the best explanation for the fact that the Reichsbank did not object to further discount of treasury notes. It held that „In view of the circumstances the Reich does not possess any other means to defray its expenditures." (Report for 1922).

Though these statements truly reflect the difficult position of the government they do not remove the objections to the general discount policy of the Bank. It is probable that an increased discount rate would have enabled the Reichsbank to market a larger portion of the treasury notes, instead of being left with an increasing percentrage of discounted notes in its own portfolio, as is shown in the following table:

TREASURY DEBENTURES IN CIRCULATION AT REICHSBANK.[8]

	Total of Debentures Outstanding	Amount held by Reichsbank	Percentage held by Reichsbank
November 1918	50 millions	19 billions	38
Dec. 31, 1920	170 millions	50 billions	29
Dec. 31, 1921	247 millions	132 billions	53
Dec. 31, 1922	1822 millions	1184 billions	65
March 31, 1923	8,1 trillions	4,5 trillions	55
June 31, 1923	24,9 trillions	18,4 trillions	73
Sept. 31, 1923	26 700,0 trillions	25 216,2 trillions	96,8

The Reichsbank assumed that in post war time there has never been a market sufficient for the absorption of the war bonds. The report for 1922 states „It does not require any particular discussion that an increase in the discount rate, in view of the present conditions, will have but a very slight influence upon the volume of credit. The need for credit by the government is inevitable and cannot be decreased by such means. On the other hand, an increase in the discount rate does not have any real significance on the volume of credit required by the business world, even if the present

---

8.   A. Lansburgh, Die Politik der Reichsbank und die Schatzanweisungen, p. 32.

rates should be multiplied; owing to the great increase in risk and chances of profit which are caused by the fluctuating value of money". It is true that an increased discount rate would not have had much effect upon the demand for credit. But this situation refers rather to the credit market than to the capital market. The capital market during that period was marked by a large influx of money and considerable flotations of new securities and bonds, and their absorption by the market. It is, therefore, probable that a part of this capital could have been attracted to the purchase of treasury notes if the interest rate had been remunerative.

The rather passive attitude of the Reichsbank towards the discount of treasury debentures was considered by the Reparation Commission as the result of the provision in the Bank Act that the „Chancellor of the Empire is the President of the Reichsbank" and that „he or his representative issues the regulations and working orders to the Directorate". The Allied governments, upon the recommendation of the Reparation Commission, demanded that the Reichsbank be given a free hand. The Reich, which at that time claimed that it was unable to meet the high reparation payments, conformed to this demand of the Allies, and, on May 21st, 1922, passed the Autonomy Act. The main purpose of this act was to free the Reichsbank from supervision by the federal government. The articles, concerning these relations read now:

(Article 27): The president of the bank and the members of the Directorate are appointed by the President of the Republic for life. The President is appointed from a list of three names which is made up by a committee of nine members, three of whom are elected by the Federal Council (Bundesrat), three by the Federal Economic Ministry (Wirtschaftsministerium), and three by the Central Committee.

(Omitted are in this paragraph the words: The Board of Directors consists of the President and the requisite number of members, and passes its resolutions by majority of votes; but ist whole proceedings are subject to the prescriptions and instructions of the Imperial Chancellor.)

Article 25: The right to supervise the Reichsbank, formerly exercised by the government, is now exercised by the curatorium which consists of the Chancellor as Chairman, the Minister of

Finance, and the Minister of Economics (Wirtschaftsminister) as vice chairman and of six other members, three of whom are appointed by the President of the Empire after consulting with the Federal Economic Ministry, and the other three designated by the Federal Council.

(Article 25 read formerly: The Imperial supervision of the Reichsbank is exercised by a board of inspectors comprising the Chancellor of the Empire and four other members.)

The most important change in the Bank Act concerns the right of note issue. The Autonomy Act provides that the principles regarding the issue of notes shall be established by the Reichsbank-Directorate after consultation with the Federal Economic Ministry.

But though the Reichsbank was now vested with the power to regulate the discount policy and the issue of notes at will, it did not change its former policy. It continued to accept treasury debentures for discount and did not attempt to induce the Reich to adopt another financial policy. This unaltered attitude of the Bank's management, and its failure to shift a part of the discounted treasury debentures to the capital market, contributed to a further depreciation of the currency. This time, too, the depreciation resulted in very serious consequences.

As in previous periods of inflation, the demand for „inflation credit" increased. Many depositors, however, had withdrawn their funds from the banks, clearly recognizing the ruinous consequence of leaving their resources with the banks. Foreign speculation in German currency had ceased and the banks found themselves with a shortage of funds to satisfy the existing demand. In this critical moment, the Reichsbank entered upon a policy which caused the final break down of the German currency at the end of 1923.

In July, 1922, the Reichsbank advocated an increased utilization of the commercial bill of exchange as a means of payment, and announced its readiness to rediscount such bills if they conformed to the legal standard. The policy was adopted by the Bank without any change in the discount rate which was then five per cent. This action of the Bank was taken at a time when the business world had gradually come to abandon the use of commercial bills for its transactions, and had introduced moving indexes for the computation of prices. These indexes were based upon the quotation of the dollar on the Bourse of Berlin, or upon general price indexes. /Naturally the new policy of the Reichsbank offered the businessman the opportunity of procuring purchasing power which he could pay back at maturity with a fraction of its original value, while he himself obtained for the goods which he bought with the aid of this credit the same purchasing power. / The great fallacy of this policy of the Reichsbank becomes apparent if one considers the fact that the Bank's discount rate was left unchanged at five per cent at a time when banks charged industrialists fifty per cent for book credit, and when loans based upon foreign exchange quotations were contracted at the Bourse of Berlin at from 10 to 15 per cent. per annum. As was to be expected, those who had the opportunity of discounting their bills at the Reichsbank, availed themselves of this means in order to obtain credit, which they then used for the construction of new buildings or expansion of their old plants. The discount policy of the Reichsbank at that time actually offered a free gift of purchasing power to those who could obtain credit from the Banks. As a result the books of the Bank showed an enormous increase of discounted bills during the period June to December 1922, as can be seen from the following figures.

Bills Discounted by the Reichsbank (in millions of mark)

June:	July:	August:	September:	October:	November:	December:
4751	8122	21704	50234	101,155	246,943	423,235

Though the quantity of notes in circulation increased immensely, the great increase in prices caused a scarcity of money units of small denominations. To remedy this situation, certain bank and credit institutions were empowered by the Reichstag to issue emergency money (Notgeld), on the condition that an equivalent amount of Reichsbanknotes was deposited with the latter. In the Fall of 1923, the issue of these emergency notes assumed such tremendous dimensions that, in a panic due to monetary collapse, all control over them was lost. Every city, town and village, and even factories and business houses issued emergency notes without fulfilling the legal requirements. The inflating affect of these emergency notes can be visualized from the fact that at the stabilization of the mark on November 15, 1923, the total of these notes amounted to 988 million gold-marks, while the aggregate of Reichsbanknotes was only 115 million gold-marks.[9]

The following tables show the increase in the issue of notes, of discounted commercial bills and treasury notes, and the decrease of the rate of exchange. In view of the tremendous depreciation, it is impossible to give an adequate graphic representation of the development. The increase in the quantity of Loan Bank notes has been omitted because these notes were almost entirely in the portfolio of the Reichsbank and the equivalent amount of Reichsbanknotes which had been issued is contained in the total of notes in circulation.

Notes in circulation: (Omitted . 000,000,000)	Com. bills: (Omitted . 000,000,000,009)	Treas. notes:	Rate of exchange:[10] (At Berlin market)
January	1,984	697	1,609	1 $ = 17,972
February	3,513	1,829	2,941	27,917
March	5,518	2,372	4,952	21,190
April	6,546	2,986	6,224	24,456
May	8,564	4,014	8,022	47,670
June	17,291	6,914	18,338	109,997
July	43,595	18,314	53,752	353,411
August	663,200	164,644	987,218	4,620,455
September	282,228,815	3,660,094	45,216,224	98,860,000
October	2,496,822,909	1,058,129,855	6,578,650,939	25,260,208,000
November	400,267,640,302			
(Nov. 11,)				2,500,000,000,000
(Nov. 15,)				4,200,000,000,000
December	496,507,424,772			

9. The inflating effect of the new credit policy of the Reichsbank was clearly demonstrated in the earlier part of 1923. In February 1923 the Reichsbank suddenly refused any further discount of bills for non-commercial purposes. It scrutinized rigidly the nature of the bills offered for rediscount and succeeded to keep the amount of discounted bills very low. At the same time it sold and bought foreign exchange in the open market. The effect of these transactions was that the foreign exchange rate was maintained almost at the same level from February to April, 1923. In April, however, the Reichsbank again changed its restriction policy on account of the ‚Ruhrkampf'. It assumed the financing of the passive resistance proclaimed by the German government against the occupation of the Ruhrdistrict by French troops in the spring 1923. In order to keep up the passive resistance the Reichsbank was forced to open again its doors to industry and commerce for the rediscount of bills and this necessity frustrated every effort to check the final break down

The inability of Germany to meet reparation payments as provided by the Commission led to the occupation of the Ruhr-district by the French army in the Spring of 1923. This invasion of the most productive section of the country rendered it impossible for Germany to make any payments whatsoever. It would exceed by far the scope of this chapter to discuss all the political and economic effects of the invasion. International negotiations were immediately initiated by the German government to obtain the nomination of a commission of economic experts to determine the amount to be paid by Germany and to fix the annuities in accordance with her ability to pay. This proposal was refused by the Allies and it was not until late in the Fall of 1923, that the solution of the reparation problem was turned over to such a committee.

The Reichsbank, during this period, was no longer master of the situation. It could not refuse to discount commercial bills and treasury notes unless it wished to cause the collapse of Germany's economic structure. Furthermore, propaganda in the Rhineland to create an independent state made it a political necessity to support the government and industry with credit. Twice, once in February and later in July, the Reichsbank attempted to check the depreciation of the rate of exchange by intervention in the market. The monetary situation drove rapidly to a climax. Immediate measures for monetary stabilization were necessary if Germany should not collapse.

Many projects were submitted to the government for a stabilization of the currency. The most important ones were those made by Dr. Helfferich and Dr. Schacht. Helfferich's proposal was the creation of an independent bank with a capital of four billion marks. This capital was to be secured by mortgages upon agricultural and industrial properties. Up to the amount of its capital, the bank should issue so called "Rentenbriefe" based upon a money unit of a "Roggen-mark" (rye-mark). These rye-marks were to be declared legal tender and the government should determine the

---

of the German currency. But it must be emphasized that this discount policy was largely due to political factors, as will be shown later.

10. These data were compiled from the annual report of the Reichsbank for 1923 and from the Statistische Jahrbuch 1923/1924.

ratio in which paper marks could be converted into these units. There was to be no more discounting of treasury debentures by the Reichsbank; a credit of 300 million rye-marks was to be granted to the government to pay off her debts and to dissolve the paper-mark. Dr. Schacht, however, pointed out the great dangers which a currency based upon an agricultural product would have, and furthermore, the impossibility of using such a currency in international trade. He also objected to an entirely independent bank without any relation to the state. His argument, here, was that a central bank ought to be managed from the point of view of the entire community rather than as a mere credit institution.

Dr. Schacht's objections were supported by many bankers and economists and led to various changes in Helfferich's project by the government. His proposal to mortgage industry and agriculture and to discontinue the discounting of treasury notes was adopted. The fundamental alterations were as follows: the independence of the new institution should be only formal. That means, that in practice the credit to commerce and agriculture should be granted by the Reichsbank, which was empowered to borrow a certain amount for this purpose from the new bank. The new currency was not based upon rye but upon gold. Finally, the government did not declare the new currency as legal tender and did not set a ratio for the conversion of the old paper currency into the new money units.

The new Rentenbank was created by enactment of the government on October 15, 1923 and was to be opened on November 15, 1923. On November 12, Dr. Schacht was appointed Federal Commissioner for currency affairs (Reichskommissar für Währungsangelegenheiten). He was authorized to attend all meetings of the federal cabinet with an advisory note. Furthermore, all measures of the federal government which could possibly affect the currency required the approval of the commissioner. Thus, the stabilization of Germany's currency and economy began.

CHAPTER V.

THE ECONOMIC EFFECTS OF INFLATION AND THE STABILIZATION OF THE GERMAN CURRENCY.

The stabilization of the German currency is one of the most interesting episodes in monetary history. Without any foreign assistance the task was accomplished in such a way as to regain the confidence of the population in the new currency and its stability. The new monetary unit became again a store and measure of economic values, and a stable means for the settlement of payments. These functions were fulfilled by the Rentenmark, the new money unit, despite its not having the character of legal tender. But what is of far greater interest to the student of banking and finance is the fact that the stabilization of the German monetary system was accomplished without the aid of precious metals used as a cover for the new notes. Based entirely upon an illiquid reserve, the economic nature of which will be discussed later on in this chapter, the Rentenmark exercised all the functions which are usually attributed to and expected of a gold standard, i. e. the maintenance of an approximately stable value of the monetary unit in relation to the general level of prices and with regard to foreign currencies as expressed in the foreign exchange rate.

The introduction of the Rentenmark as the new monetary unit was officially announced by the government as a preliminary step toward the final re-establishment of the gold standard in Germany. The amazing success of the Rentenmark as a stable monetary unit without the cover of gold to secure its value, has caused many economists to regard this experiment as a perfect proof of the validity of new monetary theories. Especially in Germany where the theory of Georg Friedrich Knapp[1] exerted a very strong influence upon economists, the opinion prevails that no modern monetary system need be based upon a gold reserve in order to make secure its stability. According to these theories a gold reserve is an economic waste in modern society where industrialization, economic development, and general education render superfluous the maintenance of a reserve of precious metals as security for the notes in circulation. The policy of note issue and the regulation of the discount rate ought not to be managed with regard to a gold reserve but must be governed by economic necessity. It must be left to the discretion of the central bank to regulate its note issue in such a way as to prevent a depreciation of the monetary unit due to an excessive issue of notes. The maintenance of a non-interest bearing gold reserve is an economic loss, which was especially great in the case of Germany where the lack of capital was so pronounced. We shall have occasion to discuss these various theories in more detail in a later chapter in connection with the Dawes Plan and the re-organization of the Reichsbank. It is necessary, however, to call to the attention of the reader those functions of the new Rentenmark which were the cause of an ardent discussion and controversy between German economists.

But before discussing the introduction of the Renten-mark and its functions as a stable monetary unit, it is necessary to analyze first the economic and psychological background of the stabilization of the German currency. Only in this way is it possible to understand the amazingly rapid success of the new monetary unit, that surprised even its originators as well as the German government, which had announced the new currency as only a preliminary step toward the final re-establishment of the gold standard.

It will be recalled that the continuous depreciation of the German currency materially influenced price calculations of

1. In his book 'Die Staatliche Theorie des Geldes' published in 1905 Knapp advances the theory that money derives its value solely from the authority of the State which vests the money unit with the function of legal tender. In a modern society, according to Knapp, bank notes are generally accepted not because they are covered to a certain percentage by gold or silver, but because the State enforces their function as legal tender.

industry and trade. As pointed out previously, these social mis-calculations were partly due to the government's regulation of rent and the abnormally low level of wages. Under normal conditions rent and interest on long term obligations represent a very sub-stantial part in the total cost of an enterprise. The government's regulation of rent during the years following the war fixed its rate at such a low level as to render it an almost negligible item in the cost of production as well as in the overhead expenses of a com-mercial enterprise. Moreover, enterprises which owned their own property and buildings were in a position to redeem their mortgages and long term obligations with a fraction of the purchasing power which the debt had represented at the time of its contraction.[2] Partly as a result of the very low cost of rent and lack of debts the entrepreneur was able to fix his prices far below the level which would still have been attractive internationally.

The effect of the currency inflation upon debtor and creditor relations in the case of long term obligations has often been discuss-ed together with the problem of reparation payments. In particuliar, the complete depreciation of government debts incurred during the Great War has been considered a very strong argument in favor of high reparation payments, when one considers the cancellation of the German internal debt as compared to the existing debts of the Allied governments. The fallacy of this argument can be shown easily. From a social point of view there had been an internal war debt of the whole German community up to an amount of about 100 billion marks. This amount was claimed by members of the same community. One must bear in mind that the State is but a symbol of all its individuals composing one entity. A government debt is therefore nothing but a debt of the entire nation to a part of the whole population. If this internal debt is cancelled the nation as

---

2. The entire depreciation of the mortgage debts as a result of the economically erroneous court decisions, mentioned in the preceding chapter, caused, in turn, the government to fix rent at such a low level as to leave to the owner of real estate, after a deduction of the necessary expenses for taxes, power, etc., an amount just sufficient to maintain the general structural con-ditions of the property. The government went even so far as to authorize tenants to demand from the landlord a monthly report about the expenditures defrayed with the receipts from rent.

a whole does not gain by it. Although it is now freed of a debt of 100 billion marks there has occurred simultaneously a cancellation of the claims of an equal total of 100 billion marks. Thus, it is obvious that Germany as a whole did not benefit by the depreciation of the debt. Her productivity was not enhanced and the general status of the country remained the same.

In the case of industrial and agricultural debts as well as all other private debts the situation is different from a social point of view. Here, the decrease in the claims of owners of bonds or mortgages did not result during the inflation in a similar increase in the fortune of the former debtor, but it resulted in lower prices for commodities. It was a gift to the buyer of the products in the market. The producer, manufacturer, and business man, who did not have to take into consideration the rent for the building or the interest payment on depreciated debts in estimating their prices, were in a position to sell their goods more cheaply by these saved payments and still have the same rate of profit on their products. And this is what generally occured. In so far as these products were then sold to foreigners they resulted in an actual loss of social substance.

Another factor which also rendered possible the low level of prices was the low level of wages. Wages are the price paid to the laborer for his services.[3] In modern industrialized countries with a stable monetary system they are continuously above the bare minimum of subsistence. Powerful l abor organizations, better general education, legal regulations and provisions protecting the interest of the laboring class defy the theory of the 'iron law of wages'. They exercise continuously a very strong influence in the direction of securing a more or less high standard of living for the laborer. But in periods of currency depreciation, wages do not increase in the same proportion as the internal value of the monetary unit diminishes. Wages are always fixed on the basis of the former cost of living and cannot therefore anticipate future declines in the value of the money unit.

---

3. The terms wage-earner and laborer include, in this discussion, all those individuals who do not derive their income from investments either in form of bonds and mortgages or in form of investments in business enterprises.

This discrepancy between nominally increasing wages and actually decreasing purchasing power assumed very drastic dimensions in Germany owing to the prolonged period of currency depreciation. By summer, 1923, this discrepancy had become so considerable that the purchasing power of the payments received by the laboring class bordered on the verge of the minimum of existence. The almost geometrically declining value of the mark rendered an instantaneous adaptation of wages impossible. In spite of the most rigorously conducted control of prices by federal and local authorities and in spite of many special regulations aiming to enforce the sale of goods for the repudiated paper mark, the government during the last few months was no longer able to carry out these policies.

The real ill-effect of the German currency depreciation is to be found in its influence upon the economic structure of Germany. This effect may be discussed under two heads. The first is the influence upon consumption and savings. Under a stable monetary system a part of the annual social income is saved for future consuption. Wage earners and businessmen do not consume the total of their income but save a part of their earnings for future uses. These savings are normally employed, either with the aid of banks or directly, for increased production. By this process social productivity is incessantly expanding, resulting in turn, in increased social income. This normal interrelation between saving and production ceased in Germany in the summer of 1922. By that time the public had lost its confidence in the currency as a store of value, and as a consequence, the saving of funds was considered an economic waste and a certain loss in view of the currency depreciation. Especially after the general introduction of moving indexes in the computation of prices by the business world, distrust of the currency spread all over the country.

From that time on the mark was no longer considered a store of value since its monetary function was merely that of legal tender. And it was only under the very strong pressure of special laws that this function could be enforced. These special laws[4] prohibited the sale of goods to German subjects for foreign currencies, the

---

4. The most important of these special laws (Sondergesetze) were: Gesetz über den Verkehr mit ausländischen Zahlungsmitteln and the Notgesetz

possession of foreign exchange or foreign currencies and the sale or purchase of foreign currencies outside of specially authorized institutions. In view of the fact that the mark no longer functioned as a store of value it is not surprising to find that a general over-estimation of goods ensued. The people endeavored to exchange their money units which they obtained for their services in the market as rapidly as possible for commodities. In consequence the velocity of money in circulation assumed such tremendous dimensions that in November, 1923, when the Rentenmark was introduced the total of Reichsbank notes in circulation represented an amount equivalent to only 400 million gold-marks.[5] This small quantity of bank notes in circulation was sufficient to serve as means of payment in a country where before the Great War six billion gold mark were in circulation.

The longer the inflation lasted the more eager became the competition among the owners of money for the purchase of the goods brought into the market. It was no longer an immediate economic necessity or an economic demand for certain commodities which determined the market demand, but solely the desire to exchange the means of payment for „tangible assets" regardless of their immediate usefulness. It did not matter to the buyer that the 'economic price' was far below his offer, if he took into consideration therisk of entire depreciation of his money in case he would delay his purchases or wait for more favorable offers. It did not matter to the buyer in the market that the price of commodities was substantially enhanced by the many agents who had put themselves between the producer and final consumer. The famous phrase of those days „the flight into tangible assets", indicates more than anything else the existing market conditions. This flight from the mark explains the tremendous velocity of money in circulation toward the end of the inflation.

---

vom 8. Mai 1923, both prohibiting the trading in foreign currencies and the speculation therein. They furthermore prohibited the contraction of sales of commodities against foreign currencies. The Gesetz über Ablieferung von ausländischen Vermögensgegenständen (23. August 1923) required the owner of foreign currencies or securities to surrender those to government agencies against payment of paper mark at the official market rate.

5. Dr. Hjalmar Schacht, Die Stabilisierung der Mark, page 76.

The other ill effect of the inflation, which from a social point is of greater importance than the influence upon consumption, was the great influence of the inflation upon the economic structure of production in Germany. The business man had recognized very early the necessity to save his funds from a total depreciation. Experience had demonstrated too clearly the advisability of investing liquid funds in the fixed capital of his enterprise. Only through such an investment policy was the entrepreneur in a position to prevent a loss of purchasing power. In consequence of this tendency to invest the funds of enterprises in fixed capital the proportion of fixed capital to liquid funds increased in favor of the former. Only the indispensable minimum of money in cash for daily payments was kept with the banks while the remainder was invested in commodities and expansions of the plant. These tendencies were very largely enhanced by the existing market conditions.

The keen competition among buyers to exchange their money in cash or bank deposits against tangible assets rendered a competition among sellers superfluous. It was a one-sided competition in the market, and consequently the price for commodities had to be so high that the existing quantity of goods was just sufficient to satisfy the highest bidding buyers. The domestic demand together with the demand from abroad created a deceptive prosperity. Rationalization of the industrial plants and commercial enterprises was therefore unnecessary. The only aim of the producer was to obtain the means for an expansion of his plants. Cost of construction was of minor importance in view of the credit which he could redeem in a short while with a fraction of the purchasing power that had been given to him in the form of credit. Especially after the Reichsbank had announced its new credit policy in the summer of 1922 a general industrial expansion began. The manufacturer did not consider the high overhead expenses of the large plants which were left partly idle because the relatively high market prices compensated these costs. Moreover the producer was always in a position to obtain additional credit which enabled him to maintain even unproductive plants. During the years 1922 to 1923 there was a period of construction and expansion of industrial enterprises for which there was no immediate need and no economic justification.

During the summer months of 1923 the general situation in Germany rapidly approached a crisis which threatened the very existence of the young Republic. Riots and plunderings were daily occurrences and the discord soon assumed great dimensions. The gravity of the situation can easily be understood by the fact that on September 27th, 1923, the German government declared a state of siege in Germany. Immediate relief had to be provided lest the country should collapse economically and politically. Many projects had been submitted to the government proposing various remedies for the situation and for a stabilization of the currency. Most of these plans, however, were based upon premises which were not realized at that time or which could not be achieved.

The problem of stabilization was twofold. First, a standard had to be found upon which the new currency could be based and which could gain the confidence of the population. Secondly, if such a new monetary system would be introduced how was it possible to secure the necessary credit for the Reich, industry, commerce, and agriculture without endangering the stability of the new currency? It will be recalled that previous attempts to stabilize the German currency had failed due to the urgent demands for credit on the part of the Reich or on the part of the economy.

So far as the basis of stabilization was concerned the difficulties were extremely great. The plan to reestablish the gold standard had to be abandoned because of lack of sufficient funds for this purpose. The supply of gold which the Reichsbank had accumulated during the war and which amounted at the end of 1918 to over two billion marks had almost vanished from the Bank. Large exports of gold in payment for food, repeated interventions of the Bank abroad to prevent a further decrease in the mark rate, and deliveries of gold to the Allies for reparation payments had reduced the total of gold and foreign exchange in the vaults of the Reichsbank to about 400 million marks in October 1923.[6] Although large supplies of foreign currencies had been hoarded by the public it was highly improbable that the population would surrender their stock of foreign currency to the government. The population did not have sufficient confidence in the management of the Reichsbank

---

6. Verwaltungsbericht der Deutschen Reichsbank, 1923 p. 32.

to submit to such a policy. Moreover, the Reich did not wish to risk the small supply of gold and foreign exchange of the Bank in another effort to attempt stabilization with the aid of interventions abroad. On the other hand there was the pressing need for credit by the Reich and the economy which naturally could not have been satisfied if the total reserves of the Reichsbank were only about 400 million gold marks. Under a stabilized monetary system the amount of credit which the Reichsbank could grant was limited by its liquid reserves. Stabilization on the basis of a gold standard or even a gold exchange standard[7] was therefore impossible.

Yet the general psychology of the German population was strongly favorable to a new experiment which would appeal to the public for securing the stability of the currency, though the new monetary unit was not based upon gold. Since 1922 long term obligations of agricultural associations based upon rye or wheat as the unit of value had always found a very open market. Emergency notes issued by the German Railways and Gold Loan notes issued by the German government which were denominated in gold mark and redeemable at maturity at a rate of 4.20 mark for one dollar had always been accepted eagerly by the population in exchange for their paper money at the official rate of paper marks for one dollar.

It is therefore obvious that the most powerful weapon in the process of stabilization was the confidence of the population in a new currency not based upon gold and nevertheless appealing to the people as a liquid and stable monetary system. If this confidence of the population in the new currency could be gained then it was possible to reduce the velocity of money in circulation. People would again look upon the money unit as a store and measure of value and would cease their „flight into tangible assets". A part of the social income would again be saved and put at the disposition of productive enterprises. Simultaneously with the reduction in the velocity of money in circulation the quantity of money outstanding would become insufficient to meet

---

7. A „gold exchange standard" is a monetary system whereby the circulating means of payment are not convertible but whereby the stable relation between this currency and gold standard systems is maintained by the central bank through buying and selling foreign exchange bills in the open market so as to maintain a fixed ratio.

the demand for means of payment. If the money unit should no longer change hands many times a day, it was obvious that the same number of transactions could only be carried on at the same price level if an additional quantity of notes were put into circulation. In this way it would then be possible to divert, in form of credit, so much new purchasing power into the market as was necessary to maintain the stable price level.

It is undoubtedly to the credit of Helfferich that he was one of the first to clearly recognize this last means as a way to stabilize the German currency. His scheme for the Rentenmark was based entirely upon the psychology of the population and their confidence was the cornerstone in the new currency. His plan called for an independent Rentenbank, free of any influence by the Reich whatsoever. This proposal for the establishment of a Bank of Issue whose management was independent of the federal government is the more noteworthy, since Helfferich represents one of the greatest advocates of the theories of G. F. Knapp. His scheme for the Rentenbank, therefore, clearly demonstrates the fundamental change in central banking theory which had been brought about by the Great War in Germany. Although the authority of the State behind the central bank is still considered essential for its functions in the community, it is clearly recognized that the credit which the Bank of Issue enjoys and the frictionless circulation of its notes as well as their value are exclusively the result of the Bank's management and policy. The theory that bank notes derive their value from their legal function alone has been disproved by actual experience.

This change in concept was generally recognized in Germany by the end of 1923, as was indicated by the court decisions reversing their former opinion that „a mark always equals a mark". It was apparent to Helfferich that the Rentenbank could only succeed if the public believed in its legal and actual independence of the Reich. And it was due to the failure of the Reichsbank after the passage of the Autonomy Act of 1922 of pursue an independent discount policy that a new Bank of Issue was proposed. The Reichsbank no longer commanded the confidence of the public which was indispensable to the success of the currency stabilization. The Reich realized the justification of Helfferich's argument and empowered, therefore, the management of the Rentenbank to pursue a policy in accordance with its own discretion. It renounced any influence upon the management of the Rentenbank. After various changes in the project of Helfferich, which had been advocated by Dr. Schacht and sustained by the German government, the German Rentenbank was created by a special Decree of October 15th, 1923.[8] The structure of this new institution is so exceptional as compared with that of any other bank of issue as to merit a detailed discussion.

THE RENTENBANK-DECREE. The capital of the Rentenbank was limited to 3200 million rentenmark and was raised through a compulsory indebenture placed upon agriculture, industry, trade and commerce, which included the banks. Half of the capital was raised by mortgages levied upon agricultural land up to four per cent of its prewar value, which was assessed at forty billion marks. For the remainder industry, trade, and commerce including the banks were indebted, the proportion of each enterprise was determined according to its pre-war value, the total value of the possessions of these three classes being also assessed at forty billion marks. In the last case a mortgage was only imposed in so far as the particular enterprise owned real estate. If this was not the case, it had to surrender to the Rentenbank special indebenture bonds up to the amount apportioned to it. Mortgages and bonds were based upon the Rentenmark which carried a fixed ratio to the United States dollar, one Rentenmark being equal to 10/42 of a dollar.

These mortgages and bonds formed the security for the new currency to be issued. The Rentenbank was authorized to issue an amount of Rentenmarks equal to the total of Rentenbriefe in its reserves. The Rentenbriefe yielded five per cent interest and could only be sold in exchange for rentenmarks. This provision was thought necessary in order to prevent a depreciation of the rentenmark. It was apparent that an interest rate of five per cent was not attractive at a time when the rate for loans, based upon the rate of foreign exchange, was between 10 and 20 per cent p. a. Should,

---

8. Verordnung über die Errichtung der Deutschen Rentenbank vom 15. Oktober 1923.

however, a depreciation of the rentenmark take place, it was thought that these rentenbriefe based upon gold would be an attractive investment. Such purchases would then reduce the total of rentenmark in circulation and automatically increase their value. The unexpectedly rapid transition to the gold mark and the great success of the rentenmark rendered an issue of Rentenbriefe superfluous.

These provisions concerning the reserve for the new currency were in clear opposition to all central bank theories and carried a great resemblance to the theory of John Law and to the assignat currency of the French Revolution,[9] two monetary systems similar in principle to the Rentenmark which had so disastrously failed in practice. The success of the Rentenmark is therefore the more surprising as the general financial situation of the Reich resembled closely those prevailing at the time when the above mentioned two currency systems had been introduced. A brief analysis of the economic dangers of a currency based upon property as the reserve for the issue of notes will contribute to a better appreciation of the great importance attached by German economists to the rentenmark experiment.

Central banks and Banks of issue have in practice and theory always adhered to the principle of a convertible metallic cover for their notes in circulation. The general acceptance of this theory of a convertible monetary system as a stable standard of value is easily explained by the nature of such a standard. If notes are issued against a legally required gold reserve and if these notes are legally convertible into gold, the value of the money unit is intimately related to the international value of gold as a money unit. Gold assumes then the character of a commodity which is shipped between countries to those places where more purchasing power is represented by a unit of weight of gold. The great scarcity of gold and its high value in connection with its relatively light weight render it profitable to ship gold when its purchasing power becomes variable between two countries. Although in reality movements of

9. Both these monetary systems were based upon real estate as a security for the notes in circulation. John Law founded, 1716, the Banque Generale which failed however a few years later due to excessive issue of notes based upon this illiquid reserve.

the precious metal are arrested, when stimulated, by changes in the discount rate and credit policy of the central bank in that particular country where gold has become a commodity profitable for export or import, the fact remains nevertheless that gold is the basic force underlying those policies which aim to bring about a readjustment of the international equilibrium. Gold is a highly liquid reserve with universal acceptability which automatically and immediately reacts upon changes in its valuation in various markets. This instantaneous reaction of the precious metal and the convertibility of the bank notes in circulation into gold always affects the reserve of the central bank in case of fluctuations in the international equilibrium, which is expressed in respective changes in the foreign exchange rate. An increase or decrease in the foreign exchange rate above or below the specie point is therefore a clear indication for the central bank to safeguard against a drainage or superabundance of gold in its reserves. The maintenance of a legally required minimum of gold and the desire on the part of the bank of issue to avoid the maintenance of too large gold reserves always induce the central bank to pursue a discount policy which avoids such extreme conditions in its portfolio.

The Rentenmark, however, lacked all these advantages of a gold standard. It was based entirely upon a reserve which was internationally illiquid. The Rentenmark derived its international value only from its purchasing power within Germany. Fluctuations in its internal value, therefore, did not set in motion any changes in the reserves of the Rentenbank but were expressed by a depreciation in foreign exchange value. Hence, the management of the Rentenbank could not regulate its issue of notes with regard to its reserve ratio as had been the policy of the Reichsbank in pre-war periods. The value of the Rentenmark depended entirely upon the policy of the Bank, and, unlike the gold standard, it bore no direct relation to other currencies based upon the gold standard.

The management of the Rentenbank assumed a great responsibility in regulating the issue of notes. Its only aid in determining its issue policy was a strict adherence to the quantity theory of money. Due to the fact that the rentenmark, by its very nature, was only a domestic currency and did not react to fluctuations in its value in the same way that a gold standard does, the only indication of an excessive note issue was the domestic price level and the foreign exchange quotation. Of these two indexes the foreign exchange rate was of far greater importance and superiority. The difficulty in relying solely upon the internal price level was due to the fact that this level does not afford any comparison between the prices in the various countries which are apt to influence the external value of a currency.

The difficulties which the management encountered in maintaining its policy were further enhanced by two provisions in the Rentenmark Decree. First, the Rentenmark was not granted the character of legal tender, although „attempts to discredit the rentenmark in public were prohibited". The acceptance of the rentenmark as a means of payment depended, therefore, entirely upon the confidence which it commanded from the population. Secondly, the Decree did not set any fixed rate at which the Rentenmark should be exchanged for the papermarks in circulation. In only provided that four Rentenmarks and twenty Pfennig should exchange for one United States dollar. But as the rate of papermarks to the dollar was not stable but increased in favor of the dollar there was no direct final rate at which stabilization between papermark, rentenmark, and dollar could be executed. Thus, the twofold task of gaining the confidence of the population and simultaneously of determining the final rate of stabilization between the papermark and the dollar was left entirely to the discretion of the management of the Rentenbank.

The Rentenbank Decree provided that the Bank should carry on its business exclusively with the Reich so far as the credit of the latter was concerned and that the credits to agriculture and business enterprises should be transacted through the Reichsbank and the four private banks of note issue. The latter obtained for further distribution ten per cent of the total Rentenmark credits. These provisions were officially passed in view of the very far spread branch system of the Reichsbank and in order to secure a centralized credit policy. However, the assumption does not seen unwarranted that this provision was passed in order to render possible a later transfusion between Rentenbank and Reichsbank so that the Reichsbank might again become the central bank of Germany.

So far as the credit policy of the new institution was concerned, the Rentenbank-Decree provided that the Rentenbank should issue at the outset notes only up to a total of 2400 million rentenmarks. Half of this amount, 1200 millions, was to be granted to the Reich as a credit during the period 1923 to 1925 in order to enable the federal government to balance the budget. Of these 1200 millions, 300 millions[10] represented a non-interest bearing loan with which the Reich was to redeem its debt at the Reichsbank; for the remaining 900 millions the interest rate was six per cent. The remaining 1200 millions were to be granted to the German economy as a credit through the Reichsbank. This was necessary, because as had been pointed out the long inflation had resulted in a great lack of circulating capital. In view of the great lack of funds among agriculturists 800 millions of the total of 1200 millions was to be granted as credit to the farming class. The rentenmark was put into general circulation in three different ways. First, the Reich used the rentenmark-credit for the payment of salaries and of deliveries in kind to the Reich. Secondly the Reichsbank offered the public an exchange of rentenmark against papermark at the official rate of exchange for the dollar. Thirdly, the Reichsbank granted rentenmark credit and issued rentenmark notes.

The administration of the Rentenbank was executed by the four following bodies: the managing board, the supervisory council, the administrative council, the general assembly. The managing board was composed of two members who were selected by the administrative council and receiv ed their instructions from the same. The supervisory council (Aufsichtsrat) consisted of 21 members, who were elected from the various professions that were indebted for the Rentenbank. Each of these classes delegated to the supervisory council as many representatives as its share in the total capital of the bank amounted to. The president of the Rentenbank was simultaneously the president of the supervisory council. The administrative council (Verwaltungsrat) was composed of 10

10. The further decline of the German currency reduced the debt of the Reich to the Reichsbank for discounted treasury notes to only 200 millions, so that the proportion of the interest-bearing to the non-interest bearing loans became 10 : 2.

members who were selected from the supervisory council, whose president was also president of the administrative council, which issued the general orders and detailed regulations to the managing board. Furthermore, the administrative council had the duty of supervising the distribution of the rentenmark credit by the Reichsbank among the various professions in accordance with their needs and in accordance with their share in the capital of the bank. The general assembly was the meeting of all those who were indebted for the capital of the Rentenbank. Each 10 million rentenmark debt claimed one vote in the election of the officers.

From the foregoing discussion of the nature of the Rentenmark and the structure of the Rentenbank it is apparent that the policy of the new Bank of Issue could only succeed if carried on along the following lines: First, the main task of the Rentenbank was to limit its credit to such an amount as was just sufficient to render possible the continuance of the country's production without increasing prices. At the same time the management had to take into account in its credit policy the various effects of the inflation upon the economic structure of Germany. The limitation of credit had to be accompanied by a careful direction of credit into the channels most important from a social point of view.

One of the most pressing problems of the German economy was agricultural credit, for which the Decree had provided a total of 800 million Rentenmarks. Unlike industry and commerce which had been able to maintain a certain quantity of liquid assets in form of readily saleable commodities or foreign currencies, the farming class of Germany had no liquid capital reserves. The money which the agriculturist had received from his products during the inflation had mostly been immobilized in its entire extent. A stabilization of the currency with its ensuing scarcity of funds and limited credit resources was therefore apt to affect the farmer much more gravely than any other group in Germany. The necessity of making possible provisions for spring orders by the farmers rendered it imperative to the Rentenbank to grant substantial amounts of credit to agriculturists.

At the same time there was to be expected a very great demand for credit on the part of industry and commerce. The nature of this demand was the inevitable result of a stabilization of a depreciated currency. At the beginning of the process of stabilization the demand for credit was substantially a continuance of the long exercised practice of one part of the enterprises to depend entirely upon bank credit for their liquid capital requirements without reducing their productive capacity to such an extent as would be in harmony with the market demand and their capital resources. It will be recalled that the credit policy of the Reichsbank had been responsible for an over expansion of industrial and commercial enterprises which depended for their existence largely upon bank credit. The long inflation period and the continuous depreciation of the markwhich had enabled the producer to redeem his bank obligations with a fraction of what he had obtained, had hampered German industry to the extent that its methods of production were inferior to those of industries in other countries. These economic mistakes became apparent with the return of a stable measure of value in the Rentenmark. Germany's production was relatively too expensive. The maintenance of large plants, whose production exceeded the demand in the market and increased the cost of production by the cost of their maintenance, the many intermediaries between the producer and the final consumer, the lack of liquid funds and the decreased purchasing power per head of the population — all these facts tended naturally to increase prices above their normal level.

It is therefore obvious that the stabilization of the German currency tended to bring on an economic crisis. Such a crisis is indispensable for the readjustment of the economic structure. Under a stable monetary system, rent and wages again become substantial items in the cost sheet of an enterprise. Banks are no longer so liberal in their credit policy as they used to be during the inflation when they were in a position to resort continuously to the Reichsbank which in case of lack of funds simply printed new notes which were then put into circulation. These credit policies cease under a stable monetary system. The Bank of Issue is legally limited in its power to issue notes and consequently in its credit policy. Only the best equipped and well managed enterprises have a chance to survive the deadly struggle for existence which accompanies the stabilization of an inflated currency. The owner of money no longer endeavours to exchange his cash reserves for 'tangible assets' regardless of his immediate need, but the individual commences again to save a part of his income for future consumption. The great overhead expenses of many enterprises which invest their liquid funds in fixed capital for which there is no demand (plants, machines, etc.) and the many intermediaries between producer and final consumer increase the price level to such a height that the existing demand is insufficient to absorb the forthcoming supply of goods.

The effect of the discrepancy between demand and supply in the market is a credit crisis. Retailers find themselves unable to dispose of their commodities owing to the high level of prices and to diminished demand. They are not in a position to meet their obligation toward the producer. As a consequence of the interruption in the circulation of goods a credit crisis ensues. Unable to continue their production at prices which the existing demand is willing to pay but which do not leave the normal rate of profit, the producer is compelled to cease further production. The stability of a currency can only be maintained if the normal relation between production and consumption is stabilized: that is if the cost of production of a unit conforms to the price which the existing demand can pay for it. A discrepancy between demand and supply must therefore be readjusted and the deflation policy of the central bank which aims to bring about this reorganization renders a credit crisis inevitable.

In view of the general conditions prevailing at that time in Germany, it is easily understood why the position of Dr. Schacht as Currency Commissioner was extremely difficult. First of all, Dr. Schacht had to regain the confidence of the German economy by limiting the quantity of means of payment in circulation, while at the same time, there was the strong demand for credit from industry and agriculturalists. A too rigid restriction of credit carried in itself the danger that before the economic conditions would be stabilized industry and the farming class would collapse on account of lack of capital.

On the other hand a liberal credit policy threatened the very stability of the new currency.

The great difficulties of the Reichsbank in pursuing its credit policy were enhanced by the inability of the German credit institutions[11] to satisfy by their own means a substantial part of the demand for credit. Their capital and resources had been mater‑ially impaired during the inflation and to a very great extent they depended after the stabilization upon the Reichsbank, for their credit policy. The latter became therefore the most important direct money lender in the German money market and consequently exercised an influence therein only paralleled by its position in the early eigthies, when it was the only credit recourse in Germany of considerably importance. This situation required the utmost energy and skill on the part of Dr. Schacht and it is to his credit that he showed himself master of this difficult situation.

THE REICHSBANK POLICY IN THE WINTER 1923/24. Owing to technical difficulties the printing of the new rentenmarks had been delayed. Nevertheless to calm the public the government wanted, the new Rentenbank to begin its activities at the fixed date, and on November 15, 1923, the bank began its activity. A mixture of hope and distrust was the attitude of the population towards this new institution. When the Rentenbank opened, there were no more than 70 million rentenmarks ready for issue, and until the end of November only 700 millions had been printed and could be put into circulation. The chief part of this amount was given to the government as credit, while the rest was offered to the public in exchange for the papermark at the official rate of foreign exchange. This rate was at that time far below that prevailing in foreign markets. In accordance with the Reichsbankdirectoreate, Dr. Schacht there-fore raised the rate considerably during the third week of November. On November 15, 1923 the rate for the dollar was raised to 1260 bil-lions, on November 15th to 2520 billions and finally on November 22nd

---

11. The diminuition of the capital and resources of the German credit institutions is reflected in the following table:

	1913 (Monthly Average)	December 1923:
Deposits in Savings Banks:	19.7 billion marks	0.1 billion marks
Deposits in Commercial Banks:	13.4 billion marks	2.7 billion marks
Deposits in Cooperative Banks:		
Deposits in Associations Banks:	4.6 billion marks	0.4 billion marks
Deposits in Insurance Co. Banks:	6.3 billion marks	1.2 billion marks

These figures are mentioned by Dr. Schacht in his book „Die Stabilisierung der Mark" p. 144.

to 4200 billions for one dollar. But in spite of this approach to the world market rate, the Reichsbank was not able to sell more than one per cent of the amount of foreign exchange demanded in the market. The rapid increase in the official rate of foreign exchange deepened the pessimistic attitude of the population towards the rentenmark.

An important change in the situation was introduced by the death of Havenstein on November 19, 1923, who was then president of the Reichsbank. Dr. Schacht was elected to this position and thus united the positions of Currency Commissioner, President of the Rentenbank and President of the Reichsbank in one person. Consequently, a much more effective policy could be pursued. Dr. Schacht realized very well the necessity of supplying industry and agriculture with credit. Although the granting of credit to the farming class is against every principle of central banking, the peculiar conditions in Germany warranted such a policy.

But another factor has to be mentioned which formed a serious obstacle to any stabilization policy, namely, the abuses of the emergency notes.[12]

In the summer of 1923, it became customary for the issuers of emergency notes to deposit these at a branch of the Reichsbank and to obtain credit for an equivalent amount which they then cashed in at another branch of the Reichsbank. Thus, they received in exchange for their own notes Reichsbank notes which had a much larger acceptability than emergency notes. Political and economic considerations had always induced the management of the Reichs-

---

12. Originally the right to issue emergency notes had been granted by the Reich to certain public bodies in order to remedy the great scarcity of notes of small denominations due to the rapidly depreciating currency. These rights of issue were granted under the provision that the issuing institution should deposit an equal amount of Reichsbank notes with the latter. During the summer of 1923 these provisions concerning the deposits had been largely neglected in the occupied territory and many industrial and commercial enterprises considered the issuance of emergency notes as a welcome means to procure additional funds without any special costs. Their issue of emergency notes was based entirely upon the assumption that the currency would further depreciate so that they would actually never be called upon to convert their issus.

bank not to refuse the acceptance of these notes, especially in the Rheinland. Such abuses threatened the effectiveness of any credit limiting policy of Schacht. Schacht therefore required the Reichsbank directorate to repudiate any further deposits of emergency notes. Furthermore, the depositors of emergency notes who had cashed in their credits were required to redeem their emergency notes. These orders of the Currency Commissioner led to ardent attacks on the Commissioner and the Rhineland industry went even so far as to threaten the erection of an independent Bank of Issue in the Rhineland if the credit calamity was not remedied in a short time by the establishment of a Bank of Issue based upon a gold standard.

It was only through a very rigid adherence to the principle of credit restriction that Dr. Schacht was able to maintain the official rate of the dollar at a ratio of 4.20 Rentenmark for one dollar. At this rate the Reichsbank, however, sold only a fraction of the foreign exchange demanded in the market. In the occupied territory where the interventions of the Reichsbank could not exercise any such influence upon the formation of the foreign exchange rate, speculation soon had driven the dollar far above the official rate established at Berlin. The following figures reflect the movements of the dollar rate in Cologne, which was at that time occupied by the French troops and where the market established its rates independently of the Reichsbank:

DOLLAR RATE AT THE BOURSE OF COLOGNE IN NOVEMBER—DECEMBER 1923[13]

(Official Rate At Bourse Of Berlin One Dollar — 4.20 Rentenmark)

November	13th	3.90	November	24th	10.25
„	14th	6.85	„	26th	11.00
„	15th	5.85	„	27th	10.20
„	16th	6.50	„	28th	9.40
„	17th	6.70	„	29th	7.80
„	19th	9.85	„	30th	7.80
„	20th	11.70	December	6th	4.90
„	22nd	10.20	„	10th	4.20
„	23rd	10.50			

13. Dr. Schacht „Die Stabilisierung der Mark" pp. 80, 81.

The above figures clearly indicate the pessimistic attitude in the occupied Rhine district toward the policy of Dr. Schacht. Owing to very large short term sales of Rentenmarks by speculators at the rates given in the table the dollar increased continuously until November 27th. At that time the credit restriction of the Rentenbank under the management of Dr. Schacht made itself felt. The speculation lacked the funds to meet their obligations. Finding themselves without the necessary credit of the Rentenbank to meet their short term sale engagements, they were forced to sell foreign exchange to the Reichsbank in order to obtain the necessary funds. The dollar rate soon decreased to the official rate of Berlin and Dr. Schacht had won his first victory over speculative attempts to discredit the Rentenmark. This firm attitude of the Rentenbank and Reichsbank had also the effect that the stock of foreign exchange in the portfolio of the Reichsbank increased by 200 million marks. Undoubtedly the strict adherence of Dr. Schacht to a plan which he deemed necessary, regardless of political and economic pressure, deserve highest credit. It was this firm unchanging policy of Dr. Schacht which helped him to gain the confidence of the public in the new currency. And it was not long before Dr. Schacht was again called upon to resist strong pressure for an extension of credit. This time it was the federal government which had experienced a financial calamity. Although it had been thought sufficient by the originators of the Rentenbank to grant the Reich a credit of 1200 millions for the balancing of its budget during the two following years, the actual need of the government had been underestimated. Already at the beginning of December 1923, the Reich had disposed of the total credit allotted to it and there was still a lack of means to defray the expenses for the remainder of the current fiscal year. Dr. Luther who was then Minister of Finance asked Dr. Schacht for further credit. But Dr. Schacht flatly refused to grant any further amount and Dr. Luther was forced to carry the budget over to the new year 1924 when the revenues began to stream in again. How critical the situation for the Reich was is best reflected by the fact that on December 17, 1923 the Reich could only pay to its employees half of their salaries in cash.

With the gradual growth of public confidence in the Rentenmark the first signs of the approaching credit crisis could be noticed.

Unemployment increased rapidly after October 1923. Furthermore, wholesale prices began to fall in December of the same
year,[14] due to the diminished demand in the market. In general the
economic conditions in Germany during the few months subsequent
to the introduction of the Rentenmark reflected a situation which
comformed to the above analysis of a stabilization crisis. The lack
of capital and the resulting high money rates are well reflected in
the following table:[15]

MONEY RATES IN THE BOURSE AT FRANKFORT a. M.
(weekly averages in per cent per annum)

	Daily Money:	14 Days Loans:	Monthly Loans:
November 1923, 3rd week	3230	4238	4740
November 1923, 4th week	765	3276	3636
December 1923, 1st week	578	1248	1512
December 1923, 2nd week	360	641	695
December 1923, 3rd week	328	391	522
December 1923, 4th week	360	459	488
January 1924, 1st week	81	255	300
January 1924, 2nd week	56	159	198
January 1924, 3rd week	36	75	149
January 1924, 4th week	15	36	36

14. WHOLESALE PRICES: (1913 — 100)			UNEMPLOYMENT: October 1923		
November	6th 1923,	129	November	1923	954.664
November	13th 1923,	132.8	December	1923	1.473.688
November	20th 1923,	141.3	January	1924	1.533.495
November	27th 1923,	133.7	February	1924	1.439.780
December	4th 1923,	127.4	March	1924	1.167.785
December	11th 1923,	124.5			
December	18th 1923,	120.6			
December	27th 1923,	122.4			
January	2nd 1924,	119.7			
January	11th 1924,	115.7			

The total of unemployment during this period and the index of wholesale
prices are compiled from the Statistische Jahrbuch 1924, pp. 265 and 299.

15. Die Wirtschaftskurve, 1924, Heft 1 pp. 75 u. 155.

The exorbitantly high rates during November and December 1923 were partly due to a predominance of speculative distrust in the Rentenmark as well as to the fact that it contained a relatively high price for risk, as is reflected by the rates in January 1924.

On account of the insufficient quantity of Rentenmark notes which were at the disposal of the Rentenbank after its opening on November 15, 1923, the Reichsbank prolonged its outstanding credits and even granted additional credit, thereby increasing the total of Reichsbank notes in circulation. In view of the fact that the greatly reduced velocity of money in circulation rendered necessary the issuance of a larger quantity of notes for the maintenance of a stable level of prices, the Reichsbank policy was economically justified. As soon as the new Rentenmark notes had been printed and were gradually issued in the form of credit, the Reichsbank should have reduced its outstanding credits in the same proportion so as to avoid an inflation of prices. Due to various factors which will be discussed in the next chapter, the Reichsbank failed to recognize the inflationary character of its credit policy. The economic situation in Germany rapidly approached a new crisis and threatened the stability of the currency. Schacht, who had been prevented by reasons to be discussed hereafter, from observing this development closely enough, found himself confronted by circumstances which required immediate measures. Other economic considerations had to be sacrificed to the primary purpose of maintaining the currency stable and undisturbed. Thus, on April 5th, 1924, Dr. Schacht issued the order to all Reichsbank branches that beginning from April 7, credit should be granted only up to the same amount as had been granted on this day.

Before discussing the credit policy of the Reichsbank during the spring of 1924 in its theoretical and economical aspects, it is deemed necessary to briefly discuss various political events and the part Dr. Schacht played in them. It was during this period that an important political event occurred which afterwards was to become the cornerstone of the reconstruction of Germany's economy; namely, the organization of the Dawes Committee and its subsequent report to the Reparation Commission.

The introduction of the rentenmark had always been considered by Dr. Schacht as an intermediary step towards the re-establishment of the gold standard and of a real gold note bank. As soon as circumstances permitted, Schacht went to London with this in mind at the end of December 1923. In London he had various conferences with Mr. Montagu Norman, the governor of the Bank of England, and several çity bankers to whome he explained the situation in Germany asking for their co-operation in the foundation of a gold note bank. He succeeded in obtaining the pledge of the Bank of England and of the leading city bankers to assist the new institution. On his return trip to Germany, Dr. Schacht also conferred with Mr. Vissering, the President of the Bank of Amsterdam, who also promised his co-operation in the new bank. But before Dr. Schacht had any opportunity to materialize his projects the Dawes Committee had begun its activities and on January 19, 1924, Dr. Schacht was officially invited by the Committee to explain his further plans. The paramount importance which the Dawes Committee has achieved in re-establishing order in Germany and in Europe warrants a brief discussion of the origin and task of this Committee, although its solution will be dealt with in a later chapter.

THE DAWES COMMITTEE.[16] The treaty of Versailles provided the nomination of a Reparation Commission whose task it was to fix by May first, 1921 the total amount of damages to be paid for by Germany and to notify the German Government of its results. The Commission was concurrently to draw up a Schedule of Payments prescribing the time and manner for securing and discharing the entire obligation within a period of thirty years from May 1921. After an investigation of Germany's resources and capacity and after hearing representatives, the Commission was authorized to modify the Schedule of Payments. It could not, how-

---

16. An excellent treatise discussing the Reparation problem from the Treaty of Versailles to the Dawes Committee is given in the book of Dr. Bergmann „The History of Reparations".

ever, cancel any payment except with the specific approval of the several Governments represented upon the Commission.

Originally it was provided that this Commission was to be composed of five members of whom one each was to be delegated by the following five nations: United States, Great Britain, France, Belgium, and Italy. Owing to a delay in the ratification of the Peace Treaty by America, the Reparation Commission was constituted without an official representative of the United States. The U. S. had, however, two „unofficial observers" in the Commission. Undoubtedly, the absence of the United States who was the least prejudiced of the Allied Powers, materially affected the relative importance of the votes. Through the absence of American, France obtained the chairmanship, a fact which led to a very sharp antagonism between the Reparation Commission and the German Government in all economic controversies. Prejudices on both sides prevented economic considerations from being given their proper weight. For almost four years the reparation problem was in the main a political issue and strongly affected by militaristic forces on one side and by political opposition on the other side.

With the beginning of the Ruhr occupation, Germany had ceased to make any further payments, claiming the occupation was a violation of the Treaty of Versailles. On October 30, 1923 the British government suggested that the economic capacity of Germany to pay reparations should be examined by experts, this means being the only way to establish order in Europe. Poincare, entrenching himself behind certain legal provisions of the Treaty ardently opposed any investigation concerning Germany's payments beyond the year 1930. Under such limitations, the American Government refused the co-operation of her experts. A conference without the United States, however, would have been quite futile. Thus in November 1923 the entire plan seemed to be wrecked.

At this critical juncture the Reparation Commission decided to take the matter up, independent of any political considerations. An opportunity offered itself through an application of the German Government on October 24, for an investigation of her economic resources and her ability to pay. The Reparation Commission granted this application and on November 30, 1923, the Commission resolved .to appoint two Committees of Experts, one of which was to consider the means to stabilize the German budget and to investigate the measures to be taken to stabilize the German currency.[17] The scope of these tasks was within the competence of the Commission. Poincaré approved the above resolution and after the consent of the United States Government had been obtained, the plan was soon put into effect.

The First Committee of Experts, later on called the Dawes Committee, met on January 14, 1924, in Paris and consisted of the following members: Messrs. Dawes (Chairman) and Young, United States; Kindsley and Stamp, Great Britain; Parmentier and Allix, France; Pirelli and Flora, Italy; Franqui and Hotard, Belgium. Immediately after the Dawes Committee had me tin Paris it began its activities. For the first time since the Treaty of Versailles the reparation problem was subject to consideration by internationally known financial authorities who were not influenced in their work by political prejudice. Politically independent experts had gathered to consider the means to be taken to re-establish order in Europe.

After the Committee had learned that Dr. Schacht, independently of their work endeavored to organize a new bank of issue, the Committee invited Dr. Schacht to Paris to explain from his point of view the conditions existant in Germany and his plans about the new bank. Schacht went to Paris and frankly told the Committee about the desperate financial state in Germany and gave a description of his plan to establish the new bank of issue. He wished to form the Bank in Berlin and to have it connected in some loose way with the Reichsbank thus utilizing the latter's organization and contact with the German economy. The capital would have to be subscribed either in Germany or abroad and would be under foreign trusteeship. These deposits would then be employed in Germany either in opening credits or issuing notes. The assets of the Bank would consist of gold exchange, notes, and paid up deposits outside

---

17. The task of the Second Committee was to investigate the total amount of German capital which had been exported from Germany by German Nationals and was now kept abroad in deposits, and the means of how to bring these funds back. The Committee was composed of: MacKenna, Great Britain; Robinson, United States; Laurrent-Athalin, France; Alberti, Italy; Janssen, Belgium.

of Germany, which could not be touched by the German or any foreign Government. Dr. Schacht described his plan not as a permanent solution but as a preliminary scheme to restore confidence in order to prepare the way for a real gold bank.

In the general structure and essential points the Committee had outlined the same plan for the organization of a new bank. The main differences being the wider scope of the Experts' plan and the matter of foreign control. The Committee issued therefore a publication to this effect.

At the beginning of February the Committee was in Berlin in order to study close at hand the condition of Germany. It was just in this period that the rentenmark showed a tendency to decline in its value. Dr. Schacht endeavored to obtain the consent of the Committee to the establishment of his new Gold Bank. In a session of the Committee on February 9, Mr. Young stated that in view of the circumstances, the Committee could not assume the responsibility of preventing Dr. Schacht from putting his plan into execution. But in order to avoid future difficulties he wished an arrangement to be made with Dr. Schacht whereby the new Gold Bank might be absorbed by the bank proposed by the experts, in case their report should be eccepted by the Reparation Commission. After a conference with the German Government, Dr. Schacht agreed and the following statement was published: „The work of the First Committee has enabled it unanimously to lay down the broad lines which it will recommend for the establishment of a new German bank of issue on a gold basis, which will exchange its own notes against those of the Reichsbank and of the Rentenbank. The general principles of this plan have been communicated to Dr. Schacht who is very clearly of the opinion, shared by the experts themselves, that if it is put into execution it will prove to be the most important step toward the definite stabilization of the German exchange and the balancing of the budget."

The final report of the Dawes Committee was submitted to the Reparation Commission on April 9, and made the basis of the London Agreement of August 14, 1924. The details of the Dawes Plan insofar as they are of importance for the present study will be discussed in later chapters.

THE GOLD DISCOUNT BANK: In view of the aim of the Dawes Committee to submit in the near future to the Reparation Commission a plan for the establishment of a new Bank of issue, Dr. Schacht modified his project. Thus, on March 19, 1924 the German Parliament passed a Law Concerning The Establishment Of The German Gold discount-Bank.[18] The main provisions of this Act and the underlying ideas were as follows:

The capital of the new Bank was composed of 10 million, which was divided into two classes, Group A and Group B, each contributing 5 million. The fully paid shares of Group A were taken over by the Reichsbank while the second serie was distributed among a consortium of leading banks upon a payment of 25 per cent.[19]

The Bank was independent of the Federal Government, and it was authorized to issue notes up to an amount of 5 million. These notes were not legal tender. The Gold-discount-Bank was prohibited by law to grant directly or indirectly credit to the Reich, to the States, or municipalities. It was provided that the notes had to be covered by at least 50 per cent in gold or foreign exchange, while the remainder had to be secured by discounted bills of exchange or cheques based upon the English Pound and maturing in three months. Owing to the rapid transition to the gold standard and to the reorganization of the Reichsbank this right of note issue was never exercised.

The administration of the Bank was exercised by a Managing Board of Directors, which was composed of three members. This Board was supervised by the Supervisory Council, consisting of at least 24 members. The president of the Reichsbank was automatically president of this Council.

The following comment of the legislature in advocating this law clearly defined the purpose and working conditions of the new institution: "The Gold-Discount-Bank is a credit institution and not a Bank of Issue. It is therefore advisable to limit the right of note

18. Gesetz über die Deutsche Golddiskontbank vom 19. März 1924. (published in the „Reichsgeestzblatt" Teil II, Seite 71.)

19. At the beginning of 1925, the Reichsbank acquired from these banks their holdings of shares of the Gold Discount Bank through exchange for Reichsbank shares, so that the institution is now owned by the Reichsbank.

issue to a small amount. The denomination of the capital, notes, and credit in English pounds is deemed wise in view of the fact that international trade between England and Germany is of great importance. As the notes and credit are solely for the purpose of facilitating international trade the denomination in a foreign currency does not appear to endanger to any degree the stability of the German currency."

In view of its principal task of facilitating foreign trade, the Bank was only obliged to discount bills of exchange arising out of the export trade. But it was also empowered to discount bills for the purchase of raw material and other commodities abroad which were imported to Germany for the purpose of later export of the finished goods.

This law became effective on April 7, when the Gold discount-Bank began its activities. It was in March 1924 that the Loan Banks (Darlehnskassen) were dissolved by the legislature. By the end of March the greater proportion of the emergency notes and other currencies issued during the inflation had been withdrawn from circulation and at the beginning of April the Reichsbank and the Rentenbank, the latter only indirectly, were the only note issuing institutions of importance in Germany.

CHAPTER VI.

THE CREDIT INFLATION IN THE SPRING OF 1924 AND THE SUBSEQUENT POLICY OF CREDIT RESTRICTION.

In the analysis of the nature of the Rentenmark as a stable currency, it was pointed out that the stability of the new money unit could be attained only by a rigid adherence to the quantity theory of money in regulating the issue of notes. The immediate success of the new currency in gaining the confidence of the population had been secured mainly by the legal limitation of the note issue. The population had been led to believe that the long period of uninterrupted note issue which had marked the Reichsbank's policy for about one decade, was to cease and that the monetary unit would therefore, maintain its stable value. Any additional issue of notes threatened to undermine this fundamental of the stabilization, the confidence of the people.

It will be recalled that in November, 1923, the Reichsbank had issued additional quantities of paper marks in the form of credit in order to relieve a monetary lack of Rentenmark notes at the disposal of the Rentenbank. Even after the total of Rentenmark credits which had been provided in the Decree had been put into circulation the Reichsbank did not cease to grant additional credits for which it issued its own notes. Such a policy on the part of the Reichsbank was dangerous from a currency standpoint. Increasing the bank notes in circulation could have but one result. It threatened the stability of the currency and delayed an economic readjustment by rendering it possible for unproductive plants to continue their existence.

In the long run the effect of credit upon prices depends upon the nature of the enterprise to which credit is granted. It is of the greatest importance for the central bank to know whether the enterprise obtaining credit is in a position to produce at prices below the marginal producer. If the business man obtaining credit is able to underbid the marginal producer, it is very probable that he will be in a position to dispose of his commodities in the market and that he will be able to redeem his debt with the receipt from the sales. Under normal economic conditions the function of analyzing the „credit standing" of an enterprise is exercised by banks. These banks are usually in contact with the parties desiring credit for a long time and are well able to determine the probability of the particular producer's availing himself of the credit economically, so as to compete successfully in the market.

During the inflation this contact between banks and customers had been lost to a very large degree. The peculiar market conditions during that period had enabled every owner of goods to sell them in the market. The productivity of an enterprise depended at that time more upon the ability of the management to obtain large bank credits which were redeemed in depreciated paper money than upon the ability to produce at the lowest cost. The contact between demand and supply had been lost entirely during those years. Even after the currency was stabilized the discrepancy between demand and supply rendered a reliable analysis of the „credit standing" of an enterprise very difficult. Although the Reichsbank granted its credits only to old established and well organized enterprises it was inevitable that the latter availed themselves of these funds both for the maintenance of their extensive plans, which at that time could not be employed to their full capacity and for the maintenance of their large stock of goods which could not be sold at the market without substantial losses. These credits therefore tended to inflate the price level.

The effect of the Reichsbank credits was considerably accelerated by the investment policy of the public bodies which had accumulated very large balances at the beginning of 1924. These funds were not always invested with the necessary prudence by the government's agencies. Instead of putting these very substantial amounts of money at the disposal of the Reichsbank or of the other large credit banks, many public institutions took particular pride in administering these funds strictly on what they termed „business principles". They endeavored to obtain as high an interest rate as possible and subsequently competed with the other credit institutions in the market, causing a liquid condition in the money market which disguised the actual credit situation. With but a few exceptions, these credits were granted by the public institutions to enterprises which offered the highest interest rate, overlooking the fact that the safety of a debt does not depend upon the high rate of return but upon the economic standing of the borrower. These financial ventures of the government's agencies (Treasury, Post-Office, Rail-Road, etc.) resulted disastrously in most cases. Considerable amounts of money were lost as a result of the inability of the illiquid borrowers to meet their obligations.

Many entrepreneurs were thus in a position to finance the maintenance of their large stock of commodities or of their unproductive plants with the aid of these credits. Instead of bringing about the necessary economic readjustment, the additional credits directed into circulation delayed this process and enhanced the dangers surrounding the stability of the currency. The effect of the excessive note issue was an inflation of the price level[1] and a depreciation in the foreign exchange rate of the Rentenmark decreased by about fifteen per cent.[2] It was only by adopting the most rigid measures within the power of the Reichsbank that the official rate of the dollar was maintained in Germany at a ratio of 4.20 Rentenmarks for one dollar. This rate could only be maintained by the Reichsbank by selling one per cent of the total of foreign ex-

---

1. The following table has been compiled from the Statistische Jahrbuch 1924, p. 265.

INDEX OF WHOLESALE PRICES JANUARY TO APRIL, 1924:

(1913 — 100)

January 2nd, 119.7	Feb. 5th 113.9	March 4th 118.7	Apr. 1st 122.0
January 8th, 119.8	Feb. 12th 115.4	March 11th 119.8	Apr. 8th 122.3
January 15th, 115.7	Feb. 19th 117.5	March 18th 121.4	Apr. 15th 124.1
January 22nd, 114.8	Feb. 26th 118.0	March 25th 130.8	Apr. 22nd 124.3
January 29th, 114.8			

2. Dr. Schacht, Stabilisierung, p. 107.

changes demanded in the market[3] and by the legal prohibition of buying and selling foreign exchanges above the official rate fixed by the Reichsbank.

In spite of these additional funds put into circulation by the various institutions the great scarcity of funds was not relieved. This scarcity of funds was natural in view of the discrepancy between demand and supply. The decreased production and the ensuing increase in unemployment together with the relatively low level of wages had diminished the demand to such an extent that the existing supply of goods for sale was far in excess of what the market could absorb. It will be recalled that during the inflation, enterprises and individuals had endeavored to exchange their technically liquid capital in the form of cash money or bank reserves for tangible assets. As a consequence there was, after the stabilization of the German currency, a very large stock of goods and very extensive plants for production without an adequate demand to absorb the prospective supply.[4]

The great tension of the economic situation at that time was further accelerated by an outside factor which increased the scarcity of funds in the money market. This factor was the German franc speculation. In February, 1924, the French franc had suddenly shown signs of depreciation and its value had decreased from one fourth of its pre-war par to one sixth. Many financial institutions and business enterprises in Germany hoped to reap large profits by speculating in the French franc, anticipating a further decline in the value of the French currency. They sold short very substantial quantities of francs to be delivered in April and May, 1924. These expectations, however, did not materialize. The franc recovered its former value after a short period and the contracts of the German speculators resulted in heavy losses to

---

3. In January this ratio had been already fifteen per cent.

4. In his book 'Ein Land ohne Betriebsmittel' Hans Fürstenberg, noted financial authority of Germany, estimated the loss of liquid capital as exceeding 100 billion marks. Germany, however, had not been impoverished by this amount but in the main a shifting of liquid funds into fixed assets had taken place. As a result Germany emerged from the inflation with large plants, and a considerable supply of goods but practically devoid of the liquid capital necessary to employ these facilities.

them which were estimated at about 400 million marks (95 million dollars).

The internal effect of the franc speculation upon the German money market was a further increase in interest rates due to a greater scarcity of funds. The complexity of the economic situation prevailing at that time in Germany can best be understood by means of the following three diagrams, representing the increase of notes in circulation, the great decline in stock prices, and the increase in the interest rates.

It will be noted that in the diagram showing the fluctuations in stock prices two phases can be observed. First an increase in prices in the second half of January and the first half of February. This was due to speculative purchases of stock stimulated by the great expansion of credit in December 1923, and January and February 1924. After the middle of February the rates declined continuously as a result of the then commencing franc speculation and the ensuing lack of funds in the money market. Especially after the adoption of a credit restriction policy by the Reichsbank the decline in stock prices became very pronounced.

The great expansion of money in circulation is demonstrated by the second diagram showing the increased issue of Reichsbank notes at the same time when the Rentenbank put very large quantities of Rentenmark into circulation.

Diagram 3 reflects the movements of money rates in the Bourse of Frankfurt a. M. during the first four months of 1924. The great scarcity of funds is reflected in the very high rates for monthly loans. It will be noted that even the rates for daily money increased to a level which clearly indicates the shortage of funds in the market.

STOCK PRICES AT THE BOURSE OF FRANFURT a/M.
(January 4th 1924 --100)

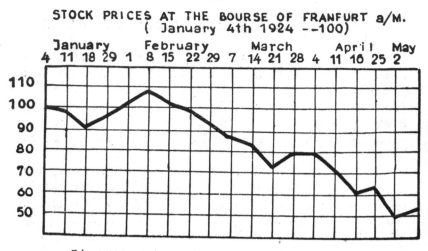

Die Wirtschaftskurve 1924, page 109

RATES IN MONEY MARKET OF FRANKFURT a/M.

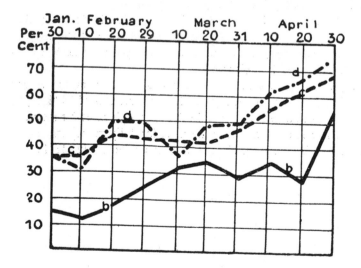

a) Die Wirtschaftskurve 1924, p.155
b) rates for daily money
c) rates for 14 days loans
d) rates for monthly loans

TOTAL OF NOTES IN CIRCULATION
(in millions of gold mark)

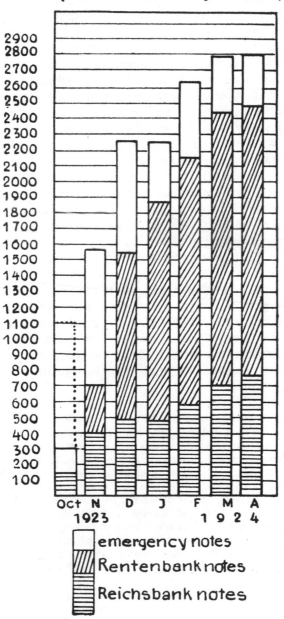

emergency notes

Rentenbank notes

Reichsbank notes

During these months, Dr. Schacht had been frequently absent from Germany and had lost sight of the occurrences during this period.[5] It was not until the beginning of April that Dr. Schacht realized the iminent danger of the Reichsbank's policy in regard to the stability of the currency. The problem which confronted the management of the Bank was whether the discount rate should be increased or whether a policy of credit restriction should be pursued. It was apparent to Dr. Schacht that under the prevailing conditions the discount rate was no longer an efficient weapon in the credit policy of the Bank. The only other alternative was therefore a drastic rationing of credit. Such a policy was the more imperative as the demand for credit had to be arrested immediately if the stability of the currency was to be maintained. Other economic considerations had to be subordinated to the necessity of maintaining the stability of the currency.

Thus, on April 5th, 1924, the Reichsbank suddenly announced that it would no longer grant credits beyond the total amount outstanding on April 7th. For the first time in the history of central banking, a central bank had pledged itself unreservedly to a rigid policy of credit restriction with all its far-reaching effects upon the economy of its country. The paramount importance which central banks have assumed during the great economic changes following the Great War and their position in the growing credit structure in modern countries justifies a theoretical analysis of these two powerful weapons of central banks in regulating the demand for credit.

---

5. Dr. Schacht frankly admits the failure of the Reichsbank to recognize the nature of its credit policy in his book „The Stabilization of the German Currency" when he writes: „I can only reproach myself for not having paid proper attention in good time to the development of the internal credit market. The commercial papers of serious organs of the press (for example the Frankfurter Zeitung as early as February and Dr. Pinner in the Berliner Tageblatt) had early called attention to the dangers of over-lavish distribution of credits with its conollary of over-rapid increase in circulation. My excuse for this neglect is to be found in a material and personal factor." p. 153. The material factor referred to by Dr. Schacht was the demand for credit by agriculture, while the personal factor was his „enforced absence at the time except for fleeting visits owing to my perpetual discussions with the Experts in Paris." p. 154.

With the steady growth of banks and their ensuing ability to create additional purchasing power by means of credit the problem of how to regulate the stream of funds directed into the economy through the central bank becomes of increasing importance from a social point of view. Banks depend in their credit policy upon the readiness of the central bank to supply them with additional funds in case of increasing demand for credit. The central bank on the other hand, has the natural desire to regulate the money market and flow of capital in such a way as to render its policy effective in periods of economic depression or expansion. Its policy is governed by social considerations and its task is to provide a distribution of the national reserves in such a way as is most conducive to the welfare of the whole community. Although the premises and effects of credit restriction as analyzed in this chapter were the outcome of post-war conditions, their underlying principles remain of great theoretical significance and warrant a detailed analysis.

It is true that the discount policy of many central banks carries in itself the potential threat of a limitation of credit should not the demand for rediscount at the central bank diminish. But such an indirect warning refers always to a special type of credit demand, as a rule to credit for speculative purposes in periods of an approaching scarcity of funds. Moreover, an increased discount rate always influences the market situation indirectly. The effects of a rise in the rate upon the demand for credit are well known. It causes a diminuition in the demand for funds, and results at the same time in liquidation of goods on the part of enterprises which cannot pay the higher rate (marginal producer). The level of prices begins to decline and tends to cause an increase in exports while imports diminish, thus resulting in a favorable balance of trade. Furthermore, an increase in the rate attracts funds from foreign markets, where the current market rate is lower. These two sets of forces (internal and external) are always active under normal conditions and set in motion those tendencies which bring about an equilibrium between the various money and capital markets of the world.

There are certain conditions which must be materialized in order that an increase in the discount rate may have the desired effect. The fundamental premise is that the gold standard (or gold exchange standard) be introduced and made effective in the most important trading countries. If such is the case the monetary unit will always move to those countries where more can be obtained in exchange for it. An increase in the discount rate would attract gold from other markets to that market where prices have fallen because of a lack of purchasing power in the market, i. e. where the money unit has now a higher value in relation to goods. The international equilibrium is then reestablished by the operation of the exchange rate which will be in favor of the country with the lower price level and will therefore cause a larger inflow of money in exchange for commodities, thus causing an increase in the total of purchasing power in that market and a diminished supply of goods.

The second premise is that the international money and capital markets react quickly to fluctuations in the price level of any one country. In case of a gold standard or gold exchange standard these movements occur immediately if the rate of exchange approaches the specie point, where it becomes profitable to export or import gold from one country to another one. If the country with the lower price level has no gold standard (or gold exchange standard) capital will only move freely between the two countries if the owner of funds has perfect confidence in the stability of the monetary system in the country in which the loans are contracted. If this confidence does not exist then the rate of interest contains a more or less high rate as price for the risk which the creditor incurs by granting the loan in an unstable currency. Slight changes in the discount rate will therefore not attract funds from foreign markets.

Thirdly, in order to achieve the desired result by an increase in the rate it is necessary that the domestic economy reacts immediately to fluctuations in the rate, by forcing the marginal producer to cease further production. The latter will be compelled to cease further competition in the market if the relation between demand and supply is such as to cause the inter-marginal producer to increase his output at a lower cost and thus to force the marginal producer out of competition. Should, however, extraordinary circumstances degrade the interest rate to a position where it no longer determines the marginal profit for the marginal producer then slight increases in the rate are without any effect upon the demand for credit.

The above analyzed premises were fulfilled before the Great War in most European countries. Fluctuations in the discount rate therefore, inevitably set in motion the respective movements of capital and changes in the relative price level which finally re-established the international equilibrium.

If owing to a currency inflation, the above mentioned premises are not active towards an international equilibrium, a discount policy has merely slight domestic effects. The lack of international confidence in the inflated currency increases the rate of interest so much as to include a substantial part as compensation for risk. This risk may be considered by foreign owners of capital so great that no movement of funds takes place no matter how attractive the rate may be. Under such circumstances it is clear that a discount rate to be effective in the domestic credit market would have to be so high as to cause very severe disturbances in the business world. In an economy, which is inflated and where the premises for an effective discount policy are absent, more drastic means must be adopted in order to arrest an increase in the demand for credit.

An increased discount rate would, in such an economy, do more harm to the community as a whole than the benefit of diminished demand for rediscount would amount to. Under such circumstances it becomes vitally important for the central bank to provide funds for productive industries and at the same time to eliminate the demand for credit by unproductive enterprises. The means by which this aim can be achieved is credit restriction, which means a limitation of the total of credits to be granted to the economy while the discount rate remains unaltered. It is a means whose influence nobody in the economy can •evade. Credit restriction has a deep effect upon the whole structure of industry and trade, including the banks.

Compared with the above analyzed limitation to the effectiveness of the discount rate, credit restriction is a much more powerful weapon in regulating the credit structure of a country. The discount rate is a means which brings about the desired decrease in the demand for credit in an indirect way. Moreover, its virtue depends upon certain premises which are not materialized in periods of severe economic disturbances. At such times the policy of credit restriction proves of far greater significance and is much more effective in promoting the desired result. It must be kept in mind, and it cannot be over-emphasized that credit restriction is not to be contrasted to the discount policy of a central bank as such but should rather be conceived of as a more powerful means to the same end in those periods when a change in the rate does not seem sufficient or is not desirable for social reasons. In a broad sense both credit restriction and changes in the rate are means to the rediscount policy of central banks, the term 'means' being used to include all means adopted by the central bans to check further demand for rediscount. The main difference between these two types lies, mainly, in the fact that credit restriction is applied when either an increased discount rate is not considered efficient enough to diminish the demand for rediscount, or where an increase in the rate would do more harm to the economy as a whole than a credit restriction.

It is a well known fact and need not be proved here that banks, in our economy, exercise a predominant influence in the money and capital markets. The increasingly large funds which these institutions dispose renders their creation of purchasing power, in the form of credits, very effective. A bank, like an individual, does not keep its funds idle but desires to derive as much profit from an investment of these funds, either in long term or short term loans, as circumstances permit. The more modern industrialization expands, the larger the funds invested in those enterprises become, the more the banks are called upon to provide the necessary funds. Our modern economy, especially since the end of the Great War, witnessed a rapidly advancing expansion of modern industry and business. Large national corporations and trusts, huge international cartels and pools are formed continuously all over the world. These tremendous enterprises require such large amounts of capital that it is only with the aid of modern banks that their needs can be provided for, either by floatation of long term loans in the capital market or by financing short term loans in the money market.

It has repeatedly been found in the preceding discussion, that the larger are the resources of a bank, the more is it in a position to lend many times as much credit than it actually disposes of in cash reserves. The proportion between the cash reserves and the total of credits granted depends upon its resources, credit standing among other big banks, and upon the type of customers to whom credit is granted. If the credit institution is well known and has considerable resources it is very likely that in case other banks have claims upon it, accrued from deposits of bills drawn upon the first bank, they will not demand a transfer of their claims in cash but will leave their funds with the former institution. The same tendency to transfer claims and not cash holds true if the customers of the bank are businessmen. It then becomes evident that banks are in a position to create purchasing power by extending credit to money seeking businessmen. The actual cash held by these institutions is considered as a reserve for those payments in cash made by individuals which occur in the normal course of business.

The creation of purchasing power is however limited by the necessity of maintaining a certain reserve without which the banks would not be in a position to meet a demand for cash. The banks hold therefore certain reserves for this purpose. These reserves may be classified under three heads: the primary reserves which include money in cash, claims upon other banks, and foreign exchange; the secondary reserves composed of bills of exchange, collateral securities for loans, and advances; and the final reserves consisting of stocks and bonds. In case the bank is required to meet larger payments than it anticipated in its policy, it uses the primary reserves. If these funds are not sufficient it can rediscount its secondary reserves at the central banks, thus obtaining new funds. This process of rediscount is the usual and normal method of banks in liquidating their funds, either to meet demand for payments or to expand their outstanding loans. From this reliance of the credit institutions upon the central banks for their liquidity the importance of a well managed and liquid central bank becomes evident. It was in this way that most central banks before the Great War tended to became „Banker's Banks" Very unwillingly and only in periods of severe depressions do the banks resort to a liquidation of their last reserves. They do so when the means of the central bank are exhausted and no other way is available. It was during the crisis of 1911 in Germany that the German banks were forced to resort to this means which caused severe losses on account of the declining rates in the market as a result of these large sales.

Thus far the usefulness of the discount rate in achieving a reduction in the demand for credit, and its limitations, have been analyzed. It is well to analyze now the nature and effects of credit restriction upon the economic structure of a country.

The primary and main effect of credit restriction is the change of the position which the central bank holds in the economy. Under normal conditions the distribution of credits is in the hands of banks. The central bank has merely the task of providing additional funds for credit institutions so that they need not wait for funds until outstanding claims mature. In periods of scarcity of money the banks depend entirely upon the central bank for additional capital. This is the normal tendency of the central banks assuming the function of a „Banker's Bank" and has no direct control over the distribution of credit into the various channels.

Such a relation between the Bank of Issue and credit institutions has the effect that the granting of credit by banks is governed by their natural desire to derive as much profit from their loans as circumstances permit. The individual bank grants its credits on the basis of the earning capacity of the capital seeking enterprise, regardless of whether this particular enterprise is of greater social importance than another industry or producer which cannot pay the high interest rate agreed upon by its competitors. An illustration: If the manufacturer of luxuries was willing to pay for a loan ten per cent interest and the general market conditions would justify the assumption that this enterprise would be able to market its products at a profit, the bank would without a doubt grant the desired loan to this manufacturer rather than to a farmer who can only produce at a profit if he would obtain credit at a rate of six per cent. The daily experience of large funds directed into the stock market, at a time when producers and farmers complain of a lack of capital at interest rates which render their production profitable, is a well known fact to the reader of commercial newspapers.

It must be admitted, however, that there are certain economic forces at work which tend to bring about an equal distribution of credit in accordance with the relative social importance of the various industries. Such a readjustment is brought about by the economic law of varying utility and desire. An individual satisfies at first the most pressing needs such as hunger, thirst, desire for clothing, dwelling, etc. If the farmer does not obtain sufficient funds to cultivate all his soil the normal production will decrease causing a shortage in the supply of a commodity which ranks first in the scale of human wants. Prices for agricultural products will therefore increase, rendering it profitable for the farmer to pay a higher interest rate and to cultivate more land. On the other hand the higher price paid for food will cause a diminuition in the purchasing power available for luxuries, thus tending to lower their prices and resulting in a lessened production of luxuries. In the long run there is this tendency toward a balanced distribution of credit among the various industries in accordance with their importance in the scale of social necessities.

In periods of great economic change or expansion it might easily occur that the competition between those desiring credit increases the rate to so high a level that socially important industries cannot obtain the necessary funds without the above stated tendencies to a readjustment. Such was the case in Germany in the spring of 1924. Young illiquid concerns which enjoyed political connections were in a position to obtain funds at high interest rates which they paid regardless of their ability to redeem their obligations at maturity while old established well-managed firms collapsed since they lacked capital, being unable to pay the high interest rates and to produce at a profit. The socially uneconomical distribution of credit resulted in higher prices and a loss of social income.

In such periods the central bank has the paramount task of enforcing a re-distribution of credit at a profitable rate to the various industries according to their social importance and relative demand for credit. A mere increase of the discount rate would not produce the desired result, because as was pointed out, an increase in the rate would in this particular case exclude just those enterprises from obtaining credit which were intended to obtain funds.

The rediscount rate has still another very important influence outside the money market. It also affects the rates in the capital market which indirectly depend upon the discount rate established by the central bank. The price for long term funds is always lower than the price demanded for short term loans. This is due to the certainty in the former case of a fixed steady return to the lender for a longer period of time. If then the rediscount rate is raised all other rates in the money market increase simultaneously. The difference between the rates in the money and capital market becomes such as to render it more profitable for owners of funds to invest their capital temporarily in the money market where the rates are more attractive. There are always owners of funds who are in doubt as to whether they should invest their capital in the money or capital market. The largest individual disposers of such capital are investment banks, and in Germany, the large credit institutions, which invest part of their funds in the capital market. These potential lenders will in case of such differences between the market rates shift their funds to the money market thus causing a proportionate increase in the rates for long term capital. This close relationship between the rates for long term and short term obligations imposes additional responsibilities upon the central bank in regulating its discount rate. In periods of economic disturbances when the central bank has the aim to achieve a redistribution of credits an increase in the discount rate would tend to raise the price of long term loans and accelerate the ill-effects of high interest rates upon the socially important industries.

All these social evils can be remedied by the adoption of credit restriction. Through this measure the central bank changes from a „banker's bank" to the largest direct money lender in the community. The credit institutions find themselves in a position where their credit policy is no longer subject to their normal principle of highest return but is materially affected by the policy of the central bank. Limited in the amount of bills which they can rediscount the banks are compelled to maintain larger cash reserves so as to be able to meet their obligations in case of increasing demand for funds on part of their depositors. Furthermore, the limitation of the bills accepted for rediscount and the fixed amount of such bills renders it necessary for the banks to adapt their distribution of credit along the same lines. Their dependence upon the Bank of

Issue for additional funds is too great to permit any independent credit policy contrary to that favored by the central bank.

If credit restriction is adopted by the central bank, the latter is in a position to divert funds into the channels described by limiting the total credit available for various industries. A similar consideration caused the provision in the Rentenbank Decree that of the total credits to be granted by the Bank 800 million marks were to be granted to agriculture. In case of credit restriction, the discount rate need not be raised but can be fixed according to the judgment of the central bank. The limitation of credit arrests an increased demand — a result which under normal conditions is achieved by a higher discount rate.

A policy of credit restriction also affects the reserve policy of banks as has been mentioned. The credit institutions unable to discount their papers at will at the central bank are compelled to adopt a cautious attitude in their own policy toward their customers. Moreover, the general distrust which inevitably follows the adoption of credit restriction by a Bank of Issue causes a credit crisis in the economy. Due to this crisis banks become still more restrained in their credit policy. They will endeavor to increase their cash reserves by liquidating their secondary reserves consisting of bills of exchange, loans on collateral, and advances on merchandise. Furthermore, the banks will then lend funds mostly on short term obligations. Thus, the daily money market will show a very great liquidity while the other markets will suffer from a lack of funds.

So far as the business world is concerned the effects of credit restriction are felt by it to their full extent. In our capitalistic system the whole economy is interrelated through the medium of credit. The retailer buys on credit from the wholesaler, who in turn purchases the goods on credit form the producer and so on. All these entrepreneurs depend in their activities upon a smooth circulation of goods from the first producer to the final consumer. If this chain is interrupted a crisis is inevitable. A limitation in the total of credit through credit restriction therefore results in credit crises. Enterprises which had financed their long term capital requirements for the maintenance of their large supply of commodities with the aid of short term funds find themselves unable to meet their obligations at maturity. Their inability to meet their due debts forces in turn their creditors either to liquidate all their reserves in form of bonds, stocks, or goods, or to go into bankruptcy. Thus, many business failures ensue from this illiquidity of concerns which often forces illiquid but not insolvent enterprises to cease their production resp. business. The diminution in the production causes an increase in unemployment, thus lessening the total demand in the market and its capacity to absorb the larger quantity of commodities forthcoming in the market as the result of liquidations. Business enterprises too become very cautious in their conditions of sale and maintain larger cash reserves with the banks.

The liquidation of stocks and bonds by businessmen in order to obtain the necessary funds causes a decline in prices at the stock exchange and renders the marketing of new issues very difficult.

The far-reaching effects of a credit restriction policy upon the business community impose great responsibility upon the central bank in pursuing such a policy. Its application is only justified in periods of extreme scarcity of money and at times when the distribution of credit by banks has resulted in a shortage or undue dearness of credit for those industries which are of great social importance. The success of a rigid credit restriction in such periods depends, however, upon a lack of international reaction to the high rates in that particular country. Otherwise, the ensuing high rates in the money and capital market will attract funds from abroad and thus frustrate the efforts of the central bank to enforce a redistribution of credit.

It should also be remembered that credit restriction affects materially the trend of business. An application of this means in a period when business is rapidly expanding and consequently when the total of credit circulating in the community is continuously growing is potentially of great danger. The effect of such a policy might easily cause a sudden abruption in the upward trend of business and do great harm to the whole community. Apparently, the effect of this powerful instrument of the central bank cannot be achieved by a higher discount rate. Should the central bank decide upon such a measure then it is imperative that it be immediately followed by a re-distribution of credits in such a way as was previously outlined.

In view of the past experience it seems, however, fair to assume that, in periods where rigid measures are necessary, a simultaneous application of both instruments (discount rate and modified credit restriction) is more in accordance with the present and probable future tasks of central banks. During the last two decades central banks have undergone a radical change in their credit policy. Throughout the 19th century and still at the beginning of the 20th century it had been considered the primary task of a Bank of Issue to safeguard the convertibility of notes in circulation and to leave the distribution of credit to the banks.[6] It will be recalled that in the case of Germany, the Reichsbank never endeavored to influence the flow of credit during the period 1875 —1912. The Bank applied the discount rate almost exclusively for the maintenance of the legally required gold reserves, without ever attempting to effect a distribution of credit in accordance with social needs. The same holds true to a very great extent of the other European central banks, of which the Bank of France, through its direct dealings with businessmen and on account of its liberty to issue notes at its discretion, probably exercised the strongest influence upon a social distribution of credit.

This rather passive attitude of central banks toward the distribution of credit in their respective countries has since the Great War been replaced by attempts to exercise a direct control over the diversion of funds by banks. The central bank no longer considers the maintenance of a certain gold reserve as its main task. Such an attitude would be too dangerous in view of the growing super-structure of credit built upon the relatively small basis of money in cash. Simultaneously with the expansion of capitalism the business cycles have the tendency toward a greater rapidity in their succession if central banks do not neutralize them. It is therefore of great social importance that means be applied to anticipate and to neutralize such fluctuations as much as possible.

In order to accomplish this task of influencing the business trend, the central bank must be in constant close contact with the

---

6. The classical example is the Bank of England which by Peel's Act of 1844 was divided into two independent branches: the Issue Department and the Banking Department.

development of business. It must continuously observe the distribution of credit and endeavor to regulate the flow and extent of credit by influencing the demand (actual and potential). The effect of changes in the discount rate upon the demand for credit have previously been analyzed and need not be repeated. A new increase in the rate, however, affects only rarely the distribution of credit. This additional task requires the application of a more drastic weapon than is represented by the discount rate. It is the application of a modified credit restriction, whereby the central bank increases the discount rate, limiting the list of eligible papers for rediscount and providing funds at a rate below the official discount rate for industries which are deemed to be of great importance and unable to pay the high rates. The extent to which the above proposed means can be applied depends entirely upon the general economic situation, and no fixed rule can be laid down.

In addition to the above analyzed tasks regulating and controlling the flow of credit, the problem of a stable price level has of recent come into the discussion of present and future central bank policies. Although the possibility and advisability of stabilizing prices is still a matter of great controversy among economists, it is generally admitted that the central bank has the task of preventing as far as possible, fluctuations of prices which are due to an excessive or insufficient issue of notes, or to an unsocial distribution of credit, whereby important industries lack funds while the stock market shows a great liquidity of money.

Summarizing the conclusions reached in the foregoing analysis it may be said that a simultaneous application of the discount rate and of credit restriction is the instrument by which the central banks will in the future regulate the distribution of credit and partly neutralize the harmful effects of severe fluctuations in the business trend.

THE CREDIT RESTRICTION AND THE ECONOMIC CRISIS. The abruptness with which the Reichsbank resorted to the policy of credit restriction found the German economy entirely unprepared. No time had been given to the business world to adapt itself to a situation such as that which arose as a consequence of the new policy. Immediate restriction was imperative for the maintenance of a stable currency and Dr. Schacht did not hesitate to pursue such a rigid policy in spite of the severe criticism which such a measure was apt to arouse from the public. The great scarcity of funds rendered a period of transition necessary during which the Bank did not adhere strictly to the set limit but permitted slight increases of the quantity of discounted bills. While the total of discounted bills amounted to 1867 millions on April 7th, 1924, this amount increased to 1953 millions on June 8th, 1924. In general, however, the fixed limit was maintained.

The immediate effect of the credit restriction was felt the harder by the business world in view of the great lack of funds which was partly due to the failure of the franc speculation. These engagements had to be met at the end of April and May and those having previously contracted the sale of francs at a rate far below its value on those dates were forced to pay very considerable differences, which amounted to about 400,000,000 million marks. A part of this amount was obtained through a liquidation of reserves in the form of stock and especially foreign exchange which had been hoarded in the early months of 1924 for speculative purposes. Due to the increasing supply of foreign exchange thus forthcoming in the market, the demand for foreign currencies decreased considerably; moreover, speculation in francs had partly been responsible for the great demand for foreign exchange during the preceding months. While in March, 1924, the daily average of the demand for foreign currencies in the market amounted to an equivalent of 400 million marks it decreased to 100 million on May 24th, (at which time the Reichsbank sold only 1 per cent of the total quantity of dollars demanded) and to 4 millions on June 4th, 1924. Thus, on June 3rd, 1924, the Reichsbank for the first time after one decade was in a position to satisfy the total demand for foreign currencies in the market which now again showed the features fo a normal market where the demanded quantity could be bought. The 3rd of June, 1924 marks the final step in the stabilization of the German currency. The great success which Dr. Schacht had achieved caused a general recognition of the justification of his policy.

The large quantities of foreign exchange offered in the market by speculators and business enterprises which were short of liquid funds enabled the Reichsbank to increase its holding of foreign exchange continuously and strengthened its position in the market. The changes in the portfolio of the Reichsbank are shown in the following table:[7]

REICHSBANK PORTFOLIO (in millions of mark)

Date	Bills and Cheques:	Loans on Collateral:	Notes Outstanding:	Giro-accounts:	Miscellaneous Assets:
Apr. 7th 1876	132	683	392	212
May 7th 1865	134	787	358	292
June 7th 1953	118	954	328	525
July 7th 1871	92	1106	320	767
Aug. 7th 1800	55	1202	356	993

It will be noted that the Reichsbank notes in circulation increased during this period by about 520 million marks. This increase is explained by the simultaneous rise in the item „miscellaneous assets" which included foreign exchange acquired by the Reichsbank in its open market operations. The total of foreign exchange in gold in the stock of the Reichsbank rose from 592 million marks on April 7th, 1924, to 1256 millions on August 7th, 1924.[8]

The effect of the credit restriction policy upon the business world was entirely in accordance with the conclusion of the theoretical analysis. Unable to obtain additional credit from the Reichsbank many enterprises were forced to obtain their funds from other sources. But as the banks were themselves limited in their resources and as the market had shown a great scaricity of funds since the beginning of the year those enterprises were forced to liquidate their reserves in the form of commodities and later on their supply of stocks and foreign exchange as far as they. So far as the liquidation of foreign currencies is concerned, which first took place, the result has already been shown. But the additional funds thus obtained proved insufficient and soon very substantial quantities of goods were sold in the market, and as even these sales did not remedy the lack of capital in the market stocks and bonds were liquidated. In consequence in all three

---

7. Die Wirtschaftskurve, 1924, page 310.
8. Dr. Schacht, Stabilisierung, page 123.

markets a great decline in prices occurred as reflected in the following table.

STOCK PRICES:[9] (Jan. 4, 1924—100)		WHOLESALE PRICES:[10] (1913—100)	
April 25th	50	April 1924	124.1
May 9th	49.5	May 1924	122.5
June 13th	45.3	June 1924	115.9
July 11th	43.1	July 1924	115.0

The relatively low level of prices undoubtedly favored large exports and the surplus of the balance of trade in favor of Germany from January to June 1924 amounted to between one billion marks and one half billion. Due to the favorable balance of trade large amounts of foreign exchange streamed into Germany and were then absorbed by the Reichsbank and explain the great increase in its holding of foreign currency.

So far as the money market is concerned the policy of the Reichsbank caused a shortage in the supply of funds and in consequence the rates for daily money and monthly loans showed very sharp increases during the month of April. At the middle of May, this movement retarded partly, due to the various measures adopted by the Reichsbank to ease the conditions in the money market. The more the credit restriction exerted its influence upon the economy the more did the rates for money in the market decrease. This was due to rapid exclusion of illiquid concerns from competition because of bankruptcies. The two following tables show the movements of the money rates during the summer 1924 in the Bourse of Frankfurt and the increasing number of business failures until July, when the culmination point was reached.

---

9. Die Wirtschaftskurve 1924, page 392.
10. Statistisches Reichsamt, Jahrbuch für 1924/1925, p. 264.

MONEY RATES IN THE BOURSE OF FRANKFURT a/M,[11]
(Ten Days Averages)

	Daily (call) Money:	Monthly Loans:
April 1st—10th	35 per cent p.a.	44 per cent p.a.
April 11th—20th	27 ,, ,, ,,	28 ,, ,, ,,
April 21st—30th	52 ,, ,, ,,	61 ,, ,, ,,
May 1st—10th	48 ,, ,, ,,	67 ,, ,, ,,
May 11th—20th	11 ,, ,, ,,	42 ,, ,, ,,
May 21st—31st	12 ,, ,, ,,	28 ,, ,, ,,

BUSINESS FAILURES IN GERMANY 1924.[12]

Month	Bankruptcies:	Official Supervision:
January	31	—
February	41	—
March	68	—
April	138	—
May	322	639
June	579	845
July	1173	599
August	855	322
Septemb.	817	245

Monthly Average in
1911 729 bankruptcies
1912 768 „
1913 811 „

The above table shows clearly the general economic conditions in Germany which were caused by the policy of credit restriction. A period of general distrust was the natural result and a credit crisis ensued, which often led to the failure of liquid and well managed concerns that were unable to obtain the necessary funds. For the larger part the credit crisis forced out of the market those illiquid enterprises which had for such a long time maintained their existence with the aid of bank credit.

However, the Reichsbank did not view this development indifferently. Immediately after announcing its policy of credit

---

11. Die Wirtschaftskurve, 1924, page 252.

12. Ibid. page 323. The „official supervision" originated in Germany in 1914 when by a special Decree passed on August 8th, 1914, an insolvent person or concern could be placed under official supervision (Geschäftsaufsicht) in order to ward off bankruptcy.

restriction the Bank endeavored to avoid any unjust hardship by ordering a re-distribution of credit according to the social importance of industries.[13] Furthermore, the management of the Bank succeeded in inducing the public bodies which disposed of very considerable funds to put a substantial part at the disposal of the Reichsbank, thus rendering possible a more efficient and centralized distribution of credit. Later on, Dr. Schacht induced the Seehandlung (the former Bank of Prussia) to grant to the members of the Bankers' Association of Berlin (Stempelvereinigung) a rediscount credit of 40 million marks and to the farming class a credit of 200 million marks. In turn the Reichsbank pledged itself to rediscount bills of the Seehandlung up to this amount if the latter should be in need.

Another very substantial aid was afforded to the business world by the Gold Discount Bank which had begun its activities on April 7th, 1924. Although it granted credit only to exporting industries, the lessened demand for credit by the importers naturally tended to ease the general credit conditions in Germany. The total of credits granted by the Gold Discount Bank in summer 1924, is shown in the following figures:

TOTAL CREDITS GRANTED BY THE GERMAN GOLD DISCOUNT BANK.[14]

(in pound sterling)

May 5th	998,695
June 7th	6511,764
July 7th	12531,065
August 7th	13751,115
August 15th	13663,391

---

13. In his book 'Stabilization' Dr. Schacht writes on page 158: „In the week which succeeded April 7th, the Reichsbank scrutinized meticulously the whole series of credits granted. The Bank's branches were instructed to consider carefully the objects for which the credits were designated, and as far as possible to divert the sums coming in from repayment of bills into channels calculated to lead to the most productive results from the standpoint of the general economic interest."

14. Die Wirtschaftskurve, 1924, page 311.

By the middle of July the crisis had passed and a period of depression prevailed. Business failures diminished as shown previously, while the total of rediscounts at the Reichsbank decreased, Funds in the money market became abundant due to a lack of eligible borrowers and to the very considerable liquidation of goods and other liquid reserves on the part of business enterprises. The table below shows the situation in the money market during the period June—August, 1924.[15]

MONEY RATES AT BOURSE OF FRANKFURT a/M.

(ten days averages)

		Daily (call) Money:				Monthly Loans:			
June	1—10	12	per cent p.a.			35	per cent p.a.		
June	11—20	10	,,	,,	,,	34	,,	,,	,,
June	21—30	10	,,	,,	,,	24	,,	,,	,,
July	1—10	11.8	,,	,,	,,	22.8	,,	,,	,,
July	11—20	9	,,	,,	,,	16.8	,,	,,	,,
July	21—31	10.8	,,	,,	,,	16.7	,,	,,	,,
August	1—10	10.1	,,	,,	,,	15	,,	,,	,,
August	11—20	9.5	,,	,,	,,	12.3	,,	,,	,,

In general the German economy showed clearly the first signs of an approaching economic readjustment. Enterprises which had been established during the inflation and which had been vegetating throughout those years with the aid of bank credit were gradually forced out of business. Slowly, the many intermediaries which had caused the increase of prices above the necessary level were compelled to cease their activities, the producer endeavoring again to gain direct contact with the wholesaler and distributor of his products. Large organizations were reorganized, reducing the supply in the market to a proportion which conformed to the existing demand. It is obvious that after such a long period of inflation a much greater interval of time is necessary to bring about a readjustment. These above mentioned tendencies toward an economic readjustment were suddenly arrested by a new set of events which occured at that time and which became the cause of the delay of the economic readjustment until a later period when its effects were more harmful to the German economy. The events referred to were the acceptance of the Dawes Plan and the resulting flow of foreign loans to Germany, the effects of which will be discussed in a later chapter.

---

15. Die Wirtschaftskurve, 1924, page 282.

CHAPTER VII.

THE REORGANIZATION OF THE GERMAN REICHSBANK UNDER THE DAWES PLAN.

It will be recalled that one of the two committees appointed by the Reparations Commission on November 30th, 1923, (the First Committee of Experts) had been entrusted with the task of considering means to balance the German budget and the measures to be taken to stabilize the German currency. In reality (though not worded so officially) its task was to investigate „what Germany could pay for Reparations without endangering the balance of her budget and the stability of her currency".[1] The Committee (Dawes Committee) was composed of businessmen and financiers of international repute who fully justified the expectations of the European countries involved that the reparation problem would be taken out of the realm of politics and would be attacked solely from a business standpoint.[2]

Because of the political tension prevailing in Europe in 1924, it is easily understood why the Dawes Plan left various questions open for future settlement. Thus, the total amount of reparation payments Germany was to meet was not definitely fixed by the Plan. Furthermore, the transfer of these payments was not to be effected in foreign currencies which Germany had to acquire and to transfer at her own risk, but it was provided that a special committee (Transfer Committee) had to effect the transfer so as not to endanger the stability of the German currency. In this way

---

1. Carl Bergmann „The History of Reparations" page 226.
2. In its letter to the Reparations Commission of April 9th, 1924, the Dawes Committee states that „the standpoint adopted had been that of business and not of politics."

the reparation payments were closely connected with Germany's capacity to pay, this capacity depending upon the balance of payments from which she would derive the necessary surplus to meet them.[3]

Keynes seems to come very near the truth when he writes that „the political solution depended upon a silent gentlemen's agreement not to look ahead of time and not to ask embarrassing questions."[4] Nevertheless, the Dawes Plan's solution of the reparations probably represents the greatest post war contribution made towards the problem of the re-establishment of stabilized economic conditions in Europe. If one bears in mind the exceedingly tense political situation in Europe when the Dawes Committee assumed its task, one will readily admit that the Plan represents the best possible solution of the problem at the time. The Plan which was submitted to the Reparations Commission on April 9th, 1924, may be divided into four main parts: The stabilization of the budget; the annuities and the required securities; the reorganization of the Bank of Issue (stabilization of German currency), and the transfer of the reparation payments. In this chapter, after a brief outline of the annuities and securities has been given, the provisions of the new Bank of Issue and their underlying theories will be discussed in greater detail. An analysis of the transfer clauses of the Plan will be the subject of a later chapter, while the stabilization of the budget is omitted in this study, since it bears no direct or indirect relation to it.

(1) THE ANNUITIES AND THE SECURITIES.[1] The Experts were well aware of the fact that in view of the economic condition of Germany at that time, it was imperative to grant to her a certain period during which she might readjust her economy. It was accordingly provided in the Plan that the Reich should make the first full payment after a transition period of five years, while

3. In Part I Sec. viii (d), the Report the Experts admits that „the funds raised and transferred to the Allies on reparation account cannot, in the long run, exceed the sums which the balance of payments makes it possible to transfer without currency and budget instability ensuing."

4. Translated from an article „Der Dawes Plan und die deutsche Anleihe" by Maynard Keynes in the German Magazine „Wirtschaftsdienst" of October 10th, 1924, Nr. 41, page 1366.

during the intervening years the annuities should be graduated according to the following provisions:

First year:	transportation tax from Railroad	200	millions
	foreign loan	800	,,
	Total	**1000**	**millions**
Second year:	Rail roads (indebentures)	595	,,
	Transportation tax	200	,,
	Industry (indebentures)	125	,,
	Receipts from the sale of preferred stocks of the Railroad	250	,,
	Total	**1220**	**,,**
Third year:	Rail Roads	550	,,
	Transportation Tax	290	,,
	Industry	250	,,
	Budget	110	,,
	Total	**1200**	**,,**
Fourth year:	Rail Road	660	,,
	Transportation Tax	290	,,
	Industry	300	,,
	Budget	500	,,
	Total	**1750**	**,,**
Fifth year:	Rail Road	660	,,
	Transportation Tax	290	,,
	Industry	300	,,
	Budget	1250	,,
	Total	**2500**	**,,**

In order to lighten the burden for the first year, a loan of 800 million marks was provided which was to be floated abroad, the receipts being utilized for the payment of the first installment, as well as to strengthen the gold reserves of the Reichsbank.

The largest item among the securities to be pledged for the annual payments were represented by the German Rail-Roads, up to then owned and managed by the Reich. The Plan called for the formation of a business corporation of the Rail-Roads but it provided that the common stock of the company was to remain with the Reich. On the Borad of Directors one half of the members represented the Reich and one half represented the reparation creditor countries. Private capital was to participate in the company with preferred stocks, the proceeds of which would pay for the capital expenditures of the corporation. Besides these preferred stocks, bonds were to be issued for an amount of eleven billion marks ($ 2.6 billions), which were to be kept by trustees as a guarantee of the payments for the annuities. These bonds were to yield five per cent interest and one per cent amortization per annum.

Besides German Rail-Roads, German industry was also pledged as security with an imposed debt of five billion marks ($ 1.190 billions), which also yielded five per cent interest and one per cent amortization per annum. It was furthermore provided that the indebenture imposed upon industry as a part of the security for the Rentenmark should be cancelled. Both mortgages imposed upon industry and Rail-Roads should be extinguished after 36 years, provided Germany had met her annual payments up to that date.

In addition to the revenues from these sources, the Plan called for annual payments from the budget and the receipts received from a special transportation tax. It also provided that the revenues from tax-receipts on beer, alcohol, and tobacco were primarily to be used for the payments to be met from the budget.

One of the peculiar features of the Dawes Plan concerning the annuities was the so-called prosperity index. This was devised so as to obtain the approval of the Allied governments who had expected considerably larger annuities. The index was based upon the following items: (1) the total of Germany's imports and exports; (2) the total of budget receipts and expenditures; (3) the total of tonnage freight carried by rail-roads; (4) the money value of consumption of alcohol, sugar, beer, and tobacco; (5) the total population of Germany; and (6) the per capita consumption. The basic figures for items (2), (5), and (6) are the averages for 1927, 1928, 1929, while for items (1), (3), and (4) the basic figures are the averages for 1913, 1926, 1927, 1928, and 1929. In accordance with increased prosperity in Germany, her payments were to increase according to the above index. The application of this index was to be applied for the first time for the year 1929/1930, but for the period 1929 to 1934 it applied only to half of the annuities and from thereafter to the full amount.

II. THE BANK OF ISSUE. The most important provision of the Experts' Plan concerned the new Bank of Issue. Originally, it had been intended by the Dawes Committee to liquidate the Reichsbank and to established a new Bank of Issue. Dr. Schacht, however, strongly advocated the reorganization of the Reichsbank as the new Bank, pointing out the great advantage which this firmly founded institution afforded as compared with a new Bank, that would have to establish these connections and experiences which the Reichsbank already possessed. In view of the old traditions of the Reichsbank, — its business connections and far-reaching branch system, — the Experts resolved to propose to the Reparations Commission the appointment of an Organization Committee to be composed of the President of the Reichsbank and one member of the Committee. The latter was to investigate whether and under what conditions it would be advisable and possible to reorganize the Reichsbank. The Committee was furthermore entrusted with the task of drawing up a Bank Law concerning the new Bank of Issue which was to be based according to the stipulations laid down by the Dawes Committee.

On July 18, 1924 the Organization Committee submitted its report to the Reparation Commission. In view of the fact that the Committee thought the organization of the Reichsbank with its 95 main branches and 350 sub-branches necessary for a Bank of Issue, and in view of the desire to attain the object of the Experts with the least possible disturbance of the national life of Germany, the Organization Committee proposed the reorganization of the existing Bank. After a careful study of the status of the Reichsbank and of the financial and economic structure of Germany, the Committee also proposed several alterations in the original provisions of the Experts' Plan for the establishment of a Bank of Issue. The report of the Committee was approved by the Reparations Commission and subsequently made the basis for the Bank Law of August 30, 1924, after the governments concerned had agreed upon the ratification of the Dawes Plan in the London Conference of August 16, 1924.

One of the striking features of the new Bank Law[5] is its external resemblance to the old Bank Act, although the new Law actually indicated an entirely new structure for the Reichsbank, which became again the central institution for the issue of notes and the regulation of credit. The Rentenbank was to be liquidated as was the Gold-Discount-Bank. Actually the Rentenbank had lost its importance as a note issuing bank already in the summer of 1924 when the Reichsbank had succeeded in regaining its old position in Germany's economy. There were still the other four private note-issuing banks besides the Reichsbank, whose separate existence were apparently unknown to the Experts until Dr. Schacht called it to their attention.[6] Due to internal political motives rather than economic need, the Experts agreed upon a prolongation of their charters.[7] Their importance was, however, very slight — the total of notes allotted to these institutions was limited to 194 million marks — on account of their legal dependence in fixing the discount rate upon that of the Reichsbank.

THE BANK LAW. Before analyzing the various provisions contained in the Bank Act of August 30th, 1924,[8] its outstanding feature the re-establishment of a gold standard in Germany requires a more detailed analysis. The re-introduction of the gold standard in Germany has undoubtedly exercised a great influence upon other European countries by causing them to stabilize their currencies upon the same basis, and to base their monetary systems once more upon a gold standard as in England. The greater importance which attaches to such a standard from the viewpoint of central banking has been the cause for a renewed and heated controversy between European economists as to the advisability and necessity of basing a monetary system upon a gold

---

5. Bank Law of August 30, 1924 published in Reichsgesetzblatt II of August 30, 1924 p. 289.

6. Dr. Schacht „Stabilisierung" p. 171.

7. Privatnotenbankgesetz of August 30, 1924 (Reichsgesetzblatt III p. 246).

8. Bank-Gesetz vom 30. August 1924.

standard so as to maintain its stability. A detailed discussion of the various theories advanced would surpass the scope of this study, whose single aim is to give a brief survey of the most important theories together with their underlying facts.

Of those participating in this controversy two men have gained wide recognition as outstanding economists and their controversial theories are of particular interest. They are Maynard Keynes of England and Gustav Cassel of Sweden. Among German economists the viewpoints of Dr. Hahn and of Dr. Schacht represent the opposing schools in that country and will also be briefly outlined. In general, however, it may be stated that all theories advanced in Europe have a close resemblance either to the views of Keynes or of Cassel.

Keynes' theory[9] of a stable currency and the maintenance of its stability without convertibility into gold is the outcome of war and post-war experience. During this period gold lost its character as the only stable monetary unit. Currencies based upon a gold standard had shown very marked signs of depreciation in their purchasing power[10] while some inconvertible currencies had maintained their pre-war parity and international value, allowance being made for an increase in prices due to a shortage in the supply of goods or higher costs of production. In all the countries where the monetary unit, whether convertible into gold or whether based upon an inconvertible standard, had maintained its relative international value, this had always been due to manipulations of the management of the central bank in regulating the quantity of notes in circulation. Keynes describes this situation as follows:[11] „Gold itself has become a managed currency and a regulated non-metallic standard has slipped in. It exists."

---

9. Maynard Keynes, Tract On Monetary Reform.

10. In his book „Deutsche Währungs- und Kreditpolitik seit Währungs-festigung" Dr. Justus Schoenthal mentions on page 98 the particularly interesting situation in Spain. From 1914 to 1924, the Bank of Spain increased its holdings of gold by six times up to a total of about 500 million dollars in 1924. During the same period it issued additional notes up to an amount of 200 pesetas per head of the population. In spite of a gold cover of 54 per cent the Spanish currency depreciated in its internal and external purchasing power to about one fourth of what it had been in 1914.

11. Maynard Keynes, Monetary Reform, p. 187.

It was especially the monetary conditions in the United States, which strengthened this argument of Keynes in favor of a „managed currency", (a monetary system, whereby the internal and external value of the monetary unit is maintained by a simultaneous manipulation of the discount rate and quantity of notes in circulation). In the United States the total of gold held by the Federal Reserve Banks increased from about 1900 million dollars in 1915 to about 4400 million in 1924. The peculiar fact is that in spite of the very material increase in the percentage of reserves to notes outstanding, the purchasing power of the dollar was in 1924 only 60 per cent of what it had been in 1914. But even this relatively low value had only been maintained by the Federal Reserve Banks by hoarding a large portion of the inflowing stock of gold without issuing any additional quantity of notes. If one does not include the gold reserve for bank deposits required by American Banking Law, the actual cover for the notes in circulation exceeded one hundred per cent. Nevertheless, the dollar has lost 40 per cent of its pre-war purchasing power.

The large supply of gold in the vaults of the Federal Reserve Banks causes Keynes to voice his fear of an international inflation should Europe return to a gold standard. Keynes writes:[12] „Confidence in the future stability of gold depends on the United States being foolish enough to go on accepting gold which it does not want and wise enough having once accepted it to maintain it at a fixed value. The position is precarious." Keynes' position may be summarized in his statement"[13] "In truth the gold standard is already a barbarous relic."

Professor Gustav Cassel's viewpoint[14] differs fundamentally from that of Keynes and he reaches just the opposite conclusions as to the future effect of the gold supply of the Federal Reserve Banks upon the international value of gold in case Europe should decide to re-establish the gold standard. Cassel admits that the real task

---

12. Keynes Monetary Reform, p. 187.
13. Ibid., p. 187.
14. This survey is based upon Prof. Cassel's book: Post-War Monetary Stabilization, and upon an article „Die neue Goldwährung" published by Prof. Cassel in the „Frankfurter Zeitung" on Jan. 1, 1926 in which Cassel takes into account the development in Europe during the preceding two years.

for the central bank in regulating the currency is the maintenance of the value of the monetary unit and thus of the general price level, and that the mere existence of a gold standard does not guarantee this effect. Experience during the post-war period has, however, clearly demonstrated that any attempt to experiment with a rationally regulated paper currency ends disastrously in practice. It was the recognition of these dangers which prompted European bankers to favor the re-establishment of a gold standard as the basis of a stable currency rather than the belief in a supremacy of gold as the basis of a stable monetary system.

This international desire to base the currency upon a gold standard is the premise upon which Cassel develops his theory of the advantages and shortcomings of a gold standard. Cassel clearly recognizes that the return to the gold standard after such a long period of inflation must be accompanied by simultaneous attempts to stabilize the international value of gold which had been lost during the post-war period. The pre-war stability of the gold standard had been due to the general existence of an international gold standard and the ensuing demand for gold for monetary purposes, caused partly by the demand of the central banks for gold reserves and partly by the demand for gold coins in circulation.

During the post-war period this demand for gold had partly been replaced by the circulation of paper currency which has brought about a depreciation of gold to about 60 per cent of its pre-war value. Due to the fact that the United States was the only country which had a convertible standard and that it had accumulated about one half of the world supply of gold, the international value of gold was determined by the value of the American dollar. This precious metal had therefore lost its function as a measure of international values. A general reintroduction of gold would therefore necessitate first the re-establishment of gold as an objective measure of value. In order to fulfill this function it is necessary that the future world production of gold should rise proportionally with the rate of economic progress of the world, which according to Cassel is about 3 per cent per annum.[15]

---

15. Cassel arrives at this rate by a statistical study of the world

As a matter of fact, the actual world production of gold has decreased below this rate of three per cent. Hence if the demand for gold would increase in the future pari passum with the general economic progress of three per cent per annum there would after a short time ensue an international shortage of gold for monetary purposes and consequently prices would fall.

It is thus that Cassel arrives at the opposite conclusion from Keynes that the re-establishment of a gold standard will not result in an international inflation due to the large amount of gold in the vaults of the Federal Reserve Banks but on the contrary will tend to deflate prices. Such a deflation can be avoided, according to Cassel, if the various central banks decide upon a system of international cooperation and concentrate the existing supply of gold in a few internationally important central banks. However, Cassel admits that a substitution of the gold standard by an internationally regulated paper currency might be practical in the future, and might even prove superior to a gold standard. Under the economic condi tions prevailing in Europe in 1924 and 1925 such paper currency lacked the necessary economic and political foundation.

Dr. Hahn's viewpoint[16] is in general similar to that of Keynes. According to Hahn, the gold standard has outlived its destination in theory and practice. Its use was justified in periods when many countries had a multitude of banks of issue without any centralized regulation or control. In modern times, a gold cover is practically meaningless because of the impossibility to convert all outstanding notes into gold if so required. Hahn denies that the convertibility of notes into gold sets in motion those quantitative changes in the price level which are attributed to the gold standard and which are considered the means which bring about an international readjustment. Such tendencies, asserts Hahn, are neutralized by

production of gold during the period 1850 to 1911 and by a comparison of the changes in the level of international prices. His conclusion is that an annual increase in the gold production of three per cent was sufficient to provide the means of payments for the expending world economy. Cassel also assumes that this rate of three per cent holds true for the future economic expansion. See Cassel, Theoretische Sozialökonomie, page 350 ff.

16. Dr. L. Albert Hahn, Goldvorteil und Goldvorurteil.

an equivalent increase in the supply of commodities, or by seasonal fluctuations which are readjusted without movements of gold.

Hahn also points out that central banks have in practice abandoned the conception of the gold standard which is embodied in Peel's Act of 1844. Thus, the German Bank Act of 1875, allotted to the Bank of Issue a fixed quantity of uncovered notes which was subsequently increased in order to meet economic needs. Moreover, the convertibility of the notes was frequently suspended in periods of drainage of gold from the vaults of the central bank. Furthermore, central banks do no longer observe passively a pouring out of gold and the automatic reaction in the internal price structure, but adopt positive means to prevent such movements of gold if they threaten the maintenance of a fixed minimum of reserve.

From all these facts, Hahn concludes that the egal requirement of a gold reserve and the limitation of the note issue are theoretically harmful and without any effect in practice. To achieve the desired result of preventing an excessive issue of notes by the central bank it is sufficient to provide that the central bank is legally obliged to sell gold in bars or foreign exchange at a fixed rate. Hahn, demands that it be left entirely to the discretion of the central bank to provide the necessary reserve of gold or foreign exchange, without prescribing any legal minimum. Such a reserve is necessary in order to maintain an international equilibrium as well as for international payments. It is Hahn's opinion that the Rentenbank conformed to the requirements of modern currency theories and that the reorganization of the Reichsbank upon a gold standard was unnecessary and of potential danger.

Compared with the three theories analyzed above, Dr. Schacht's viewpoint is different because of its emphasis upon practical necessities which distinguishes the President of the Reichsbank from the theorists. Dr. Schacht had always been an adherent of the gold standard, and considered the Rentenbank merely as a preliminary step toward the final reestablishment of the gold standard. In his opinion the Rentenmark was not a means for the settlement of international payments which had to be made in gold or foreign exchange. Only a bank based upon a gold reserve and disposing of a considerable stock of foreign exchange was in a position to provide the necessary means for international payments. Moreover, the President of the Reichsbank clearly recognized that his task could not be to defend the permanence of a monetary system which was but an experiment at a time when there was a very pressing need for foreign capital in Germany. In view of the international distrust of a monetary system the stability of which depended entirely upon the management of the Rentenbank, an influx of funds from abroad was very improbable, if the Rentenmark currency would have been maintained. It was the recognition of an international psychology with regard to the gold standard which induced Dr. Schacht to favor the reintroduction of the gold standard in Germany. One will recall that Dr. Schacht after taking office in November 1923, held various conferences with the Bank of England and bankers in London as well as with the Bank of Amsterdam about a month later in order to obtain their cooperation in the establishment of a Gold Bank in Germany.

In the light of actual conditions there cannot be any doubt that Dr. Schacht and Professor Cassel rightly advocated the reintroduction of the gold standard in Europe. The potential danger of a managed paper currency outweighed by far the disadvantages of the maintenance of gold as a reserve and the ensuing payment of interest which could be saved in case of a pure paper currency.

Undoubtedly the Experts have been prompted by similar considerations in their demand of the reorganization of the German monetary system on a gold basis. Nevertheless, the Experts were not uncompromising believers in the stability of the gold standard as is reflected in the following provision of the Plan: „Gold is only a measure of value, and over a long period of years may be an uncertain and defective one. We, therefore, propose that a reduction or increase in the figures both as regards the standard and the supplementary payments should be made automatically in correspondence with changes in the general purchasing power of gold, whenever such changes amount to more than ten per cent."[17]

(1) Note Privilege of the Reichsbank. Article One of the new Bank Law determine the independence of the Reichsbank and reads: „The Reichsbank is an institution independent of the government of the Reich, vested with legal personality and having

---

17. Report of the Experts, Part I Sec. VIII, c.

the task to regulate the circulation of money within the area of the Reich, to facilitate settlements of payments and to utilize available capital." Thus the Reichsbank was wholly removed from any influence of the Reich upon its credit policy. This clause represents one of the important principles inserted by the Experts into the German central bank system. For half a century, the German Reichsbank had always been considered an institution which must by its very nature be closely connected with the government if the interest of the public was to be safeguarded. The Autonomy Act of July, 1922 had proved in reality to be but a formal separation of the Reichsbank from the supervision of the Reich, without affecting the previous relation between Reich and Reichsbank so far as discount of treasury debentures was concerned. In Germany the standpoint had always been maintained that the central bank had public functions and thus must be under the supervision of the Reich.

The Experts, however, deemed it essential that the new Bank must be independent of any governmental influence in order that the stability of the currency be secured. It was deemed necessary that the Reichsbank should be granted its note privilege for a long period. An agreement was reached between the Organization Committee and the Reich that the new Bank should be granted the privilege of note issue for the next fifty years, whereby the Reich renounced its right to withdraw this charter during the above period. Reichsbank notes were granted the exclusive character of legal tender. As a compensation for this privilege the Reichsbank on its part agreed to the following proposal:

The Reichsbank should assume of its own liability the redemption of 252 million gold marks Dollar Treasury Notes which were due on April 1926. Secondly, concerning the existing debt of the Reich to the Bank of an amount of 235 million marks, the Reichsbank agreed to convert a part of this loan of 100 million marks into a permanent loan bearing two per cent interest and maturing only after the termination of the note privilege. The remainder of 135 millions was to take the form of a loan yielding 3 per cent p. a. and to be repayable in fifteen equal instalments over a period of fifteen years.

(2) Capital of the Reichsbank. Originally it had been provided by the Experts that the capitalization of the Bank of Issue should amount to 400 million marks. The Organization Committee departed, however, from this sum and decided upon a capital of 300 million marks which it considered to be sufficient. This resolution was adopted in view of the scarcity of capital in Germany and in view of the very liquid condition of the Reichsbank which was deemed to justify the limitation of the capital to the above amount. It was provided that the old shares of the Reichsbank should be converted in the proportion of two old shares for one new one. For the remainder of the 210 million marks, new shares were to be issued at a par value of 100 marks each.[18]

(3) Organization of the Reichsbank. A fundamental change in the organization of the Bank, as compared with its structure before this law was passed, is to be found in the influence granted to foreigners upon the policy and management of the Bank. This influence was exercised by two bodies within the Reichsbank, namely, the General Board and the Commissioner for Note issue, and one outside body, i. e. the Transfer Committee represented by the Agent General for Reparation Payments. In this chapter we shall deal mainly with the functions of the two internal bodies (General Board and Commissioner for Note Issue), while the influence exercised by the Agent General will be discussed in the next chapter concerning the transfer problem.

The main reason for the introduction of foreign control upon the management of the Reichsbank was the desire on the part of the Experts to render impossible the recurrence of a new inflation caused by excessive issues of notes.[19] It had already been recognized by the Reparation Commission that the payments of annuities could only be made under a stabilized currency, and the reader will recall that the original task assigned to the Dawes

---

18. Of these additional shares, only about 33 millions were issued. The portfolio of the Reichsbank contains at the present not-issued shares for 177 million marks.

19. Dr. Schacht cites in his book the reply of Owen D. Young to his objection of foreign control over the Reichsbank: „If we trust this Bank with all the money these reparation sums represent, we must at least have the right to a certain insight into its affairs." Stabilization, p. 167.

Committee had been to investigate means of stabilizing the German currency. In order to secure a safe bank policy the Experts not only required the insertion of certain provisions into the Bank Law, but also demanded the right to exercise control over the continuous application of these clauses by the management of the Bank. Another important reason for these provisions concerning foreign control, is to be found in the necessity to reestablish international confidence in the stability of Germany's currency. German industry and trade threatened with collapse because of the lack of capital and credit. The necessary funds, however, could only be supplied from foreign loans, the internal resources being quite insufficient. Control over the policy of the Reichsbank was, however, a necessary requirement to induce foreign capital to flow into Germany.

The organization of the Reichsbank has the following general features.

The administration of the Bank is exercised by a Managing Board of Directors (Reichsbankdirektorium), which is composed of a President who acts as Chairman, and the requisite number of members. In particular the Managing Board directs the currency, discount, and credit policy of the Reichsbank. The President of the Bank an the members of the Board must be German Nationals. The President is elected by the General Board (Generalrat) by a majority of at least nine votes, at least six of which must be cast by German Nationals. Such an election in order to be valid requires the signing of the appointment by the President of the Reich. Should, however, the President of the Reich refuse his approval to two successive nominations, a third election legally appoints the President of the Reichsbank without the requirement of the signing of the deed by the President of the Reich.

The shareholders meet annually in the General assembly, wherein they receive the reports of the Managing Board. In these meetings they elect a Central Committee (Zentralkomitee), whose rights are much limited as compared with those conferred upon this body by the former Bank Act. The Managing Board consults their opinion only in matters which it thinks fit. From the Central Committee three deputies are elected for the purpose of consultation by the Directors in special matters. Both the Central Committee and the Deputies must be German Nationals.

The General Board,[20] as the third body in the organization of the Bank, is composed of fourteen members, seven of whom must be German Nationals, while the other seven members must consist of one British National, one French, one Italian, one Belgian, one American, one Dutch, and one Swiss National. The President of the Reichsbank is one of the German members and at the same time the Chairman of the General Board. At each of the meetings, (at least once every month), the General Board examines the reports submitted to it by the President and the Commissioner for Note issue. The assent of the General Board is essential and required in the following cases: If the ratio of the reserves is to be reduced below the legally required minimum of 40 per cent; if the redemption of the Reichsbank notes into gold is to be resumed; and if the ratio of the collateral loans is to be altered.

Originally the Experts had planned immediately to introduce full convertibility of the Reichsbank notes into gold. Dr. Schacht, although an adherent of the gold standard, ardently opposed this project, pointing to the fact that there was not a single country in Europe which at that time had legally established complete redemption of its notes into gold. The Organization Committee later on decided to propose the postponement of redemption. Thus, Article 52 prescribes that the conversion of notes into gold should not come into effect until a concurrent resolution of the Managing Board and General Council has been passed. The legal provision that the Bank sells foreign exchange at any time renders the currency for practical purposes as effective as a gold standard.

The General Board has, furthermore, the task of appointing one of its foreign members, or a foreigner who is a national of those countries represented in this body, as Commissioner of the Note Issue. His election requires at least nine votes including a minimum of six foreign votes. The elected Commissioner by virtue of his oppointment becomes a member of the General Board if he had not been in this body before his election, in which case the member of the same nationality has to resign from this Board.

---

20. The General Board has the position in the Reichsbank which had formerly been held by the Bank Curatorium.

(4) The Bank's Sphere of Business. The scope of operations which the Reichsbank is empowered to undertake is so important as to justify their reproduction in full: The Reichsbank is authorized:

(1) To buy and sell gold and silver coins or bullion as well as foreign exchange.

(2) a.[21]

„2 a. To discount, buy and sell Treasury Bills of the Reich which have a currency of not more than three months and which are backed by a person of known solvency in addition to the Reich.

The amount of Treasury Bills of the Reich discounted or bought in accordance with this provision or accepted as collateral in accordance with figure 3g may not at any time exceed the amount of 400 million marks. This amount will not rank as note cover within arxicle 28."

(b) To buy, to sell or discount bills of exchange maturing no later than 90 days, bearing at least three names of known solvency and cheques also bearing at least three names of known solvency. The requirement of a third name may be dispensed with in cases in which the safety of the bill of exchange or cheque is secured by collateral or in some other manner.[22] The volume of such papers may not exceed 33 per cent of the total bills held. All bills must relate to bona fide commercial transactions.

(3) To grant interest-bearing loans up to 90 days against the following collateral securities (Lombarddarlehen):

(a) Gold and silver (minted or unminted).

(b) Fully paid common or common priority stock or priority obligation of German rail-roads whose lines are in opera-

---

21. On July 8, 1926 an amendment to the Bank Law was passed, resolving the insertion of the following sentence in this paragraph:

This amendment was approved by the Reparation Commission on May 29, July 3, 1926 (Decisions No. 3249, 3286) and published in the Reichsgesetzblatt II July 13, 1926 page 355.

22. The Experts' Plan had originally called for discount of papers bearing the indorsement of at least three solvent vouchers. In view of the fact that the custom of the Reichsbank to discount directly through its branches the bills of exchange of small traders and in view of the experience which it had developed and which showed that the losses had been infinitesimal, the Organization Committee had proposed that 33 per cent of the total of discounted bills may bear only two signatures. This concession was then embodied in the Law.

tion, as well as debentures of agricultural, commercial, or other German land credit institutions under federal supervision, and debentures of German corporate mortgage banks, up to 75 per cent of their market value.

(c) Bearer obligations of the Federal Government, of a German State, or a domestic commercial corporation or interest-bearing obligations, the interest of which is guaranteed by the Federal Government or by one of the States up to 75 per cent of their market value. The maturity of the above mentioned obligations must not exceed one year. Loans guaranteed by such collateral may be granted to banks of known solvency only.

(d) Interest-bearing bearer obligations of foreign states as well as state guaranteed foreign railway obligations, up to 50 per cent of the market value.

(e) Merchandise warehoused within the country up to two thirds of its value. The Bank may with special authorization of the General Board take as collateral long-term obligations of the Federal Government for loans maturing in 90 days or less if there are two guarantors liable for the obligation outside of the collateral, both of whom must be doing business within Germany, and one being a bank. It is, however, stipulated that secured loans for which long-term obligation of the Federal Government are collateral may not exceed the paidup capital of the Bank plus its reserves.

(4) To buy and sell the securities mentioned under 3c; the purchase of such securities for its own account is permitted only in so far as it is essential to maintain its current business with its customers.

(5) To handle collections for institutions, of fiscal bodies and private persons; to make payments and transfer for their account. provided the Bank has received countervalue.

(6) To buy for customers' account, securities of any kind as well as precious metals, provided the counter value has been received, and to sell the same, provided delivery has been made.

(7) To receive money without interest or deposits in gold.

In general, we may fairly state that the Reichsbank was authorized to carry on all those kinds of operations which usually fall within the scope of a central bank's activities. A special feature of these clauses is that they prevent an excessive amount of government paper from getting into the Bank's portfolio.

Article 24 of the Act provides that the Bank shall purchase any quantity of gold at a fixed price of 1392 reichsmark for one pound (500 gramm) gold of 1000/000 finess. This clause has lately found much opposition among German financiers and economists. It fixes the upper limit of the value of the German currency and exposes it to fluctuation in the value of gold in other countries, i. e. it renders it dependent upon a depreciation of some other currency. Although it is not very probable that the value of gold will depreciate in the next future, this limitation of the mark in its upper value might some day become of great significance. Experience since the Great War has shown that the value of gold is also exposed to great depreciations just as the value of any other commodity. Furthermore, it must not be overlooked that the Reich renounced its right to pass any ammendment to the Bank Law without the approval of the Reparation Commission. Should therefore, the value of gold in some country depreciate and other countries through legislative measures prevent a concurrent fluctuation in the value of their currency, the mark will inevitably depreciate, too. In view of the psychological circumstances which caused the adoption of this clause and in view of the re-established international confidence, the assumption seems justified that this provision might be amended some day with the approval of the Reparation creditors.

As far as credit to be granted by the Reichsbank to the Reich is concerned, Article 25 limits this amount to 100 million marks, and prescribes the maturity of these loans at no later than three months. The Reichsbank was, however, authorized to grant loans to the German rail-roads and to the German Post office up to an amount of 200 millions. Outside of these amounts the Bank was forbidden to grant directly or indirectly any credit to the Reich, States, municipalities, or foreign governments.

Paragraph 26 regulates the relation between the Bank an the Agent General for Reparation Payments. These relations are described as those of a bank to its customers. The Reichsbank establishes a special deposit account for the Reparation Payments to be paid in by the Reich for the credit of the former.

So far as note issue is concerned, article 27 provides that „the preparation, the issue, the withdrawal and cancellation of banknotes is effected by the note department under the control of the Commissioner. The Commissioner shall be empowered and it shall be his essential duty to insist upon the carrying out of such of the provisions contained in the law and in the constitution of the Reichsbank as referred to the excersion of the right of issue of notes and the preservation of the cover in gold for the notes in circulation. Without any object in view, the Commissioner shall have the right to have furnished to him all statistics and documents which he may deem useful for the accomplishment of his task. He may be present at all meetings of the Managing Board. He or his assistants are bound to observe complete secrecy in respect to all affairs and arrangements of the Bank which have come to their knowledge.“

The above clause shows clearly the great controlling influence which the creditor countries exercised upon the issue of notes and maintenance of a fixed minimum gold reserve through the Commissioner for Note Issue.

Another very important provision concerns the legally required cover for the issue of Reichsbank notes. Article 28, which prescribes a minimum cover of 40 per cent consisting of at least three quarters in gold and for the remainder in foreign exchange, represents a compromise between banking and currency principles. The reader will recall that the Bank Act of 1875 had provided a cover of at least 33 per cent in gold; thus the required cover of foreign exchange is a new item in the reserves. Originally, the Experts had proposed that the issued notes be covered by only 33⅓ per cent in gold, while a reserve of 12 per cent in gold was to be required for deposits with the Reichsbank.

A legally required cover for deposits is an old principle in American banking law, but unknown to German law. This difference in principle is an outgrowth of banking development in these two countries, a fact whose full importance Experts did not seem to realize. Thus, when the Organization Committee proceeded with its work, it recognized that the adoption of such a measure into the Law was very difficult and its success very doubtful in view of the possibility of an accumulation of a deposit of two billion marks by the Agent General. German banks do not keep any deposits with the Reichsbank other than a bare minimum, for the purpose of clearing their payments throughout Germany. The other parts of the deposits belong to the Reich, railways, Post Office, Commerce and States. In view of the great fluctuations in all these deposits, especially those of the Agent General, it was of utmost difficulty to provide an automatic system of gold reserve. The Organization Committee also realized that any attempt to this effect might have very serious consequences. Thus, the following clause was adopted:

„The new Bank will be required to maintain at least a reserve of 40 per cent against its notes in circulation. At least three fourths must be in one form of gold in its own vaults or with foreign banks of issue at the free disposal of the Reichsbank, the pound of fine gold being reckoned at 1392 mark. The balance of the 40 per cent must consist of „devisen" which is defined as (a) foreign bank notes, (b) bills of exchange running no more than 14 days, (c) foreign cheques, (d) deposits with any bank situated in a foreign financial centre and known to be solvent. Against the balance of 60 per cent the Reichsbank will be required to hold eligible bills of exchange or cheques.

Under special circumstances and with the consent of the general Board the reserve percentage may be allowed to drop below 40 per cent. In case the reserve percentage remains below 40 per cent for more than a week, the Reichsbank will be required to pay a deficiency tax to the government according to the following scale:

In the case of a cover between 37 an 40% . . . 3% annually
In the case of a cover between 35 and 37% . . . 5% annually
In the case of a cover between 33 and 35% . . . 8% annually
In the case of a cover less than $33\frac{1}{3}$%   8% and one per cent additional tax for every per cent below $33\frac{1}{3}$% per cent. Whenever a deficiency tax is to be paid, the discount rate must be raised by one third of the tax rate to be paid and to at least five per cent.

Although the Law did not require a legal reserve of 12 per cent gold for deposits, it prescribed a special cover of 40 per cent to be composed of demand deposits of the Reichsbank with other banks and maturing no later than in thirty days. (Article 35).[23]

VI. Distribution of Profits. The Law prescribes that the Reichsbank has to maintain a reserve fund, and as long as this fund amounts to less than 12 per cent of the notes in circulation, 20 per cent of its net profits are to be added to its reserves. It was provided that the shareholders are entitled to a cumulative dividend of eight per cent per annum, which has to be paid after the reserve fund requirement has been met. Of the balance of the net profits, the government will receive an important share in lieu of taxes. Of the first 50 millions one half goes to the government and one half to the shareholders; of the second 50 millions $\frac{3}{4}$ go to the government and $\frac{1}{4}$ to the shareholders; if there remains any further balance the government receives $\frac{1}{10}$ and the shareholders $\frac{1}{10}$.

Liquidation of the Rentenbank.[24] The Experts' Plan called for the immediate liquidation of the Rentenbank after the reorganization of the Reichsbank. But in view of the very complex and severe economic conditions prevailing in Germany, the Organization Committee found it necessary to depart considerably from the lines laid down by the Dawes Committee. Especially the great crisis through which the agricultural class was then passing rendered it improbable that their loans would be met at maturity, and a period of three years was considered necessary for the liquidation of this credit. Thus the Organization Committee came to the following arrangement:

In view of the bonds and debentures imposed upon German industry as security for the Dawes annuities, it had been deemed necessary to release these industries from the mortgages and

---

23. It will be noted that the Bank Law of 1924 does not allot a contingent of uncovered notes to be issued by the Reichsbank as had been legally permitted by the Bank Act of 1875. This reserve clause, therefore, undoubtedly represents an outlived and economically unwarranted restriction in the issue policy of the Reichsbank.

24. Gesetz über die Liquidierung der Rentenbank vom 30. August 1924 (Reichsgesetzblatt II S. 252).

debentures imposed upon them by the Rentenbank Law. It was thus decided to increase the remaining mortgage upon agriculture from 4 to 5 per cent of the assessed pre war value, and to decrease the interest rate from 6 to 5 per cent. The capital value of these mortgages was estimated at between 1700 and 2000 million marks. The circulation of rentenbank notes in June was in round figures: 1200 millions credit to the Reich; 800 millions general credit to the Reichsbank; 70 millions general credit to the other four private note issuing banks.

These notes are redeemed in the following manner. With regard to the 1200 millions credit to the Reich the latter had agreed to redeem it in annual instalments of 60 millions for 10 years. These 60 millions were guaranteed by the Reich as revenue from the interest of the mortgages imposed upon agriculture. The Reichsbank would handle over to the Rentenbank the assets for the 800 millions, which the Rentenbank was to collect during the next three years.

Besides the self liquidating 870 millions, the debts of 1200 millions of the Reich would be liquidated as follows:

From the government	annually 60 millions
Interest from mortgages estimated at	annually 85 millions

and in addition all the profits payable to the Reich from the Reichsbank.

At the same time the attention of the Organization Committee was called to the fact that there was very considerable need for farmer's credit, the lack of which threatened the collapse of agriculture. It was strongly urged that some portions of the means of the Rentenbank be utilized for this purpose. In order to relieve this situation the Organization Committee entered into the following arrangement:

The Rentenbank has the task to concentrate upon the liquidation of its notes and is not authorized to undertake any other business. An agricultural credit institute (RENTENBANK KREDITANSTALT) was founded to which the Rentenbank would transfer its balance standing on September 30, 1924 and which was estimated at about 150 millions. In addition each year, after 60 millions had been applied for the redemption of the outstanding rentenmark currency, an amount not exceeding 25 millions shall be paid to the Rentenbank Kreditanstalt if available.

It was furthermore provided that the Golddiskontbank should be liquidated through acquisition of all outstanding shares by the Reichsbank in the form of an exchange of shares of the Golddiskont Bank for those of the Reichsbank at the ratio of one to one.

CHAPTER VIII.

THE EFFECT OF FOREIGN LOANS UPON THE ECONOMIC READJUSTMENT OF GERMANY.

The ratification of the Dawes Plan marked the last step in the stabilization and reorganization of the German monetary system. It is but natural that the following year marked a period of readjustment and reconstruction of the economic disorganization brought about by the currency inflation. Especially the restoration of international confidence in the German economy and the gradual upbuilding of normal credit and financial conditions were directly attributable to the confidence which the Dawes Plan inspired. However, the economic readjustment of Germany did not take place without a period of severe depression and disturbances, a fact which is not surprising in view of the conditions prevailing in Germany in 1924. One factor was of particularly great influence upon her economic development during the following years, i. e. the flow of foreign loans. They have been indispensable for the reorganization of industry and commerce and have also been responsible for a delayed readjustment of the economy as will be shown later on in this chapter. One cannot understand the events without analyzing carefully the effects of the stream of foreign loans upon the Reichsbank and upon the German business world.

It will be recalled that the Dawes Plan had provided for the flotation of a German External Loan of 800 million marks[1] which was to serve the twofold purpose „of assuring currency stability and financing essential deliveries in kind during the preliminary period of economic rehabilitation". The negotiations concerning this loan did not terminate until October 11, 1924 and delayed the

---

1. The rate of issue was 92% at 7 per cent interest and maturing 1949. The nominal amount issued was 960 million marks.

ratification of the Bank Law until that date.[2] In the light of modern currency theories the dual character of the loan was not without danger from the standpoint of the central bank. A simultaneous use of these funds for reserve purposes and financing deliveries in kind tended to inflate prices through the additional purchasing power which the Reichsbank had to grant the government in order to effect these purchases. Such an increase in prices was detrimental to the transfer of reparation payments in cash and to a reorganization of the economy which required a deflation policy in order to neutralize the inflationary effects of the foreign loans.

The influence of an inflow of funds from abroad upon the domestic price level depends upon how these amounts are employed by the borrower. The process by which international loans are contracted and the ways in which they may be disposed of by the debtor are as follows: A (German) entrepreneur obtains a loan from a (New York) bank. The creditor will then authorize the debtor to draw foreign bills of exchange against him up to the amount of the loan. These funds are then at the disposal of the borrower who may avail himself of his present claims in various ways. If he happens to be an importer of goods from this or any other country he may draw a bill of exchange upon the (New York) bank and thus pay for the merchandise. In this case the total of money in circulation (in Germany) has not increased, other things being equal, while the supply of commodities in the market has now become larger. As a consequence, the prices of goods will fall and foreign buyers will be attracted by the lower price level.

On the other hand if the borrower does not import goods for which he pays with bills drawn upon his foreign credit he may dispose of his funds by selling his bills either in the open market or by exchanging them for domestic currency at the central bank. The effect of these foreign loans upon the domestic price level will then depend upon their final employment. If they are acquired by an importer of goods with the aid of bank-credit for the purpose of effecting payments abroad the domestic price level will remain unaltered. The import of goods will augment the existing supply but will be compensated for by the additional purchasing power

---

2. Law of October 10th, 1924 published in Reichsgesetzblatt II, page 238.

which the seller of the bills obtained. Should the importer buy the bills without employing additional bank credit for this specific purpose, then the effect will be the same as in the first case. The total quantity of commodities being larger than the total of money remaining unchanged will result in a decline of prices.

However, if the foreign credits are not employed finally for the import of an equivalent quantity of goods then the effect will be an inflation of prices. The enterprise which has obtained foreign credits and which has sold its claims to the central bank represents additional purchasing power in the market. It competes in the market on the basis of banknotes which are covered by foreign exchange or even gold, if the central bank has converted the claims abroad into gold, but without an equivalent rise in the social output of goods. Apparently the larger quantity of money now in the market will then increase the price level for the unchanged supply of commodities. The effect of foreign loans upon prices will thus be an inflation. Such a result can be avoided if the central bank, simultaneously with the issue of new notes against the foreign exchange, retards the total of credits outstanding by an amount sufficient to maintain the original balance between demand and supply in the market.

The influence of foreign loans upon the domestic price level above analyzed holds only if they are of a long term nature. Otherwise, the redemption of the debts after a short interval of time will set in motion tendencies in the opposite direction before any material change in the price structure occurs. Thus the large inflow of funds tended to exert quite an influence upon the German economy and the final effect depended upon the utilization by the borrowers. The foreign debts can only be repaid, without harm to the community from a surplus of social income, viz. savings resulting from postponing a part of present consumption for future uses. The actual use of these credits during the first year the plan was in operation, was however not in accordance with those principles which economic prudence required. As a matter of fact the flow of foreign loans although having contributed to increased production had also been the cause of a further delay of the economic readjustment which had commenced to take effect after the credit restriction of the summer of 1924.

In order to understand the frequent economic abuses of these loans it must be kept in mind that Germany lacked at that time a capital market of any appreciable extent, such a market being of utmost importance in supplying the necessary long term funds. The funds in the capital market are the result of savings and in view of the totally depreciated savings during the inflation it is obvious that the reestablishment of a capital market required many years. As a consequence the German business world depended almost entirely upon foreign markets to provide the necessary funds. At the outset the overwhelmingly large part of these loans represented short term funds deposited by foreign owners of capital with German banks for the purpose of taking advantage of higher rates in the German money market.[3]

Many entrepreneurs availed themselves of these funds for purposes detrimental to the nature of the credit. In many cases the borrower reorganized his plan in order to be in a better position to compete in the market. Others used their credit to finance a further maintenance of their unproductive plans, unwilling to undergo the pecuniary sacrifices which a rationalization required. The effect of such an investment policy was a renewed illiquidity of many enterprises which were not in a position to redeem their debts unless an additional amount of long term funds should be forthcoming in the capital market. But as the domestic sources for new capital were negligible in comparison with the demand, liquidation of these short term debts was only possible if sufficient capital flowed in from abroad. It is therefore obvious that a crisis was inevitable at the time that the maturing debts could not be transformed into long term obligations and the illiquidity of money enterprises would thus be revealed. And it was not before long (the summer of 1925) that a new crisis broke out which finally led to the economic readjustment of Germany.

Aside from loans contracted by private enterprises, many states, municipalities and other public bodies who had not been able during the inflation to finance the expansion or renovation of their properties, desired to float bond issues abroad in order to

---

3. The total of short term funds deposited with the German banks in winter 1924—1925 was estimated at about 2.5 billion reichsmark.

obtain the necessary funds. In order to understand the situation, attention must be called to the fact that German power companies, street cars, subways, and similar enterprises are owned and managed either by the states or by municipalities. A clear distinction had therefore to be drawn between loans contracted for the purpose of financing such productive enterprises or loans asked for the financing of unproductive construction, i. g. hospitals, parks, playgrounds, etc. While in the first case the interest payments and amortization of the debts could be defrayed with the profits of those enterprises these payments could in the second case only be met by imposing additional taxes. Such an increased tax burden would approach the limit to which the German economy could be subjected without jeopardizing social productivity.

The lack of sufficient business prudence on the part of the public boards tended to lead to a contraction of debts which could not be redeemed by earnings from the investments but only by means of taxation. These loans also tended to increase the interest rate for business enterprises by the greater competition for foreign loans which was carried into the foreign markets. The Reichsbank clearly recognized the true nature of these loans and owing to the initiative of Dr. Schacht, the federal government appointed a Federal Advisory Board for foreign loans (Reichsberatungsstelle für Auslandsanleihen).[4] This board has the task of investigating the nature of the enterprise for which a loan was desired by public authorities and to analyze its productivity. It examined the conditions of the loans, the interest rate, etc. Undoubtedly the establishment of this federal board has been of great aid in preventing public boards contracting debts which might have had grave consequences.

The far-reaching effect of the inflow of foreign funds had also a very material influence upon the conditions in the money market and simultaneously upon the Reichsbank.

So far as the moneymarket was concerned, the conditions prevailing therein were far from normal. Throughout the later part of 1924 and during the whole of 1925, the money market showed a very great liquidity. The causes for its development were manifold.

---

4. Decree of November 1st, 1924. Reichsgesetzblatt I, p. 276.

First, the economic depression which had taken place in August 1924 continued and as a consequence the demand for short term money was declining. Secondly, banks and business enterprises kept large cash reserves which in turn made for a liquid money market. Thirdly, the large funds accumulated by public boards were offered for short term investments and enhanced the existing liquidity. And last but not least, the very substantial amounts of foreign short term funds sought employment in the money market. Owing to these tendencies, the money market was very liquid and the declining rates rendered the dependence of borrowers upon a rediscount by the Reichsbank very slight. Especially the foreign funds, which were employed by the borrowers for financial purposes, increased the independence of the market over the central rates in the market of Berlin during this period.

be used immediately by the debtor and were then placed upon the money market, thus, contributing to the prevailing liquidity.

The following table demonstrates the movement of the money bank. In many cases loans had been contracted which could not

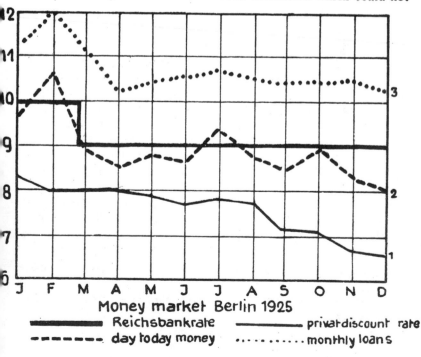

Money market Berlin 1925

———— Reichsbankrate ———— privat discount rate
------- day today money ·········· monthly loans

As was pointed out, the influx of foreign funds exercised a very considerable influence upon the policy of the Reichsbank and upon its position in the German economy. From the standpoint of the currency, the question automatically arose how the Reichsbank was to gain control over the instreaming funds. It was obvious to the management of that institution that such an investment policy could not continue without ill effects upon the whole community. In the first place, the contractions of loans abroad and the practice of exchanging the ensuing claims for German currency tended to thrust the Bank aside as a credit institution. The credits granted by foreign markets took the place of the commercial credits otherwise granted by the Reichsbank. In the place of a considerable and concentrated portfolio of domestic papers, the Bank's holdings declined and it was forced to buy foreign bills of exchange.

The second result was that the Bank was compelled to issue notes for the additional foreign bills and thus to increase the total of notes in circulation. This tendency for the first few months after the ratification of the Dawes Plan, could not be prevented by the Reichsbank. A refusal on part of the latter to buy foreign exchange at the par rate of 4.20 Reichsmark for one dollar would merely have increased the value of the mark up to the specie import point, where it would have been profitable for the owner of foreign bills to undergo the expense of importing gold to Germany. Under the Bank Law of August, 1924, the Reichsbank was, however, compelled to purchase any quantity of gold offered at the rate of 2784 Reichsmark for one kilogram gold. The high foreign exchange quotation of the mark would have merely handicapped the importer of goods, who had to acquire foreign bills at the high rate, without preventing the increase of prices which would ensue from these loans.

The Reichsbank was fully aware of these tendencies without being able during the autumn of 1924 and winter of 1924—1925 to prevent directly such a course. The short term nature of the larger part of the inflowing funds rendered it imperative for the Reichsbank to accumulate a sufficiently large stock of „devisen"[5] in case

---

5.. The term „devisen" includes: foreign bank notes, bills of exchange, foreign cheques.

the opposite movement should commence and the redemption of the debts cause an increased demand for foreign exchange. It has been shown how the Bank endeavored to influence the contraction of loans with regard to public boards. In December, 1924, the Reichsbank made similar efforts to influence the policies of the German credit institutions.[6] In the latter case, however, the bank did not have the desired success as was revealed in the crisis of 1925.

Before discussing the credit policy of the Reichsbank, it is well to mention first a few minor phrases of the Bank's policy, which had a certain bearing upon the credit situation. The primary effect of the instreaming funds was a substantial increase in the Bank's holding of foreign exchange. It was thus enabled to meet every demand for foreign currencies and maintained throughout the par value of the mark at the rate of 4.20 Reichsmark for one U. S. dollar. The following table reflects these tendencies and their effect upon the gold reserves and the note circulation.

HOLDINGS OF GOLD AND FOREIGN EXCHANGE BY THE REICHSBANK (in million marks).[7]

	Gold	Foreign Exchange eligible for reserve[8]	Notes in circulation	Dollar Exchange rate in Berlin
Nov. 7, 1924	694	231	1863	420
Dec. 6, 1924	696	232	1941	420
Jan. 7, 1925	781	260	1901	420
Feb. 7, 1925	845	282	2106	420
March 7, 1925	985	328	2308	420
April 7, 1925	1003	334	2447	420
May 7, 1925	1014	338	2601	420

6. „At a banquet of the Central Association of German Banks and Bankers on December 15th, 1924, I urged that short credits should only be taken up for short transactions, and that the risk of having to repay such credits in foreign currency, which might not be obtainable from the Reichsbank on credit, would then have to be paid in cash, should be kept in mind." Dr. Schacht, Stabilization, p. 219.

7. Die Wirtschaftskurve 1924 p. 419 and 1925 p. 209.

8. This item is published since the new Bank law permitted the maintenance of a note cover of 10% in foreign currencies and 30% gold.

It is evident from the above table that a very large part of the instreaming foreign currencies were converted by the Reichsbank into gold and caused a not quite adepuate increase in the quantity of notes in circulation. It must be admitted that a part of the additional notes issued by the Reichsbank at that time were conditioned by expanding business activity. In view of the potential danger, that at the maturity of many short-term debts the demand for foreign currencies might easily assume very great dimensions, the Reichsbank deemed it wise to accumulate these instreaming funds. Furthermore, the short term nature of these debts rendered utterly dangerous a policy of further limitations in order to neutralize the inflating effect of these loans.

In spite of the great liquidity in the money market the general credit situation showed a less favorable picture. Banks and private owners of funds were reluctant to invest their money in commercial papers but preferred to use them for daily loans. It must be kept in mind that the restriction of credit, introduced in April 1924, was not suspended. Such a suspension was impossible in view of the almost negligeable market for commercial papers which would have imposed the whole burden upon the Reichsbank. Furthermore, the enforcement of an economic reorganization had still to be continued and it is understandable that the Bank endeavored to promote such a readjustment as far as possible by adhering to its policy. The prevailing lack of funds rendered it necessary to gradually modify this policy. The credit institutions especially were greatly handicapped from the pursuance of an independent liberal credit policy. They depended too much upon the Reichsbank for additional funds and could not use their funds for investments beyond the limit allotted by the Bank for rediscount, without running the risk of suddenly finding themselves in a position where they would be unable to liquidate their assets if an emergency arose.

The Reichsbank subsequently adopted various means to ease the situation. As early as September, 1924, the Reichsbank announced its willingness to rediscount commercial papers which still had 90 days to run until maturity. This provision facilitated considerably the credit policy of the banks. During the summer of 1924 the Reichsbank had rediscounted only those papers maturing in no later than eight weeks. The banks had thus been forced to keep the discounted papers for a period of 4 to 5 weeks in their own portfolio before being able to obtain additional funds by means of a rediscount of their assets. The new policy of the Bank enabled the credit institutions to expand their total of credits.

In October, 1924, the Reichsbank advocated in various publications an increased employment of commercial papers by the business world as a means of payment in order to relieve the lack of funds. The management of the Reichsbank was of the opinion that there were sufficient reserves in the business world to finance the circulation of these papers at least for the greater part of their maturity. In this way the period for which the Reichsbank would normally have to hold them would have been materially reduced. Owing to the investment policy of many business enterprises, however, the market did not dispose of these necessary reserves. The effect of the official recommendation to avail of the commercial papers as means of payment was in reality that the bill was used not as a means to finance current transactions but to finance the maintenance of large stocks of commodities. In part, the great abuses by employing the bill as a means for the above mentioned purpose contributed to the severity of the credit crisis which broke out in the summer of 1925.

Another measure, adopted in October 1924, with the aim of easing the strain of the total credits allotted to the German credit institutions. The banks were enabled to enlarge their credits substantially. A more important step toward the re-establishment of normal credit conditions was the effort of the Bank to promote the formation of an open discount market. Throughout the autumn and winter of 1924/1925, the Reichsbank had made very active efforts to re-establish an open discount market in Berlin, without departing from its policy of credit restriction. At the outset the banks were reluctant to employ their funds in the purchase of bills because of the much higher rates which they could obtain in other branches of banking. It was not until March of 1925 that the Reichsbank persuaded twelve of the main banking houses in Berlin to buy acceptances in the open market. The banks agreed upon such purchases only after the Bank had promisedto rediscount additional papers of these banks beyond their rediscount allotment up to about one half of their capital stock and reserves, which amounted to about 330 million marks additional credits.

Probably the most important measures adopted by the Reichsbank were those aiming at a centralized control over the employment of funds accumulated by public banks. Amongst the most important of these institutions are the following ones: The „Reichs Kredit-Gesellschaft", all the stock of which was owned by the „Vereinigte Industrie-Unternehmungen A.G.", which in turn was a holding company with a capital of 120 million marks, owned by the Reich. The latter created this institution so as to manage its interests in industrial enterprises. In view of the very substantial part which the Reich had among certain German industries (especially Potash and Coal industries) this institution had at times received very considerable deposits from the Reich.

The „Verkehrs-Kredit-Bank" was an institution established by the German Rail-Roads after the latter became a business corporation as had been provided in the Dawes Plan. The Railroads originally used this bank for the purpose of financing the purchases of material and goods. After a short time, however, the Verkehrs Kredit Bank expanded its activities, accepted deposits and commenced open market operations. This institution had at certain periods several hundred millions of mark at its disposal.

Another institution of very substantial size was the „Rentenbank Kredit-Anstalt". The functions of this institution have been dealt with in connection with the liquidation of the Rentenmark credits, as provided by the Dawes Plan. In view of its limited and legally prescribed investment policy, which was fully in accordance with actual need and not detrimental to the Reichsbank policy, its acticities were not objected to by the Reichsbank.

The „Preussische Staatsbank" (State Bank of Prussia), generally known as „Seehandlung" acts as an agent for the Prussian State and at times is the depository of very substantial sums. The „Deutsche Giro-Zentral" acts to a great extent as a central bank for the „savings-offices" (Sparkassen). With increasing growth of savings deposited at these offices, the sums over which the Deutsche Giro Zentrale disposed became of great importance from the standpoint of centralized regulation of funds. Similarly, the German Post-Office which maintains a transfer-account system in all its branches disposed of funds which at times exceeded one half of one billion marks.

The principal public banks above enumerated transacted a very considerable amount of business during the year. These transactions involved very substantial amounts and it is apparent that their operations in the open market had an important bearing upon the general financial and credit situation in Germany. It could not be a matter of indifference for the Reichsbank to observe how these institutions invested their funds in the open market, without taking into consideration the general economic structure and the necessity for a concerted policy of these banks and the Reichsbank. Gradually the public banks developed to a point where they seriously rivalled the private banking system both in deposits and lending capacity.[9]

Such a banking structure proved itself an obstacle to an effective Reichsbank policy. Especially in 1925, these banks have taken a more significant turn with the sudden accumulation of large surplus funds at the command of the public authorities and deposited with those institutions. It was a most unnatural situation that at times when the whole German economy experienced a shortage of working capital, the public offices and banks found themselves in the possession of exceptionally large funds. The desire on the part of public officials who were in charge of the administration of public funds, to obtain high rates for loans has often led to the granting of loans to institutions which would not and often did not meet the ordinary test of banking judgment. Many public scandals ensued when the liquidation of these loans could not be achieved.

Public opinion was aroused and the investment policy of many public institutions was severely criticized. Gradually the Reichsbank succeeded in inducing these public banks to invest substantial parts of their funds in bills bought by the Reichsbank. In this way the latter was able to rediscount a part of its holdings at these institutions and to grant additional credit to the German economy. An agreement was reached in the spring of 1925 between the Reichs-

---

9. The Reichs Kredit Gesellschaft showed, according to its annual balance sheet of June 30, 1925, total deposits to an amount of 350 millions Reichsmark, the Seehandlung showed in its bi-monthly report of August 31, 1925, total resources of 900 millions; the savings offices united in the Deutsche Giro Zentrale disposed of deposits of nearly 1600 millions in December 1925; and the German Post Office had about 500 millions in its transfer accounts.

bank and the Post-Office whereby the latter put its funds — approximately 500 millions Reichsmark — at the disposal of the Bank. It was provided that the Post Office should always maintain an account of at least 30 millions at the Reichsbank. Of the remainder, one third was to be invested by the Post-Office in bills eligible for rediscount at the Reichsbank, while the remaining two thirds were to be employed for the purchase of public bonds, or be granted as loans to banks owned by the various states.

Similar agreements were concluded with the Reichs-Verkehrs-Bank and the Seehandlung. Furthermore, the Reichsbank exerted a strong influence upon the savings offices in order to compel the latter to reduce their interest charges to the rates established by the German Bankers Association (Deutsche Banken-Vereinigung). The Reichsbank endeavored in particular to induce these savings offices to invest a part of their funds in mortgages instead of short term papers. It is obvious that such a concentrated regulation of credit rendered possible a distribution of funds in accordance with social principles. It also rendered cheaper these funds for productive enterprises by eliminating the competition of illiquid concerns.

DISCOUNTS OF REICHSBANK OCT. '24 — SEPT. '25
(in million marks)[10]

	Bills & Scheques	Loans on Collateral	Bills Rediscounted at Public Banks	Total
Oct. 7, 1924	2176	15	201	2392
Nov. 7, 1924	2327	15	255	2597
Dec. 6, 1924	2170	8	502	2749
Jan. 7, 1925	1884	8	600	2490
Feb. 7, 1925	1647	47	585	2279
March 7, 1925	1663	8	606	2277
Apr. 7, 1925	1487	7	611	2105
May 7, 1925	1492	8	535	2035
June 6, 1925	1522	4	536	2062
July 7, 1925	1587	6	459	2052
Aug. 7, 1925	1706	24	490	2220
Sept. 7, 1925	1701	14	532	2247

10. This table has been compiled from: Die Wirtschaftskurve 1924 bis 1925, and Wirtschaft und Statistik 1924—1925.

It will be noticed that, aside from periodical fluctuations, the total rediscount of the Reichsbank, including those amounts discounted at public banks, remained almost the same. The decline in the total of bills held by the Reichsbank in the spring of 1925 was due to various economic depressions which narrowed the circle of eligible papers. On the other hand the increase in discounts in the summer of 1925 was caused by the credit actions of the Reichsbank with regard to various large concerns which were forced into liquidation.

In connection with the rediscount policy of the Bank, mention should be made of the Gold Discount Bank. Originally it had been provided in the Dawes Plan that this institution was to be liquidated (after the reorganization of the Reichsbank) through an acquisition of the outstanding shares of the Bank. In order to provide additional credits for the import and export industries, the administration of the Reichsbank deemed it wise to re-open the Gold Discount Bank. This policy was stimulated by the desire to avail of an institution which accepted interest bearing deposits[11] and through which open market operations might be executed. In April 1925 the Gold Discount Bank resumed its activities in the market. The interest rate for credits to import and export industries was fixed at 7 per cent on May 19th, and later on lowered to 6% in October 1925.

It was stated previously that the large sums which were streaming into Germany from abroad had delayed but not suspended the readjustment crisis. The foreign loans had enabled the business world to continue its production by means of the inflowing funds. The discrepancy between production and demand which had been at the bottom of the credit crisis of the summer of 1924, was not remedied. Before discussing the economic development during this period, it might not be amiss to give a brief survey of the credit policy of the German credit institutions. The following table reflects the relative development of the various items in the bimonthly balance sheets of six of Germany's Great

---

11. Article 23 of the Bank Law prohibited the acceptance of interest bearing deposits by the Reichsbank.

Banks[12] who possess about three fourths of the total banking strength of Germany.

BI-MONTHLY BALANCE SHEETS OF 6 GREAT BANKS.[13]

Date	Dec. 31, 1913	Dec. 31, 1924	Febr. 28, 1925	Apr. 30, 1925	June 30, 1925	Aug. 31, 1925	Oct. 31, 1925
Total amount in million marks	7838.8	3892	4319				
ASSETS IN PER CENT OF TOTAL AMOUNTS:							
Money in cash and account with Reichsbank	4.59%	5.0	1.97	2.17	3.34	2.41	2.12
Claims on other banks and bills	26.8 %	38.13	34.92	34.84	33.98	38.58	33.84
Loans on Stock market, collateral advances	20.71%	9.15	10.38	10.14	9.44	9.57	10.57
Other assets	45.91%	43.22	48.45	43.28	49.28	50.49	49.55
LIABILITIES IN Per CENT OF TOTAL AMOUNT							
Short term obligations:							
due no later than in 7 days	54.22%	55.22	54.34	59.08	57.38	55.68	52.74
Due no later than 3 months	16.63%	25.75	28.58	26.07	28.18	29.18	32.35
Due after 3 months	2.44%	1.60	1.69	1.07	1.36	2.24	2.30
Other liabilities	2.14%	1.45	0.98	0.63	0.50	0.44	0.61
Capital and reserves	19.02%	15.98	14.40	13.15	12.58	12.46	11.99

This item includes: securities, stocks of enterprises in which the respective bank is stockholder.

In the above figures the material change in the various items from 1913 to 1925 is clearly seen. Among the assets it is especially noteworthy that the cash reserves show a continuous decrease. This is due to the more frequent use of banks by the public which enables the credit institutions to maintain a smaller per centage of money in cash. This decrease is compensated for by the higher

12. These institutions include: Deutsche Bank; Dresdner Bank; Darmstädter Bank; Disconto-Gesellschaft; Commerz- und Privatbank; Mitteldeutsche Creditanstalt.

13. Die Wirtschaftskurve 1925, pp. 179, 328, 437.

percentage of claims upon other banks and the larger holdings of bankers' acceptances. On the other hand, the loans on collateral and advances on merchandise show a sharp decline of almost 50% of what they totalled in 1913. Among the liabilities, similar changes can be noticed. While short term obligations due in less than 7 days remained almost unchanged, the obligations due in less than three months increased to almost double the per centage of 1913. This increase was partly at the expense of deposits due after 3 months, and partly balanced by the reduced capital and reserves. In general, the balance sheets reflect a very cautious and liquid credit policy.

The economic development of Germany during this period took a course which led from what appeared to be prosperity at the outset to a credit crisis in the spring of 1925, lasting until the autumn of that year when a period of depression began. It was natural that, due to the influx of funds, price increased while business failures and unemployment declined.[14]

However, in February 1925, the first signs of the approaching crisis appeared. Many bankruptcies and insolvencies in various industries took place. Similar to the conditions which precipitated the summer of 1924, these failures were the direct result of the discrepancy between production and demand. In spite of a very large supply of goods and a considerably expanded industry, the crisis was inevitable because of the nature of the demand and the employment of credits. The demand for credit was not prompted by a desire on the part of the business enterprises to start a better

---

14. The following table shows this development.

Month	Wholesale Prices	Bankruptcies	Official Super-vision	Unemployment
Sept.	126.9	817	418	588,485
Oct.	131.2	520	377	573,496
Nov.	128.5	599	196	435,312
Dec.	131.3	572	204	436,607
Jan.	138.2	760	232	593,024
Feb.	136.5	700	216	540,460
March	134.4	744	283	465,071

The figures have been compiled from Die Wirtschaftskurve 1924 pp. 323; 1925 p. 363; and Statistisches Jahrbuch 1924.

round-about-process in order to decrease the cost of production. On the contrary, the institutions requesting credit desired to maintain their expansive plants and uneconomic enterprises, despite the decreasing demand in the market, at prices which would render possible the employment of these enterprises.

The demand had decreased and the owners of goods wanted credits in order to finance their stocks. Consequently the granted loans soon became „frozen" assets from the standpoint of the creditor-bank and led to a crisis. A decline in prices, which was but the natural tendency in such periods, was prevented in Germany by the activities of the many price-cartells which artificially maintained a price level far above the normal one. As a result of this fallacious price policy the entrepreneur was led to base his new production on the existing price level and thus continued to make an erroneous estimation of the cost of production which accelerated the severity of the crisis. In addition to these tendencies it must be remembered that the many intermediaries between producer and final consumer were responsible for the maintenance of plants and stocks of commodities in excess of what actual need required. One can easily visualize the situation from the following figures which show the relative number of incorporated enterprises in 1914 and 1925.[15]

	Stock Companies	Companies with Limited Liability
1914	5486	7925
1924	17074	26790

The relative changes in the short term liabilities of business enterprises between 1914 and 1924—1925 are reflected in the following table,[16] which represents 57 industrial stock companies existing before the war:

---

15. Deutsche Bank, Jahresbericht 1925, p. 17.
16. Die Wirtschaftskurve 1925, p. 431.

Number of Stock Companies

Short term liabilities in per cent of their capital and reserves	June 1914	June 1924	June 1925
up to 10 per cent	25	14	9
10—25 per cent	12	11	13
25—50 per cent	6	15	9
50—100 per cent	11	11	19
More than 100 per cent	3	6	7
	57	57	57

The tendencies in 1924 and 1925 were to engage a much greater per centage of short term credits, whereas in prewar periods long-term capital had been employed. These figures are typical of the investment policy of business enterprises during the years 1924 and 1925. The above mentioned enterprises had a combined capital of 240 million marks in 1925. The following diagram shows the relative change in their total of short term and long term obligations.[17]

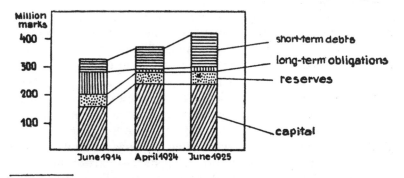

17. Die Wirtschaftskurve 1925, p. 433.

Shortly after the first signs of the crisis had been felt the need for economic readjustment revealed itself in a severe crisis which ensued in the summer of 1925. A drastic example of the unsound investment policy is afforded by the Stinnes Concern. Originally, a coal mining entrepreneur, Hugo Stinnes took advantage of the currency depreciation by acquiring a great variety of enterprises for which he paid with bank credit. At the end of 1923, this concern combined enterprises representing almost every industry in Germany. During the inflation the financing of these enterprises was not a problem because of the liberal credit policy. After the death of the founder of this concern, Hugo Stinnes in 1924, and when the credit crisis began, the impossibility of providing sufficient funds to reorganize the various enterprises became apparent. Instead of reducing the concern to those institutions which were in a liquid position, the character of which would render possible a uniform production of a few commodities from the mine to the finished product, thus forming a „horizontal" concern, the successors of Stinnes pursued another policy. They maintained the concern in its inflated form and thus were compelled to distribute the relatively small credits which they obtained among liquid and illiquid concerns.

The collapse of this conglomerate of enterprises was inevitable and occurred in the summer of 1925. The great expansion of this concern rendered, however, a gradual liquidation of the various assets necessary if very grave disturbances in Germany's „heavy industry" were to be avoided. Recognizing this fact, the Great Banks prompted by the Reichsbank, formed a consortium for the purpose of liquidating the assets of the Stinnes concern. Similar actions had to be taken in the assistance of other concerns which also lacked funds for reorganization. It was natural that the necessity of the Banks employing a substantial part of their funds with these enterprises reduced the resources which would have been applied to the aid of other enterprises.

The credit crisis began to assume a severe form. Wholesale prices showed a very sharp decline due to the forced liquidation of goods. Likewise toward the end of 1925, business failures increased, frequently causing the collapse of perfectly solvent but, owing to circumstances, illiquid enterprises. These effects are shown in the following table:[18]

1925	Wholesale prices 1913 = 100	Business Failures	Business Supervision
January	138.2	700	232
February	136.5	700	216
March	134.4	744	283
April	131.0	660	208
May	131.9	755	311
June	133.8	709	308
July	134.8	797	359
August	131.7	718	372
September	125.9	887	430
October	123.7	1139	588
November	121.1	1320	838

The maintenance of the high price level until July was due to two factors. One, the activities of the price-cartells has already been mentioned. The other factor was the custom of paying debts in bills which were not redeemed at maturity but prolonged. In this way, many business enterprises delayed the liquidation of their merchandise until the outbreak of the crisis forced the liquidation. It will be noticed that the price level from August to November shows a very sharp decline.

A good realization of the situation may be obtained from a study of the movement of stock prices during the year 1925.

---

18. Die Wirtschaftskurve 1925, p. 363 and Statistische Jahrbuch 1925.

The following diagram shows their fluctuations in the Bourse of Berlin.

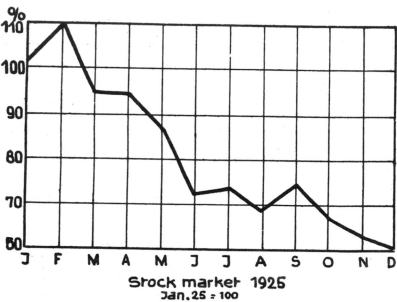

Stock market 1925
Jan. 25 = 100

There the real nature of the economic situation was revealed first. In March, stock prices began to decline, a tendency which continued throughout the rest of the year. The scarcity of funds, the low level of earnings by business enterprises had contributed to the fall in stock prices which at the end of 1925 was about 40 per cent of what the stocks had been worth at the end of 1924 and about 40 per cent of their value on January 4th, 1924. Undoubtedly, the internal value of the stock was, at the end of 1925, higher than the market quotations. But a pressing lack of funds prevented a readjustment of prices at that time.

It would have been of great influence if the Reichsbank had been able to enforce at that time a reorganization of the German economy. The stabilization of the currency had been successfully accomplished, while the reorganization of production had been delayed by the credit inflation in the spring of 1924 and by the flow of foreign funds in the winter of 1924—1925. In the summer of 1925, the Reichsbank was no longer in a position to exercise a rigid control over the credit market. It had lost its contact with the money market where the prevailing rates were below the official

Bank rate. Furthermore, the increasing deposits at the Great Banks enabled the latter to provide the required funds for the economy. The credit crisis had eliminated many demands from the money market and the banks were thus able to provide ample funds.

Another factor which lessened the influence of the Reichsbank was the instantaneous reaction of foreign capital to increases in the German market rates. The Bank realized that it had no longer the means to effect a firm policy of credit restriction and decided to stimulate the readjustment by other means. It eased the strain of credit restriction so as to enable banks to expand their credit for productive enterprises.

CHAPTER IX.

THE ECONOMIC READJUSTMENT OF GERMANY IN 1926.

At the close of 1925, the German economy was near a severe crisis. This condition was not caused by the failure on the part of the banks to provide ample credit for industry and commerce, but it was attributable to the inherent discrepancy between production and existing demand in the market. It had been pointed out in a previous chapter that the economic structure of the German economy had been dislocated and expanded beyond the demand during the inflation. Twice, the necessary economic readjustment had been delayed by outside factors. The first time it had been due to the credit policy of the private and public banks in the spring of 1924, which was directly responsible for the continuance of an investment policy by business enterprises wholly contrary to normal conditions. Later on, when the Reichsbank had adopted a policy of credit restriction and the deflation crisis had begun to throw the first shadows ,the flow of funds from abroad after the ratification of the Dawes Plan had again rendered possible the financing of enterprises by means of the instreaming credit. However, the foreign loans could only delay but not prevent the outbreak of the crisis.

The discrepancy between demand and supply became apparent in the summer of 1925, when the continually declining demand in the market rendered it impossible for many enterprises to sell their products. Moreover, many enterprises which had availed themselves of the credits for the purpose of reorganizing their production had gradually eliminated the unproductive competitors. The latter were thus unable to continue their production and to meet their debts. In consequence of this struggle to survive in the considerably narrowed market a credit crisis ensued. A feeling of general distrust was felt. which was but the natural result of the increasingly large number of business failures. Especially after the Stinnes concern had gone into liquidation, the producers were very unwilling to sell on credit except to firms of the highest standing. Banks became very reluctant to grant credit, moreover, as a substantial part of their funds was tied up in the liquidation of the large concerns. Instead they preferred to invest their liquid funds in other kinds of business which were of short term nature and offered a high degree of liquidity. Such a credit policy was but natural in view of past experiences.

The process of reorganization through the elimination of unproductive producers is well reflected in the increasing number of business failures and the rise in unemployment as shown in the following table.[1]

BUSINESS FAILURES AND UNEMPLOYMENT
OCT. '25/DEC. '26.

1925	Unemployment	Business Failures	Business Supervision
October	364,784	1139	588
November	673,000	1320	838
December	1498,000	1598	1317
1926			
January	2030,000	2013	1428
February	2056,000	1920	1573
March	1946,000	1871	1481
April	1782,000	1302	923
May	1744,000	1046	691
June	1741,000	913	477
July	1652,000	701	366
August	1548,000	493	228
September	1394,000	467	147
October	1308,000	485	148
November	1370,000	453	121
December	1759,000	427	105

1. Die Wirtschaftskurve 1925, pp. 363, 384, and 1926, pp. 48, 4, 117, 354.

This process of elimination reached its height in February 1926, after which a period of depression commenced. It was a development indispensable to the readjustment of the German economy as well as to the credit situation. In both cases burdens left over from the inflation had to be removed in order to give room for rationalized and cheapened production. Unproductive users of credit, who, for the two preceding years had depended upon credit for their existence without being able to redeem these debts with their products which the market did not absorb, were driven out of the market. In this way the banks were able to put the remaining funds at the disposal of productive enterprises.

The period under discussion marks an era of economic readjustment and reorganization. This tendency of rationalization was in particular responsible for the great unemployment, which increased toward the end of the year despite an expanding production in the second half of 1926. Thus, in the coal mining industry the total production in December 1925 was 5 per cent less than in January 1925, while the number of laborers employed had declined during this period by 15 per cent.[2] In turn, this process of rationalization rendered possible a cheaper production and in consequence an enlarged absorption by the market. Although, wholesale prices decreased in the course of the year, attention must be called to the fact that the index for the cost of living did not decline correspondingly, because of a slower adjustment of retail prices to the general fall.[3]

By the end of March, 1926, the German economy had passed the state of a crisis and a period of depression ensued which lasted until about July of the same year. This change was manifested in a decline of business failures and a relatively stable price level. It was undoubtedly due to the diminished domestic demand during the crisis and subsequent depression that the balance of trade became favorable for Germany. The excess exports of 460 millions above the total of imports was due rather to a diminution in the

---

2. Die Wirtschaftskurve 1926, p. 5.
3. WHOLESALE PRICES 1926.*

J	F	M	A	M	J	J	A	S	O	N	D
140.9	138.76	137.50	135.78	136.20	134.8	134.4	133.7	136.65	136.67	137.75	136.80

* Die Wirtschaftskurve 1926, pp. 123, 358.

importations than to increased exportations. Another indication of the depression prevailing during the second quarter of 1926 was the decrease in the total of protested commercial papers, which decreased from a total of 32,000 protested notes in January 1926 to 9,438 in May, representing an amount of 47 million reichsmarks respectively 11.5 millions.

In the second half of the year, business began to expand. The credit and capital market reflected this movement which will be discussed at length in other sections of this chapter. Stock prices reached new heights which they had not approached since January 1925, when the great slump had commenced. Especially, the coal mining industries profited by the coal strike in England. The most essential fact, however, is the gradual conversion of short term debts into long term obligations by those enterprises which had employed bank credit in preceding years so as to reorganize their enterprises and thus were at a shortage of working capital. These errors in their investment policy were now remedied by the absorption of their stock issues and the flotation of bonds by the market. In general, the year 1926 marks a period of stabilization of the German economy. The financial and economic structure of industry and commerce was put on a basis where it could gradually build up to the position which it had enjoyed before the Great War. However, it must be kept in mind that this process of rationalization was just the first step in the building up of the German economy.

It is but natural that the economic disturbances during the period under discussion should have very grave effects upon the money and capital markets. However, the development in these two markets showed a movement fundamentally different from that in summer 1924. It will be recalled that at that time the credit crisis had provoked a scarcity of funds which had caused a very pronounced increase in the market rates. Compared with this movement the conditions in the money market during the period August 1925 to December 1926 were of a most unusual nature, as can be seen from the following diagram:

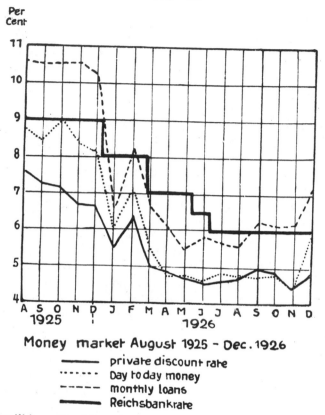

Money market August 1925 - Dec.1926

——————— private discount rate
· · · · · · · Day to day money
– – – – – monthly loans
━━━━━━ Reichsbankrate

It will be noticed that the rates for daily money which averaged about 9 per cent in August 1925 were as low as 5.5 per cent in March 1926 and declined further in the course of the year. Similar declines occurred with regard to monthly loans where the respective rates were 10.80 in August, 1925, and 7.73 in March, as well as private discounts which decreased from 7.76 to 5 per cent during the same period. It must, however, be remembered that these rates, which already compare favorably with pre-war periods,[4] were

---

4. The relative figures for 1913 and 1926 were als follows:

	1913 (average)	1926 (fourth quarter)
Day to day money	4.12 per cent	5.30 per cent
private discount	4.98 per cent	4.73 per cent
Reichsbank rate	5.88 per cent	6.00 per cent
Net return of bonds	4.50 per cent	8.20 per cent

Verwaltungsbericht der Reichsbank, 1926, page 4.

partly the result of a slight scarcity of funds. The actual rates were in many cases still below these official figures, and it was only due to the pouring out of funds into foreign markets where the prevailing rates rendered possible more profitable investments, that the price for day to day loans in the German market maintained itself at about 5 per cent.

If one were to compare this decline in the rates with the increase in the market quotations which followed the credit crisis of 1924, it seems that the credit conditions in Germany during the period August, 1925, to December, 1926, had considerably improved and that the attitude of banks in their credit policy had become much more liberal.

In reality, however, the situation in the German money market was the reflection of a rigid credit policy on the part of the banks. In order to understand this apparent contradiction it is necessary to relate briefly the credit policy of the banks, although this will be discussed at length later on in this chapter.

Soon, after the outbreak of the credit crisis in the summer of 1925, German credit institutions became very reluctant in their credit policy. Realizing that many enterprises had merely been able to exist with the aid of bank credit, although being financially illiquid from a banker's point, the banks refused to grant any credit, except to firms of the highest standing. Their attitude was the more necessary as a large proportion of the banks' funds were tied up in the liquidation of large concerns which had fallen into financial diffeculties because of their erroneous investment policy. Consequently the number of eligible borrowers diminished so considerably that the relatively small funds at the disposal of the credit institutions were in excess of the demand. The liquidity on the money market was sustained by the conversion of the short term debts of business enterprises into long term obligations. The amounts thus obtained through the flotation of bonds and obligations were not employed for expansion or constructions but for the redemption of previously contracted short term debts which had been availed of for the purpose of long term investments. As a result of these repayments, funds were again put into the money market, where they increased the existing supply of credit available.

On the other hand, the liquid conditions in the money market exercised a very profound influence upon the capital market. During the first two years after stabilization the relatively slight difference between money and capital rates was not sufficient to overcome the lack of incentive on the part of the possessors of funds to invest them in long term obligations. At the beginning of 1926, however, this relation changed fundamentally. The confidence in the stability of the German currency was fully restored and the low rates prevailing in the money market in connection with the difficulties of placing funds therein, rendered investments in long term obligations sufficiently attractive. In many cases banks and enterprises which had obtained foreign deposits and loans, faced the difficulty of investing their funds in remunerative paper. These amounts were then directed into the capital market for temporary investment. This temporary investment of a large part of the funds in 1926 in long term obligations must be kept in mind. Although savings which were the natural source of funds for the capital market, had gradually increased, as will be shown later, the German economy was not yet able to absorb the forthcoming long term obligations.

As a consequence, the market for long term obligations showed great activity throughout the year 1926. Especially, the States and municipalities were in a position to float in the market new issues which compared favorably with those abroad. Industry and commerce still depended upon the foreign markets, although the domestic market absorbed a very substantial part of their new issues of shares. The two following tables give the relative figures for 1925 and 1926.

FOREIGN LOANS (In millions of Reichsmark).[5]

	1925	1926
Loans of the States	138.6	270.6
Loans of Municipalities or Provinces	256.0	249.5
Loans of public or semi-public enterprises	364.5	371.7
Loans of private enterprises	470.7	736.5
Loans of various church organizations	25.1	47.1
Total	1254.9	1675.4

5. Agent General for Reparation Payments, Report November 1927, p. 90.

DOMESTIC ISSUES (In millions of Reichsmark).[6]

	1925		1926	
	Bonds*	Shares	Bonds*	Shares
First Quarter	337.0	219.0	436	99
Second Quarter	346.0	142.0	956	120
Third Quarter	158.0	151.0	827	305
Fourth Quarter	187.0	149.0	1053	374
Total	1028.0	661.0	3272	898

This item contains mortgages issued by real estate credit institutions.

It will be noticed that in the first table the loans contracted by other than private enterprises abroad increased only immaterially, while those of private enterprise rose from 470 millions to 736 millions. So far as the domestic market is concerned the proportion was the reserve. Of the 1153 millions floated by other than real estate credit institutions in the domestic market, during the period January—October 1926, roughly three fourths were issued by States and municipalities (863 millions), while about one fourth (289.8 millions) was obtained by private enterprises.[7] It will also be noticed that in 1926 the quarterly issues moved in the opposite direction from 1925, a fact which clearly indicates the business cycle during these two years. Particular attention must be called to the revival of the market for mortgages in 1926, when the total of Pfandbriefe, i. e. mortgage letters issued by mortgage banks, amounted to about 1100 million reichsmarks.

In the long run, the money and capital markets had to look to the savings of the country as their main source of supply. With the reestablishment of confidence in the stability of the currency and with the gradual reorganization of the German economy the saving of the country showed a steady growth. A large amount of savings also accrued from the rationalization of industry and improved methods of administration. The growth of savings since ratification of the Dawes Plan is shown in the following table:

---

6. Ibid. p. 91.
7. Agent General for Reparation Payments, Report of Nov. 1926, p. 57.

SAVINGS-DEPOSITS (In millions of reichsmark).[8]

	J	F	M	A	M	J	J	A	S	O	N	D
1925	482	553	621	682	742	796	846	901	948	996	1559	1631
1926	1799	1937	2044	2155	2258	2362	2469	2591	2712	2831	2956	3090

It was but natural that the great liquidity in the money market and the prevailing low rates greatly stimulated the activities of the stock market. Such a diversion of funds into the stock market was the more natural as the prices for stocks had in the course of the credit crisis fallen far below their initial value. The liquidation of reserves by many enterprises and the reluctance of banks to grant credit for the purpose of financing purchases of stocks had attributed to this decline in their value, so that on January 2nd, 1926, the index for stock prices was 58.31 per cent of what it had been on January 2nd, 1925. With increasing liquidity in the money market banks naturally sought more remunerative employment for their funds, which held true likewise for individuals. Foreign investments especially in German stock, as well as American purchases of shares in German shipping companies,[9] accelerated the upward tendencies of prices.

The continuous rise of stock values throughout 1926 is easily perceived in the following diagram:[10]

---

8. These figures are compiled from the following reports of the Agent General for Reparation Payments: May 1925 p. 47; November 1925 p. 67; June 1926 p. 33; November 1926 p. 56; December 1927 p. 115. The figures for the period January—Oct. 1925 include only Prussia, while the rest includes Germany.

9. The rise in stock prices of German ship companies due to these purchases from abroad are reflected in the dotted line in the diagram.

10. Die Wirtschaftskurve 1926, pp. 144, 379.

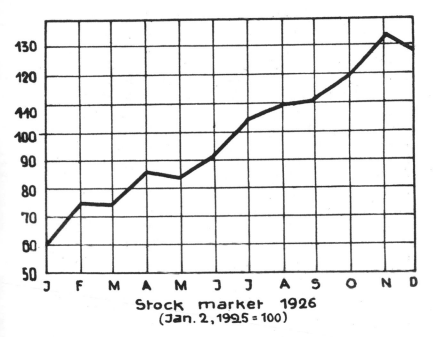

Stock market 1926
(Jan. 2, 1925 = 100)

In the later part of the year stock prices reached new heights and exceeded by far their initial value. Undoubtedly the rates of many stocks at the end of 1926 were less a reflection of probable dividend returns than a discounting of possible speculative profits.[11] This speculative wave reached its crest toward the end of October and

11. The following table gives a comparison of the dividends of 164 firms the stocks of which are quoted on the Bourse of Frankfurt a. M.:

	Paid by . . . firms in		
	1913	1924	1925
No dividend	13	54	47
1²/₃ — 4½ %	10	13	12
5 — 7.5 %	47	42	36
8 — 10 %	51	50	59
More than 10 %	43	5	10
	164	164	164

Die Wirtschaftskurve 1926, Heft 2.

middle of November, when the increasing scarcity of funds in the money market, due to seasonal factors, caused a slight decline in stock prices.

So far as private and public banks were concerned their policy was conditioned by the prevailing situation in the money market, which in turn had reacted as the result of their policy in 1925. A very substantial part of their loans granted in 1925 had been redeemed by the borrowers with the receipts from foreign loans or flotations of domestic issues. Furthermore the demand for credit had materially diminished on account of the rigid elimination of borrowers who were not of the highest standing. As a consequence, the German credit institutions found themselves in a position where they had to look out for other profitable investments of their funds. A part of their funds was directed into the domestic money market or invested abroad. Many banks availed themselves of the large funds at their disposal for the repayment of loans previously obtained from foreign banks.

On the other hand the low rates prevailing in the money market and the difficulties frequently encountered in loaning their funds even at these low rates induced many banks to invest to some extent in the capital market. Long term issues, which a few months ago had not found accomodations in the domestic market were now readily absorbed by banks. It should again be emphasized that these investments were only of a temporary nature. The relative superabundance of funds induced credit institutions to invest a part of their funds in the stock market.

From the standpoint of the Reichsbank, the general credit policy of the banks was of far greater importance. In this case, the banks endeavored to invest their funds in commercial papers of the highest standing because of the greatly reduced numbers of eligible borrowers: This policy of the banks naturally tended to absorb the greater part of the offerred supply which then remained in the portfolio of the credit institutions, thus causing them to be independent of the Reichsbank. While in 1925 the general demand had been for a more liberal credit policy by the Bank and further modifications of credit restriction, the demand for rediscount in 1926 fell far below the amount allotted for this purpose by the Reichsbank.

The following table shows the changes in the status of the six great Banks during 1926:

BI-MONTHLY BALANCE SHEET OF 6 GREAT BANKS
(In millions of mark).[12]

	31.12.'25	28.2.'26	30.4.'26	30.6.'26	31.8.'26	31.10.'26	31.10.'13
(in 7 days:	1092	1064	1154	1270	1297	1354	—
ɔsits due (in 3 months:	886	1087	1092	1085	1198	1305	676
(later:	30	43	35	57	83	66	390
ɔtance liabilities:	233	241	243	239	249	283	1295
⸴y in cash:	248	109	120	145	127	149	228
ıs on other banks:	643	631	592	703	731	762	323
of exchange:	1249	1243	1383	1397	1339	1413	1896
⸴ on stocks & securities:	2675	2672	2785	2975	3086	3420	3934
⸳ assets:	2385	2471	2535	2485	2614	2880	3416

It appears from the foregoing figures that after a short period of interruption at the beginning of 1926 the volume of credit reported in the statements of the private banks resumed the expansion which had been foreshadowed in the first half of 1925. On the liability side, the time and demand deposits increased by about 600 millions of reichsmark during the first ten months of 1926. On the asset side, as might be expected, the main item of increase was in loans on stocks and bonds which showed a total growth of roughly 650 millions, or 50 millions more than the rise in deposits. This difference was compensated for by a decrease in the cash reserves. Advances on merchandise, discount of commercial papers, and bankers acceptances show only very slight increases, which took place in the second half of the year as a result of expanding production and business activity.

Compared with 1925, the accumulated public funds of the Reich and the States were in 1926 less important in their size and influence upon the money market. This was due to a federal program to reduce the tax burden which, coupled with rather large expenditures, especially for unemployment relief, exerted a powerful influence in the direction of reducing the total of public funds. The

---

12. Die Wirtschaftskurve 1926, Appendix.

maintenance of a large cash balance for working purposes of the Reich was rendered superfluous by an amendment to the Bank Law which became effective on July 14, 1926, and which authorized the Reichsbank to rediscount treasury notes up to a total of 400 million reichsmarks. The public banks, however, still exercised a strong influence upon the money market, which was partly due to the increased deposits and partly to the gradual discontinuance by the Reichsbank of rediscounting a part of its portfolio with the public banks. The latter were, therefore, compelled to invest their funds in the open market, where they offerred strong competition to the private banking institutions and to the Reichsbank.

As a result of the fundamental changes in the general credit situation, the Reichsbank's relation to the market underwent a very material change. During the summer of 1925, the policy of credit restriction had been opposed by industry and commerce which suffered a lack of credit. The continuance of this policy was suspended in practice by December 1925. Early in January, 1926, the Reichsbank publicly announced the termination of its credit restraining policy which had been in effect since April 1924. It was but the official acknowledgement that the Reichsbank had lost its great influence upon the credit circulation. The diminished demand for credit in connection with the increasing funds at the disposal of the credit institutions had enabled the banks to satisfy the demand for credit without resort to the Reichsbank. In recognition of this tendency, the Bank lowered its discount rate on January 12th, 1926 from 9 to 8 per cent, and the rate for collateral loans from 11 to 10 per cent.

Despite this reduction, the total of discounted bills continued to diminish. Such a development could not be viewed indifferently by the Reichsbank, which faced the problem of regaining its control over the credit situation. This problem was the more pressing since, by a provision in the Bank Law, commercial papers contributed a very substantial part of its legal reserve for the notes in circulation. It is, therefore, apparent that the situation in the money market tended to exercise a material influence upon the note issuing policy of the Bank. It had to face the question of whether it should meet the difficulty by reducing the total of notes in circulation, or by reducing its discount rate to such a level that the contact with the money market might be reestablished. Or finally, whether it should leave the total of notes unchanged, decrease the discount rate slightly and increase its reserves of gold and foreign exchange. Each of these three alternatives was apt to affect the economy in a different way, and the administration of the Bank finally decided upon a policy of strengthening the reserves of gold and devisen.

A brief analysis of the nature and potential effects of the three different measures specified above will help understanding the Bank's decision to increase its holdings of gold and foreign exchange.

As has been pointed out, the first alternative was whether the Bank should diminish the note circulation. This could have been done in practice by withholding the quantity of notes instreaming at the redemption of granted credits to the extent to which the total discounts diminished. Such a policy would, however, disregard the fact that at that time the demand for credit at the Reichsbank did not have any direct relation to the actual demand of the economy. The great difference between the Bank's rate and that prevailing in the market had the natural tendency of diverting a part of the demand for credit from the Reichsbank to the open market. In consequence the lower amount of discounts at the central bank could not serve as a dependable indication of the actual situation. The Bank clearly recognized this fact and in spite of a continuously decreasing portfolio of commercial papers, the notes in circulation increased due to factors to be discussed later.

The second alternative was to lower its discount rate to such a level as would bring it in direct contact with the market rate, at the same time, however, leaving the total issue of notes unchanged. The natural effect of such a policy would be an increased competition on part of the private banks and public credit institutions for the small quantity of prime papers offerred in the market for discount. Consequently, the market rates would have decreased below the rates which prevailed therein without the competition of the central bank. Banks and owners of funds would then been attracted by the high rates in the capital market. Such a policy would also have produced two tendencies which the Reichsbank wished to avoid. First, the low rates in the money market which would have resulted from a reduction in the Bank's rate, would have stimulated an increased speculation in the money market, a potential tendency which the Reichsbank regarded unfavorably. Secondly, the central bank wished to prevent a diversion into the capital market of funds which were of only temporary nature and which would cause grave disturbances therein if withdrawn later on because of a greater demand in the money market.

The last alternative was to decrease the rate slightly and to acquire additional gold and devisen for its reserves. This policy resulted in a continuous diminution of bills being held and in a loss of its contact with the money market. Moreover, the strong competition of the banks for the bills offered in the market had the effect of making inferior the quality of bills discounted at the Reichsbank to those held by the credit institutions. In view of the general conditions, it must be admitted that the Bank could not have pursued any other policy than that which it actually adopted — increasing the acquisition of devisen and foreign exchange.

The effect of this policy upon the various items in its portfolio is shown in the following table:

Portfolio of the Reichsbank (in millions of reichsmark).[13]

Monthly			Gold	Devisen	Bills and Cheques	Collateral Loans	Other Assets	Notes in Circulation	Bills Rediscounted at public banks
1925	S.	7th	1144	352	1701	14	532	2559	
	Q.	7th	1175	321	1636	14	555	2609	
	N.	7th	1207	361	1474	10	786	2679	
	D.	7th	1207	402	1594	5	676	2734	503.6
1926	J.	7th	1208	403	1738	3	745	2732	520.5
	F.	7th	1256	419	1411	5	779	2563	484.2
	M.	6th	1405	468	1160	4	906	2730	413.5
	A.	7th	1491	481	1228	8	1011	3061	198.1
	M.	7th	1492	348	1220	7	838	2941	149.1
	J.	7th	1492	356	1240	6	617	2795	

13. Die Wirtschaftskurve 1925 p. 460; 1926 p. 464.

Monthly		Gold	Devisen	Bills and Cheques	Collateral Loans	Other Assets	Notes in Circulation	Bills Rediscounted at public banks
J.	7th	1492	344	1273	8	620	2893	
A.	7th	1493	487	1127	8	721	2972	
S.	7th	1519	483	1281	8	666	3102	
O.	7th	1616	511	1378	11	612	3139	
N.	7th	1737	413	1348	11	711	3185	
D.	7th	1755	479	1268	143	605	3290	

In the foregoing table, it will be noticed that the total of gold during the fifteen months under discussion increased by about 600 millions. Although, the holdings of devisen as reported rose only by about 127 millions, a very substantial part is contained in the item „other assets"; it should be remembered that this item also includes rentenbanknotes held by the Reichsbank. In view of the reduction of rentenmarks in circulation during this period, the inference seems justified that the item „other assets" contained about 300 millions more devisen (the equivalent of the withdrawn rentenbank notes) at the end of 1926 than in September, 1925.

The great decrease in the discount of bills and cheques is clearly visible. These reductions gain importance if one bears in mind that since May 30th, 1926, the Reichsbank ceased to rediscount a part of its portfolio with the public banks. It will be recalled that these rediscounts were as high as 595 millions in October, 1925. The basic causes for the very substantial increase in the total note issue will be discussed in another section of this chapter. This item has been included, here, to show the almost similar growth of notes and holdings of gold and devisen. The following diagram shows the effect of the accumulation of gold as contrasted with the decrease in the total of discounted bills and cheques.

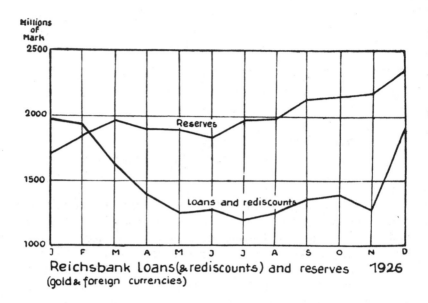

Reichsbank Loans(& rediscounts) and reserves 1926
(gold & foreign currencies)

At the beginning of 1926, the Reichsbank faced the task of providing credit for agriculture. The latter having been mortgaged for the security of the Rentenbank and pressed by lack of funds had to bear a heavier burden than it had ever experienced. The lack of sufficient credits in the autumn 1925, had forced the farming population to sell its products at low prices, so as to obtain liquid funds. The Reich, States, and many banks recognized the necessity to protect the farmer from further losses and, furthermore, the need of increased farm production, which required large amounts. Although the Reichsbank was legally in no position to grant long term loans to agriculture, it employed the Gold Discount Bank for this purpose. It will be recalled that the outstanding shares of the latter had been acquired by the Reichsbank, and that this institution had resumed its activities in April, 1925. In spring, 1926, the Gold Discount Bank being so induced by the Reichsbank, bought obligations of the Rentenbank Credit Anstalt, running from three to five years, up to an amount of 250 million reichsmarks, this total being reached by November 30th, 1926. In this way the landowners were enabled to repay 293 millions of the agricultural bills (rentenmark loans), which were due at that date.

The Gold Discount Bank, furthermore, rediscounted at the open market its own notes for an amount of 100 millions, for which it then acquired so-called Pfandbriefe. These „solar notes" of the Gold Discount Bank were readily absorbed by the market as the Reichsbank had announced its readiness to rediscount them, if so required. Such a policy of financing long term obligations with short term papers on the part of the Reichsbank (viz. Gold Discount Bank) seems contrary to the principles of sound central banking. This measure was without danger in view of the relatively small amount involved, and the large funds at the disposal of the Reichsbank. In addition to these sums, the Reichsbank acquired thru the discount of public banks obligations of the Rentenbank Credit Anstalt for an amount of 113 millions and 55 millions[14] for its own pension funds.

From the Reichsbank standpoint the greatest problems were those offered by the continuous inflow of foreign loans. In September 25th, 1926, Dr. Schacht, at a meeting of the Central Committee of the Reichsbank[15] gave warning of the dangers of an unlimited contraction of loans abroad. He attributed almost the entire increase in note circulation, which amounted to no less than 300 millions in the period from July 23rd to September 23, to an increased conversion of devisen into marks, accruing from inflowing foreign funds. His attitude to such a credit policy and its effect upon the currency and economy were summarized by Dr. Schacht in a speech before the Enquete commission of the Reichstag on October 21, 1926.[16] In view of the contrast of the opinion held by the President of the Reichsbank to that which had been generally advanced by bankers on the annual meeting of the German Bankers Association in September, 1925, a brief reproduction of Dr. Schacht's arguments seems justified.

---

14. Reichsbank, Verwaltungsbericht 1926, p. 10.
15. Die Bank 1926, October Issue, Article: Die Reichsbank im September.
16. Reports of the Subcommittee on Money and Credit of the Official Committee of Inquiry into German economic conditions.

At the outset of his speech, Dr. Schacht admits the great dependence of the German economy upon foreign loans. However, a continuance of too hasty and often unnecessary contraction of loans is of iminent danger from the viewpoint of the Bank's credit policy, of the German economy, and of the reparation problem. So far as the Reichsbank is concerned, the latter could not view indifferently a continuous diminution in the quantity of bills offered for rediscount while at the same time the total of foreign exchange converted at the Bank into reichsmarks exceeded by far the amount required for purposes of reserve. By this process, the Reichsbank would tend to become merely an institution to convert foreign exchanges, instead of functioning as a central bank.

From the point of view of the economy, the danger lies in a steadily growing burden of interest payments and amortization of foreign debts. The individual entrepreneur, contracting these obligations is very frequently unable to produce goods which will ultimately cause an influx of devisen necessary for the redemption. Instead they nourish the incorrect belief that the German economy will provide the devisen at the required moment, an assumption which amounts to self-deception. A favorable balance of trade for the purpose of obtaining the necessary foreign exchanges can only result from increased production for foreign markets. In reality, however, the loans obtained abroad have merely increased the domestic production.

Finally, this loan policy tends to picture a possibility to transfer the reparation payments which exists for the moment, but which will disappear after a short time, when the influx of foreign funds diminishes.

As a matter of fact, the actual state of conditions is that German individuals contract loans abroad, obtain claims for the amounts contracted, which are then converted into reichsmarks and which are finally acquired by the Agent General for Reparation Payments for the purpose of transferring the obtained annuities. The net result is then that the burden upon the German economy increases while there is no provision for the repayment of the debts. The Reichsbank, however, was not in a position to alter the effect of these tendencies by its discount policy, asserted Dr. Schacht.

As was pointed out, Dr. Schacht's arguments were in opposition to the opinion prevailing among bankers, and were severely criticized. His opponents[17] pointed to the international mechanism of the foreign exchange rate which would always prevent an upsetting of the equilibrium in the relative price level. A conversion of the devisen would result in higher prices in the domestic market, causing increased imports and decreased exports, whereby the increased imports would cause a larger demand for devisen, diminuition of reichsmarks. This would in turn result in greater exports as well as lessened imports, due to the lower price level of the domestic market. The inference generally drawn was that the contraction of foreign loans would ultimately result in increased exports and would thus provide the necessary foreign exchanges. This concept of the bankers overlooks, however, that the pre-war equilibrium between the various countries was not yet reestablished and that changes in the relative debtor-creditor relations and new tariff walls prevented such an instantaneous reaction of the foreign exchange rate to internal price changes.

Another important feature in the Reichsbank policy was the withdrawal of the Bank's support of the reichsmark in the foreign exchange market on August 26, 1926. Until then the Reichsbank had maintained the par value of the mark at the rate of 420 marks to one dollar by buying and selling dollars in the market at this rate, thus attaching the value of the mark firmly to the dollar. This policy was responsible for the fact that banks often preferred to sell foreign exchange to the Reichsbank instead of rediscounting their bills. As long as the dollar rate maintained its fixed value such a practice was without risk. This practice in connection with the great supply of devisen in the portfolio induced the Reichsbank to abandon its policy. As a consequence the normal forces of demand and supply were again permitted to regulate the rate. As shown in the following diagram the mark maintained a slight premium for about six weeks and then moved to a slight discount. Although the Reichsbank remained the main buyer and seller of foreign exchange in the market, the quotations may be taken as a fair reflection of the value of the reichsmark as represented in foreign currencies.

---

17. Verhandlungen auf dem Bankiertage on September 20th, 1925.

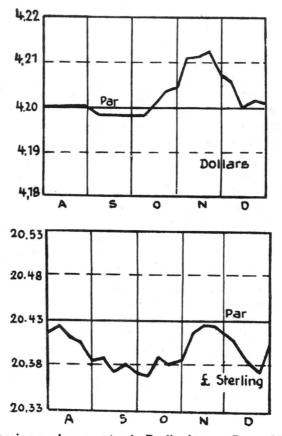

Foreign exchange rates in Berlin Aug. — Dec. 1926

While the foreign exchange rate indicates the stability of the external value of the mark, the internal stability was manifested in a fairly stable level of general prices, if one takes into account the changes in prices abroad. This relative stability of prices was maintained, although the volume of the currency in circulation increased continuously. The expansion of the currency coincided with the growing expansion of business activity in the second half of 1925. The assumption seems justified that the velocity of money in circulation diminished, in consequence of the lessened credit pressure. The growth of circulation is shown in the following table:

TOTAL OF CURRENCY IN CIRCULATION (in million marks).

Month		Reichsbank-notes	Rentenbank-notes	Other Currency[a]	Total
1925	Sept.	2649.1	1713.1	718.9	5081.1
	Oct.	2802.9	1542.6	734.4	5082.9
	Nov.	2770.9	1480.3	753.2	5004.4
	Dec.	2960.4	1475.7	772.4	5208.5
1926	Jan.	2648.8	1450.2	764.8	4863.8
	Feb.	2822.3	1354.4	784.0	4941.7
	March	3159.6	1108.4	800.3	5068.3
	April	3085.9	1156.8	809.4	5052.1
	May	2878.8	1373.1	813.9	5065.0
	June	2971.2	1378.8	829.1	5188.1
	July	3106.5	1363.4	831.3	5301.2
	Aug.	3225.1	1260.0	834.9	5320.0
	Sept.	3251.1	1369.2	855.4	5475.7
	Oct.	3325.8	1317.6	870.7	5514.1
	Nov.	3374.5	1190.0	867.5	5441.0
	Dec.	3735.5	1164.0	930.2	5829.7

This item is composed of notes of private banks of issue, which amounted to between 158 to 191 millions, and the remainder consisting of small coinage issued by the Reich.

The changes in the elements composing of total of notes in circulation have been no less marked than the changes in the total itself. It will be noticed that Reichsbank notes had more and more assumed their place as the principal element in the currency. Their total growth was about 1100 millions during the entire period. Reichsbank notes replaced rentenmark in circulation to the extent of roughly 600 millions. The other 500 millions were put into circulation towards the end of 1926, and ensued from increased productivity and greater demand for money due to seasonal factors. It will also be noticed that Reichsbanknotes increased by about 300 millions more than the total net growth of the total German currency. The changes in the total clearly reflect the business trend during this period. From September to December 1925 the increased note issue indicated the approaching crisis. During January and February 1926 a decreased circulation is apparent because of the credit crisis and the ensuing curtailment in the total of credits granted. After this interval, there came a period of depression from March to June without any material change in the demand for currency. The next four months (July to October) mark a period of economic recovery, while the growth of the circulation in November and December 1926, was partly enhanced by seasonal factors.

CHAPTER X.

THE ECONOMIC DEVELOPMENT OF GERMANY 1927—1928.

During the last two years 1927 to 1929 the German economy has made powerful strides toward regaining its past position in the world market. The stabilization of the currency had been successfully completed by the end of 1924 with the ratification of the Dawes Plan, while the stabilization of economic life did not take place until 1926. Reference has been made in a previous chapter to the causes for this delay in readjustment. It was but natural that the process of rationalization and reorganization which began in 1925 and continued throughout 1926 could not be completed in so short a time. Too much productive power had been destroyed and dislocated during the war and then by the currency inflation to render possible a complete recovery in such a short period. Germany has since then changed her position among other nations from that of a creditor to that of a debtor country.

The economic development of Germany during this period has clearly demonstrated that normal forces have gradually come into the foreground and have asserted themselves in many parts of the German economy. The violent and severe disturbances which had attended the stabilization of the currency and later on the rationalization of the economy are matters of the past andGerman production, trade and finance have taken on an aspect of steadiness during the past two years.

The first signs of the approaching business expansion had become manifest in the second half of 1926 and had expressed itself in a revival of the capital market, credit expansion by banks, slight increase in prices, and decrease in business failures. At the same time, the figures of production of the basic industries (coal, iron, steel,)[1] had shown a continuous growth. This rise in productivity continued throuhout 1927 with a moderate recession in 1928. Doubtless, the very substantial inflow of funds from abroad had been largely responsible for this upward movement of the business cycle. The funds thus directed into the capital and credit market had rendered possible an increased productivity, as the rates of the credit market approached the level of international rates. It was to be expected that the low rates caused an increased borrowing and stimulated an expansion of business activity.

On January 12, 1927, the Reichsbank had lowered its discount rate to 5% in order to regain contact with the market and had through its low rate accelerated the tendencies toward expansion. It must be pointed out that the industrial and commercial growth of 1927 was confined mainly to the internal market. As a consequence of the rising domestic demand, imports continuously increased without an equivalent rise in exports. The total deficit of the trade balance for 1927 amounted to approximately 2600 million reichsmarks without taking into account the deliveries in kind which would bring the total to about 3 billion reichsmarks.[2] These large excess imports were mainly caused by the poor crop yields of German agriculture in 1925 and 1926, which had rendered necessary large imports of foodstuffs. Again as in previous years the deficit in the trade balance was met with the receipts of foreign credits granted to the German economy.

Toward the end of 1927 the capital market showed the first signs of an approaching scarcity, although business expansion continued. It became evident that the German economy was not yet in a position to provide the necessary reserves for a great expansion. As a result of the lack of sufficient credit, the business world resorted to an increased use of commercial papers as a means

---

1.

	Pig iron	steel	coal
	(in thousands of metric bons)		
1925 average	841	1004	11.100
1926 „	803	1019	12.100
1927 „	1092	1356	12.800

2. According to the revised figures of the Statistische Reichsamt for 1927.

of payment.[3] At the same time banks withdrew a substantial part of their credits circulating in the stock exchange and invested these funds in short term paper. The rates in the money market were at the end of 1927 from one to two per cent higher than at the same period in 1926.

The general economic development during the two years of 1927 and 1928 is reflected in the following figures, representing wholesale prices, unemployment and business failures during this period.

WHOLESALE PRICES, BUSINESS FAILURES, UNEMPLOYMENT 1927—1928.[4]

	Wholesale Prices		Business Failures		Business Supervision		Unemployment (in 000)	
	1927	1928	1927	1928	1927	1928	1927	1928
J	135.9	138.7	473	753	90	160	1827	1333
F	135.6	137.9	457	706	112	222	1669	1238
M	135.0	138.5	537	778	127	259	1121	1010
A	134.0	139.5	403	619	164	242	870	729
M	137.1	141.2	451	702	122	202	649	629
J	137.9	141.3	407	765	91	292	541	611
J	137.6	141.6	418	663	129	325	452	564
A	137.9	141.5	395	547	132	301	420	515
S	137.1	139.9	355	551	92	241	355	577
O	139.8	140.1	455	691	69	268	346	671
N	140.1	140.2	582	687	115	287	605	1030
D	139.0		605		175		1188	

In the spring of 1928, a moderate recession took place which lasted almost all the year. Prices of commodities, as shown in the foregoing table, developed relative stability, and the number of business failures, although considerably higher in 1928 than in 1927,

---

3. While the monthly average of bills of exchange in Berlin was 5.38 billion reichsmarks in 1926, according to the receipts of the stamp tax, this amount had risen to 71.129 billion reichsmarks in November 1927. See Die Wirtschaftskurve 1928, p. 349.

4. These figures are derived from the annual publications of the German Statistische Reichsamt and Die Wirtschaftskurve 1927 to 1928.

was far below the monthly average of 1925 and 1926 which amounted to 932 and 1023. The same holds true for „business supervision" which averaged monthly 492 in 1925 and 653 in 1926. So far as the figures for unemployment are concerned, mention must be made of the continuing increase in productive efficiency. While the total volume of output increased in 1927 by 13%, the corresponding rise in the number of labores employed rose by only 3.5%.[5] In addition to the above figures, the index of production, published by the German Institute for Economic Research show the following decline in general business activity.

Index of Production.[6]

(Coverning 14 commodities; July 1924 to July 1926 = 100)

1925 average	106.8
1926 „	100.8
1927 „	123.7
1928 April	124.6
„ May	121.5
„ June	118.8
„ July	117.5
„ August	117.8
„ September	117.2

The general expansion of business activity and industrial production had the beneficial effect of increasing wages. It was but natural that labor which had received very low wages since stabilization, wished to share in the savings ensuing from the rationalization of industry. In the autumn of 1927, the German government raised the salaries of those employed in the civil service and soon these increases were followed by similar ones adopted by all branches of the public service, States, municipalities, provinces, Post Office and Railways. These increases in wages were made the basis of similar demands on the part of the laborers employed in industry and commerce. Owing to the general business activity, these demands were met and the official wage tariffs increased by about six per cent until May, 1928. Such expansion of the purchas-

---

5. Die Wirtschaftskurve 1928, p. 6.
6. Compiléd from the Vierteljahreshefte zur Konjunkturforschung, published by the Institut für Konjunkturforschung.

ing power of the consumer class, if accompanied by greater efficiency, viz. larger social output, is conducive to a higher standard of living and enlarges the absorptive capacity of the market. Doubtless, the increased wages and the ensuing greater demand in the market have been a factor determining the trend of business activity.

However, many enterprises frequently, owing to price cartels, endeavored to evade the burden of increased wages although the rationalization actually rendered possible price reductions. As a consequence prices were not reduced in accordance with decreased cost of production but in many instances were even raised in proportion to the increased wages. These policies had the effect of neutralizing the beneficial result which might otherwise have been derived from higher wages. Such increases in prices tended to cause a decrease in exports, a fact which was the more regrettable since the financial burden of the reparation payments made it of paramount importance that Germany's exports should exceed her imports.

It is evident that increased business activity and expanding production must be adequately supported by the money and capital markets in order to carry on the larger volume of transactions. The violent fluctuations which took place during the period under discussion in the capital, money, and stock markets make it necessary to give a separate analysis of these three markets, although it must be kept in mind that they are mutually interrelated and have a direct bearing upon each other. Low money rates tend to divert funds into the capital and stock market, while high money rates attract funds into short term investments.

It will be recalled that in the autumn of 1926, the money market had shown great liquidity. A continuous stream of foreign loans supported this condition and gradually the prevailing money rates approached the international level. Despite a reduction of its discount rate to 6%, the Reichsbank had not regained its contact with the market. At this juncture, the Bank adopted two measures, hoping to exert again its former influence upon market conditions and to curb the inflow of foreign loans. Induced by the administration of the central bank, the Minister of Finance suspended on December 4, 1926, the exemption of German issues placed abroad from the „capital income tax“, a measure which will be discussed at length in the section dealing with foreign loans. The immediate effect was an arrest of the contraction of foreign loans, abroad, which in view of the capital income tax could be placed more cheaply in the domestic market.

In the next year, the Reichsbank lowered its discount rate on January 12th, 1927, from 6 to 5 per cent.[7] Both, the capital income tax and the low discount rate, resulted in an almost complete interruption in the flotation of issues abroad. On the other hand, the low money rates which were supported by the Reichsbank's discount rate, rendered it profitable for many enterprises to redeem their foreign obligations with credits obtained at home. Large funds were invested in foreign markets, where the rates were higher than in Germany. Especially, the relatively high rates offered in France and Belgium, where the currencies had previously been stabilized, attracted large sums from Germany.

Toward the end of March the situation in the money market suddenly changed. The flotation of a federal loan of 500 million reichsmarks in February, 1927, exhausted the capital market almost completely and the demand for funds in the money market increased. Consequently, money rates rase above the Reichsbank rate and remained above the Bank's rate until late in autumn of 1927, when contact was again re-established. The conditions in the money market can be illustrated by means of the following diagram:

---

7. In connection with this reduction, mention should be made of some of the rates of other central banks. The Bank of England maintained its rate at 5% until April 21, 1927, when it was lowered to 4½%. The Bank of France and the Bank of Belgium reduced the rate from 6 to 5½% on April 27th. The Federal Reserve rate in New York stood unchanged at 4% since August, 12, 1926.

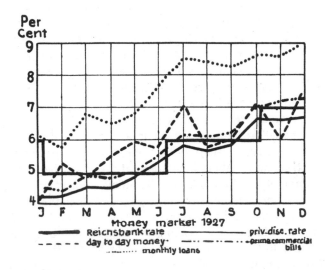

Money market 1927

Although the inflow of foreign loans was resumed late in the summer and throughout the remaining period, it will be noted that the rates reveal a substantial tension. This was due to the necessary business expansion which maintained the rates at a relatively high but stable level. The decline in the market rates in January 1928 was due to heavy borrowing at the Reichsbank in December for seasonal expansions, and the maturity of these debts in February and March. The funds at the disposal of enterprises prior to the maturing of the debts were then put into the open market, causing the periodical decline in the rates.[8]

The renewed imposition of the capital income tax upon the foreign buyers of German issues had a particularly grave effect upon the capital market. In February 1926, the German capital market had evidenced a revived capacity to absorb a substantial portion of new share and bond issues. Even after small cities had been able to float issues of considerable amounts in the market and

---

8. According to Die Wirtschaftskurve 1928 p. 360 the credits granted by the Reichsbank in November and December 1927 matured as follows: one third prior to January 15th, 1928, 19 per cent no later than January 31, 1928, 33 per cent in course of February and 15 per cent during March.

at favorable terms, it was expected that a federal loan of 500 million reichsmarks would be readily absorbed by the market. The interest rate was five per cent, which because of the re-imposition of the capital income tax reduced automatically the yield to the foreign investor to 4½ per cent. As a consequence, only a few subscriptions from abroad were placed in the German market, which was compelled to carry the entire loan by itself.

The reserves were only just sufficient to absorb this issue, thereby exhausting entirely the funds available in the investment market. The ensuing scarcity of funds, expressing itself in an increased demand for short term credit at the Reichsbank, put such a heavy strain upon the Bank that the official rediscount rate could not be maintained. The situation was such that the Minister of Finance finally found it necessary to resort to the very unusual procedure of voluntarily increasing the coupon rate of government bonds from 5 to 6 per cent. At the end of March the investment market was practically lacking in funds and thus incapacitated for a very long period of time.

The following table gives a survey of the issues placed in the domestic market during the period 1924 to 1928:

DOMESTIC ISSUES 1924 — 1928 (in millions of mark).[9]

Period	Bond Issues	Issues of New Shares	Shares of new Corporations
1924, total	176.30	66.00	113.88
1925, total	144.60	593.76	114.12
1926, total	1306.00	1242.66	90.38
1927, 1st quarter	831.80	361.2	19.80
„ 2nd „	53.70	390.3	34.20
„ 3rd „	7.80	128.1	68.70
„ 4th „		144.4	16.83
1928, 1st „	139.40	364.2	18.20
„ April—May	270.70	162.3	25.90
„ June—Aug.	77.5		
„ Sept.—Nov.	80.25		

9. The table is compiled from figures published in Die Wirtschaftskurve 1928 pp. 147, 256, 359. The amount of new share issues during the last period could not be ascertained by the author.

It was not until the beginning of 1928 that the investment market showed again signs of an increasing capacity. Resources were limited and during the summer of 1928, the market was again incapable of absorbing large issues.

The following table gives a survey of the issues placed in the domestic market during the period 1925—1928.

DOMESTIC BONDS ISSUES 1925 — 1928 (in million marks).[10]

Period	Loans of Reich, state and municipalities	Public and semi-Public enterprises	Private Enterprises
1925, 1st quarter			21
2nd „		5	42
3rd „			24
4th „	15	17	26
1926, 1st „	88	9	9
2nd „	369	8	77
3rd „	180	2	102
4th „	167	26	141
1927, 1st „	523	10	86
2nd „	133		97
3rd „	33	5	6
4th „			
1928. 1st „	149		
April	207		
May	63		
June—August	77.5		
Sept.—Nov.	80.25		

Not until the beginning of 1928, was the capital market again able to absorb new issues. The total amount of 207 millions placed in April, 1928, is the highest sum absorbed in bond issues by the market during any one month throughout the preceding four years.

The rapid expansion of credit which took place during 1927 carried with it the danger of speculation in stocks. It will be

---

10. The figures for the period 1925 to 1927 are derived from the annual publication of the Statistische Reichsamt, while those for 1928 are from Die Wirtschaftskurve 1928. The figures for 1928 are totals for all three items.

recalled that the rise in stock prices at the end of 1926 had been largely due to speculation rather than to the anticipation of future earnings. In many cases business enterprises endeavored to recover a part of their losses, incurred in the general process of rationalization and reorganization, by speculative purchases in the money market. The great liquidity in the money market and the prevailing low rates were a great stimulus to the upward movement. In addition to these domestic tendencies, there were very substantial purchases of German shares and securities by foreign investors, mostly confined to speculative buying and selling.

The rapid and long-continued rise in stock prices, due to their speculative nature, was a threatening element in the German economy. The diversion of funds in great amounts into the stock market and the export of realized profits by foreign investors could not be viewed indifferently by the Reichsbank. Although the Bank had left its rediscount rate for collateral loans unchanged at 7 per cent, the lowered rate of 5 per cent for commercial paper was accepted by the Bourse as an indication of easier credit conditions. As a consequence, stock prices continued their upward movement throughout the period between January and April, 1927. By April the large demand for funds in the stock market had driven the market rate well above the Reichsbank rate and resulted in increased borrowing from that institution.

At this juncture the Reichsbank decided to apply some drastic measures against the Bourse in order to regain its contact with the market rate. It exerted considerable pressure upon the Berlin credit institutions and suddenly on May 12th, 1925, the latter made public the following announcement.

„The members of the Berlin Bankers Association (Berliner Stempelvereinigung) have agreed to gradually but appreciably reduce the funds loaned for report (margin purchases) and lombard purposes and for other advances on securities. They will, therefore, begin by making a reduction of 25% in the funds available for report and advance purposes on the Bourse by the date of settlement at the middle of June and will undertake further reductions on subsequent dates of settlement. The same procedure will be adopted towards cultomers. It is expected that the lenders of money not belonging to the said association will take similar action.“

The theory of the Reichsbank had been that a contraction of credit on the stock market would increase the funds in the banks without exerting pressure upon the credit facilities for commerce and industry, an aim which could not have been achieved under an increased discount rate. This policy was, furthermore, actuated by the thought that a higher discount rate would tend to attract additional short term funds from abroad, which attraction the Bank wished to avoid.

The suddenness of the above mentioned measure which came wholly unexpectedly to many bankers in the provinces and many cities in the Reich had a catastrophic effect. Stock prices began to decline to a great extent and the losses incurred on the day following the above announcement, on the „black Friday", May 13th, were estimated at three billion marks. Many provincial banks and business enterprises were met unprepared for such a decline in stock prices as set in and were forced into bankruptcy. The drastic measure of the Berlin Banks evoked severe criticism on the part of the commercial press.[11] The movement of stock prices during the year 1927/1928 is well reflected in the following diagram:

---

11. The general view of the press is well represented in the following comment of Die Wirtschaftskurve (published by the Frankfurter Zeitung) in the June issue of 1927: „This action was unskillful and rather unnecessary for the normal function of the credit market, and has had an effect which could have been avoided. It has resulted in a collpase of a speculation which is of great importance for the support of the credit and capital market with funds, and the faults of which could have been remedied by simpler means without causing such losses to the economy." p. 147.

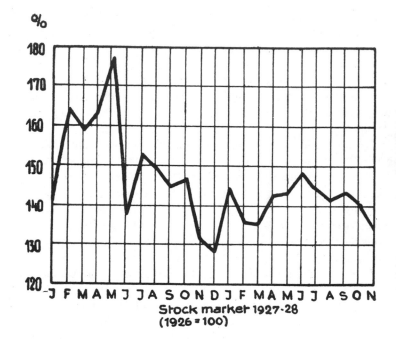

Stock market 1927-28
(1926 = 100)

The desired effect did not fully materialize. As will be noticed in the diagram, stock prices soon began to rise again and by July had recovered half of their losses. A new decline in prices occurred at the middle of November 1927, when stock prices reached the lowest point in that year. In December prices increased again and remained almost stable throughout 1928 with but little activity in the market. The decline of stock prices in the second half of 1928 was caused by liquidations and withdrawals of funds by American investors, attracted by the high rates in the New York market at that time.

Repeatedly in the preceding discussion reference has been made to the almost uninterrupted inflow of foreign funds into Germany since 1924. It has been pointed out in a previous chapter that these loans were of primary importance in the upbuilding of Germany during the last few years. The only period when foreign funds of long-term nature did not stream into Germany was during the first few months of 1927. As was pointed out the re-imposition of the capital Yield tax[12] in December 1926 in connection with the low rates prevailing in Germany had arrested a further inflow of funds from abroad. However, the absorption of the domestic reserves by the federal loan of 500 million marks had increased the rates again to such a level that a renewed import of capital was considered profitable. This movement did not start until after June 3rd, 1927, when the Minister of Finance announced that he was willing to recommend again tax exemption „if the loans are to be used for desirable economic purposes and if their conditions correspond to the conditions of the money market".[13] This measure was immediately followed by a renewed inflow of foreign loans, which increased rapidly. The issues placed abroad in the month of October, 1927 amounted to about 525 million marks. These loans continued throughout the next year, and by the end of October 31, 1928, the amount of loans contracted abroad was as follows:

FOREIGN LOANS 1925—1928 (in million marks).[14]

	1925	1926	1927	Jan. 1 to Oct. 31, 1928	Totals
Loans of States	138.6	270.6	267.3		676.5
Provincial or Communal Loans	256.0	249.5	112.5	193.2	811.7
Loans of public and semi-public enterprises:					
a) of the Reich	161.7	25.2	336.0	152.3	675.7
b) of the States, provinces, communties	202.8	351.5	205.7	530.8	1290.8

12. By law of March 20, 1920, the German Reichstag had passed the German Capital Yield Tax (Kapitalertragssteuer) which is merely a prepayment by the domestic investor of 10% of his federal income tax. Due to the fact that a foreigner is not in a position to make any allowances for the German capital income tax when filing his own tax return, it is obvious that this discrimination had always proved a serious obstacle in negotiating foreign loans.

13. Report of the Agent General for Reparation Payments December 1927, p. 89.

14. This table is compiled from Die Wirtschaftskurve 1925 to 1928.

	1925	1926	1927	Jan. 1 to Oct. 31, 1928	Totals
Loans of private enterprises	472.0	742.0	597.3	354.5	2165.8
Loans of various church organ.	25.1	57.6	4.1	29.8	116.6
Totals	1256.2	1696.4	1522.9	1261.1	5736.6

The total of foreign loans during the period 1925—1928 was 5736 million marks, leaving out of account the German External Loan of a nominal 960 millions which was issued in 1924 under the Dawes Plan. Of the above total about 38 per cent (2165 millions) were obtained by private enterprises for the purpose of reorganizing their structure. The remainder of about 6 per cent, leaving out the loans of the various church organizations was received by public authorities and public or semi-public enterprises. The frequent uneconomic employment of these funds and the ensuing danger for the economy as a whole were made the subject of an exchange of notes between the Agent General for Reparation Payments and the German Minister of Finance.[15] It would exceed the scope of this study to discuss, here, the ensuing controversy. Suffice it to say, that the German government in 1928 adopted the policy of granting permission for the flotation of bond issues abroad by public authorities only in such cases where an economic use of these funds was assured. The Federal Advisory Board for Foreign Loans laid down very definite rules and was thus in a position to prevent abuses.

Although the stream of foreign loans has been of great importance in the re-creation of capital in Germany, it is obvious that the main source must come from the reserves and savings of the community. So far as savings are concerned, this item shows a continuous growth during the last few years. While the total deposits in savings-offices (Sparkassen) in Germany amounted to merely 400 millions at the end of 1923, these deposits had increased by October 1928 to 6598 million marks and thus formed a very substantial source for the further creation of capital. The following

---

15. Report of Agent General for Reparation Payments 1927.

table shows the uninterrupted rise in savings during the years 1927 to **1928.**

SAVINGS DEPOSITS 1927—1928 (in million marks).[16]

	J	F	M	A	M	J	J	A	S	O	N	D
1927	3381	3572	3718	3854	3965	4022	4122	4245	4340	4444	4543	4665
1928	5046	5326	5486	5645	5780	5921	6074	6252	6372	6548		

In addition to these savings deposited with the Sparkassen, there were substantial amounts deposited on savings account with Berlin banks, which pay a slightly higher interest rate than the savings-office. These savings deposits, are not reported separately in the bi-monthly balance sheets of the banks and cannot therefore be exactly ascertained.

Of paramount importance to the credit market are the private banks. Among these the six German Great Banks represent three fourths of the total banking strength in Germany and their balance sheets afford valuable information about the creation of capital and the growth in the volume of credit. These six banks showed an aggregate portfolio of bills and treasury notes of 2332 million marks on October 31, 1928 as compared with 2100 million marks on June 30, 1914. Their combined assets amounted to 9765 million marks on October 31, 1928, while the corresponding figure for December 31, 1913 was 7838 millions. Although these figures compare favorably with the pre-war figures, mention should be made of the relatively small amount invested in bankers' acceptances, an item which amounted to only 399 millions in October 1928 as compared with 2157 millions outstanding on June 30, 1914. This was due to the lack of an effective private discount market in the post-war periods.[17]

At a superficial glance the German banks seem to have regained or even surpassed their pre-war position in the German economy. Such however, is not the case. In the first place a very large proportion of the deposits are of foreign origin and of short

---

16. Die Wirtschaftskurve 1927 and 1928.

17. These figures have been derived from Die Wirtschaftskurve 1925, 1928.

term nature.[18] It is especially the short term nature of the banks' deposits which greatly impairs the position of the banks in the German economy. One must bear in mind that the German credit institutions before the war had the function of supplying long term credit (investment-capital) for industry and commerce. To a very large extent, the banks had pursued the policy of loaning a part of their deposits, which were savings, for this purpose and later on transforming this credit into long term obligations of that particular enterprise through the flotation of bonds or new share issues among its own depositors. The inadequacy of the banks' deposits of a long term nature has led to a substitution of foreign funds instead of those of the banks.

The following table represents the bi-monthly reports of six Great Banks at various dates between 1924 and 1928.

BALANCE SHEET OF SIX GREAT BANKS
(in million of marks).[19]

	Jan. 1 1924	Dec. 31 1926	Dec. 31 1927	Cct. 31 1928
Cash and amounts due from banks and bankers	565	1048	1361	1226
Bills and treasury notes	42	1556	1858	2332
Loans and advances total	609	4024	4994	6207
a) on stock exchange				1786
b) other				4421
Time and demand deposits	1058	5970	7503	8932
Acceptance Liabilities	2	316	384	399
Contingent Liabilities				957

18. According to an estimate published in Die Wirtschaftskurve 1929, 1. Heft, the amount of foreign funds deposited with eight large Berlin banks totalled 43 per cent of the total deposits of 10.4 billion marks.

19. Die Wirtschaftskurve 1924—1928.

On the other hand the commercial banks experienced in the last few years an increasingly strong competition from the public banks. Numerous banking institutions were created by the various states, provinces, and municipalities. Their banking strength should not be underestimated and on October 31, 1928, 21 State and Provincial banks including the „Seehandlung" (Bank of Prussia) had outstanding loans for 1761 million marks and deposits amounting to 2831 million marks.

The Reichsbank's policy during the year 1927 was under the influence of two dominant forces — the movement of foreign funds and the contradictory conditions in the money market. At the end of 1926, the Banker's rate had lost its contact with the market, where funds had been offered below the official discount rate. In order to re-establish this contact the administration lowered its rate on January 12th, 1927 to 5%. This reduction was also prompted by a desire on the part of the central institution to arrest a further inflow of foreign short term funds. The actual development soon reversed the situation for the Reichsbank. It will be recalled that the federal loan of 500 million marks, placed in February, had entirely exhausted the reserves of the market and caused an increase in the market rate above the official discount rate.

The Reichsbank, however, did not raise its rate to 6 per cent until June 10, 1927, mainly because it assumed that if it had acted sooner, foreign short term funds would have been attracted by the higher rate and would have accelerated the speculative movement in the stock market. In the interval the Reichsbank had no control over the market. The lower Bank rate attracted increased borrowings at the central institution and in the course of five months its portfolio of discounted bills, cheques, and collateral loans had increased by 665 million marks. On the other hand, the Bank's holding of gold and foreign exchange had diminished during the same period by about 1000 million marks. This was due to a variety of causes. In the first place the rising business activity was mostly confined to the domestic market and resulted in large excess imports over exports which had to be paid for with devisen, obtained from the Bank. Furthermore, the redemption of short term debts abroad by various German institutions enhanced the demand for foreign exchange.

It was not until the discount rate was raised to six per cent on June 10, 1927, that this outflow of gold and devisen was arrested. The renewed inflow of foreign funds which took place soon after this increase in the official rate, brought additional gold and foreign exchange once more to the Reichsbank. The Reichsbank pursued, however, the policy of acquiring only such odd amounts of devisen which represented the day's excess in the market. As a consequence, buyers of foreign bills had to look to the Reichsbank for the currency required for these large supplies and resorted to discount bills at the Bank when necessary. The institution's holding of bills thus continuously increased, attended by a proportionate growth in the total notes in circulation. By the end of September, 1927, the total of discounts and the quantity of notes in circulation was as high as 2746 million marks respectively 6100 millions, marking the highest points since stabilization. The Reichsbank, accordingly raised its discount rate to 7 per cent. In spite of this increase, the Bank's rate was still below the market rate and contact was not re-established until early in January, 1928. In connection with the increase in the discount rate it is deemed well to cite here from the annual report of the Reichsbank, the latter's attitude in regard to the accumulation of gold and its policy of note circulation:[20] "Any heavy increase in the currency circulation even with full cover is bound prejudicially to affect the development of prices; experience shows that any rise in prices, even if due to quite natural causes in connection with the supply of commodities or the conditions of production is regarded by wide circles of the population as a symphony of inflation. The cover percentage cannot, and should not, therefore be taken by the Reichsbank as the sole criterion of its policy. To do so would be to lead industry along faulse paths. The currency circulation of a country must be kept at all times in a proper proportion to the extent of the country's economic activity. The test for the volume in circulation is the development of the general level of prices particularly in comparison with the development in other gold currencies."

---

20. Annual report of the Reichsbank, 1927, p. 78.

The changes in the various items of the Reichsbank during the year 1927 are demonstrated in the following table:

REICHSBANK PORTFOLIO 1927 (in million reichsmarks).[21]

1927		Gold reserves	Eligible devisen	Bills, cheques	Other assets	Reichsbank notes in circulation	Rentenbk. notes in circulation	Total note circulation
J,	7th	1831	513	1694	575	3436	1108	5411
F,	7th	1834	293	1378	598	3274	1114	5477
M.	7th	1844	202	1604	457	3347	1095	5589
A,	7th	1851	192	1924	520	3460	1060	5637
M,	7th	1850	127	1931	485	3504	1033	5661
J,	7th	1815	87	2338	465	3689	1017	5746
J,	7th	1802	58	2318	492	3667	1008	5855
A,	7th	1805	62	2351	493	3770	1007	5866
S,	7th	1853	157	2498	511	3800	988	6122
O,	7th	1852	156	2603	537	4004	896	6103
N,	7th	1852	298	2388	619	4220	780	5950
D,	7th	1861	279	2392	502	4044	716	6059
D,	31st	1864	282	3128	499	4564		

Special attention must be called to the gradual increase of Reichsbank notes in circulation which notes assumed once more the main function in the circulation. The total of rentenmarks is continuously diminishing in accordance with the provisions in the law providing for the liquidation of the Rentenbank.

In connecton with the devisen policy of the Reichsbank, the influence of foreign loans upon the exchange rate of the mark deserves special analysis. It is evident that as long as the German money rate is sufficiently high to attract foreign funds, the value of the mark in terms of imported currencies, in the shape of bills of exchange, must necessarily be at a premium and vice versa. A very good demonstration of these tendencies is afforded by the relative fluctuations in the private discount rate in Berlin and the movement

---

21. This table is derived from the annual report of the Reichsbank 1927 and Die Wirtschaftskurve, 1927.

of the foreign exchange rate of the mark as shown in the following diagram:

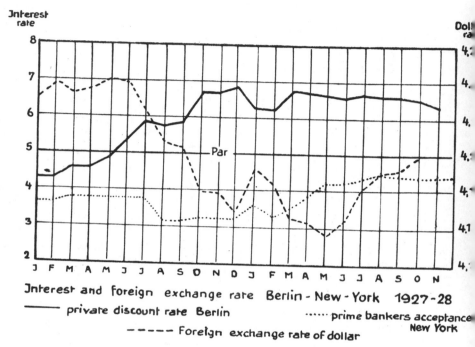

Interest and foreign exchange rate   Berlin - New - York   1927-28
——— private discount rate Berlin   ······ prime bankers acceptance
                                                        New York
      − − − − − Foreign exchange rate of dollar

It will be noticed that during the first six months when the Reichs-bank rate was close to the New York rate, the mark was at a discount. This was due to the insufficient supply of devisen as compared with the large demand during that period. Soon after the Bank's rate was increased, foreign funds streamed in again and the mark was at a premium. The relative movement of the two rates confirms the previous conclusion that the disparity of the rates was of powerful influence in attracting foreign funds.

During the year 1928, the Reichsbank has been able to exert its influence over the money market more effectively than during any other period in the preceding four years. Its discount rate was in close contact with the market rate throughout the entire period and was again an efficient weapon in the Bank's control over credit. This development marks a stabilization in the general credit conditions of the country, which underwent such violent fluctuations in the years following the adoption and suspension of credit restriction policy. The following diagram reflects this close contact of the discount rate to the credit market during the year 1928:

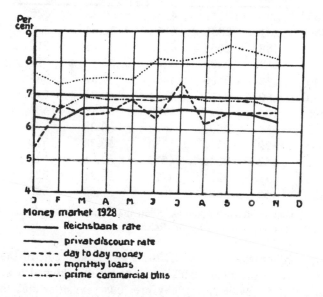

Money market 1928
——— Reichsbank rate
——— privat discount rate
– – – – day to day money
·········· monthly loans
–··–··–·· prime commercial bills

A similar stability can be noticed in the institution's short term credits, consisting of discounted bills, cheques, and collateral loans. These items moved proportionately with the trend of business and are therefore a valuable indication of the re-establishment of stable economic conditions in Germany. Normal forces had again asserted themselves and the fluctuations of earlier periods have given way to a comparative steadiness in the money market, although the prevailing rates were still relatively high.

This stability in the Bank's relation to the market can be easily seen from the following table:

REICHSBANK PORTFOLIO 1928 (in million marks).

1892	Gold	Foreign Exchange eligible as cover	Bills and cheques	Reichsbank notes in circulation	Legal cover for Reichsbank-notes %	Rentenbank notes in circulation	Total circu-lation (a)
J	1865	296	2372	4251	50.83	626	5375
F	1888	281	2336	4268	50.84	630	5389
M	1930	188	2652	4513	46.95	616	5662
A	2040	167	2492	4409	50.10	609	5576
M	2040	274	2469	4486	51.57	589	5654
J	2083	250	2477	4674	49.94	578	5574
J	2199	183	2516	4569	52.16	561	5672
A	2248	194	2603	4673	52.28	570	5808
S	2396	179	2576	4830	53.38	570	5903
O	2532	163	2348	4672	57.71	543	5708
N	2623	173	2211	4724	59.21	524	5721
D	2729	155	2627	4930	58.52	530	6276

(a) includes: Reichsbanknotes, Rentenbanknotes; notes issued by private banks, and coins issued by the Reich.

Throughout the year 1928, the short term credit of the Bank represented by the item „Bills and Cheques", showed a stability which did not prevail during any previous year after stabilization. The slight fluctuations in the total were due merely to seasonal influences. It will also be noted that the quantity of rentenmarks in circulation continued to decline and was replaced by additional Reichsbank notes. Before analyzing further the very substantial increase in the gold reserves, reichsbanknotes, and total circulation in the second half of the year, it is necessary to insert here a brief discussion about the movement of the foreign exchange rate in 1928 and its effect upon the note issue of the Bank.

During the years 1925 to 1927, the gold stock of the Reichsbank was mainly enlarged either, by an acquisition of foreign currencies in the domestic market by the central bank and subsequent imports of gold from abroad, or by converting the obtained foreign currencies into gold in their respective central banks. In the summer of 1927, when large funds were streaming in from abroad the Reichsbank lowered its purchasing price for gold to the legal minimum of 2784 reichsmarks per kilogram of 1000/000 fine gold. This action had the effect of placing the foreign exchange rate, at which it would be profitable to import gold into Germany, somewhat lower than it had been at the price previously paid for gold by the Reichsbank. In general, it may be said that until 1927, the movement of gold to Germany was the result of corresponding conversions of foreign currencies by the Bank.

In 1928, the margins between imports and exports narrowed continuously thereby removing from the market a substantial part of the demand for foreign currencies while the inflowing loans from abroad maintained the supply well above the demand. As a consequence, marks were at a premium and many other currencies were quoted as below parity with the reichsmark. The two following tables show the relative movements of the dollar and the pound sterling.

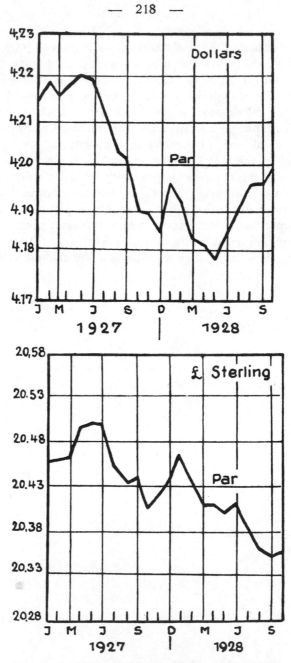

Foreign Exchange Rates in Berlin 1927—1928

During the second half of 1928 the sterling rate declined so abruptly that it became profitable for bankers to export gold from England and to sell it to the Reichsbank. Such a process, although in its last analysis nothing but an ordinary banking operation, was in marked contrast with earlier movements of gold which had been due to transactions carried out by the Reichsbank, when it acted on its own initiative and converted its acquired foreign currency into gold. This development may therefore be taken as a sign of the reassertion of normal forces in the relation of the mark to the value of other currencies.

This movement of the mark rate in the second half of 1928 explains the great increase in the gold holdings of the Reichsbank during those months. It was due to the importation of gold that the quantity of Reichsbank notes in circulation increased, causing a simultaneous increase in the total circulation. Judged by the domestic price level and the foreign exchange rate movements, this expansion in the note circulation was without any inflationary effect.

Although the general conditions in the money market in 1928 in connection with the successful control over credit by the Reichsbank rate seem to indicate a return of stable credit conditions in Germany, such a conclusion would be premature. It must constantly be kept in mind that the German economy has not yet achieved a state of economic reorganization in which the continuous pressure of the reparation payments would not be a potential threat to its stability. The transfer problem in its practical aspects will be discussed at length in the next chapter. Nevertheless, it is deemed necessary to call at this point attention to this pressure upon the Reichsbank policy, which revealed itself fully in the course of the first seven months of 1929.

At the end of 1928, the German currency was one of the stablest currencies. The large gold and foreign exchange holdings in connection with the close contact between the Reichsbank rate and market rate were generally taken as a sign of economic stability. It was frequently overlooked by foreign observes that in the last analysis the productive expansion during the years 1927 —1928 and the reparation payments were financed by foreign loans. By the end of 1928, Germany was not yet capable of bearing the reparation burden without a further inflow of funds from foreign markets.

CHAPTER XI.

THE TRANSFER PROBLEM UNDER THE DAWES PLAN.

The Dawes Plan divided the redemption of the annual payments into two distinct parts: — first, the raising of contributions within Germany, and secondly, the transfer of these sums by converting the German currency obtained for reparations into foreign currencies. With regard to the annual payments the Plan provided certain taxes and debentures to be levied upon industry, railways, and the budget of the Reich. As long as these contributions do not exceed the annual savings of the German community, their internal accumulation does not involve any substantial difficulty. However, the conversion of such large amounts into foreign currencies encounters many practical obstacles which raise the question what measures must be taken in order to transfer these funds to the creditor countries.

One of the essential features of the Dawes Plan was the establishment of a Transfer Committee, under the chairmanship of the Agent General, which was entrusted with the task of transfering the annuities obtained from Germany to the creditor countries without endangering the stability of the German currency. The Dawes Committee clearly recognized that in the long run such payments could only be met from a surplus in the trade balance. Doubtless, the lack of such a protective clause under the system, prior to the Dawes Plan, had partly been responsible for the German currency depreciation. Under the new system, Germany is required to deposit the annuities at the Reichsbank to the credit of the Agent General for Reparation Payments. In view of this necessity to safeguard the stability of the currency, the problem of the Transfer Committee is to determine what conditions must be established in order that these transfers can be effected in the long run without jeopardizing the stability of Germany's monetary system.

Experience during past years does not offer any solution to this problem. Foreign loans have rendered possible not only the cash transfers of the Agent General, which amounted to 798 million marks, but they have also financed the deficit in the trade balance,[1] which amounted to 8444 million marks for the period October 1924 to October 1928. It is obvious that Germany cannot indefinitely borrow money abroad. The loans contracted must gradually be repaid and the question arises as to how the reparation payments can be met in the future. One must bear in mind that modern countries must continuously expand and progress so as not to lose their position in the world economy. An external debt of the dimensions of the Reparation payments is apt materially to influence the future development of Germany. It is the aim of this chapter to analyze the transfer problem in its theoretical and practical aspects and to examine objectively the possibility of Germany's making such payments over such a length of time. Political influences and jealousies have for many years past balked a general recognition of the economic problems involved in reparations. Much has been done by the Dawes Committee and many economists of great repute in putting the economic aspect of the war debt again into the foreground of the discussion.

In order to understand the past and present part of the Agent General in the transfer problem it is well to reproduce here the provisions of the Dawes Plan concerning the establishment of a machinery for the transfer of the annuities.[2]

---

1. According to an estimate of the Reichsbank in its report for 1928 p. 6, the total of foreign long term loans during the past four years amounted to 7 billions while the short term credits are estimated at more than 6 billions, from which must be deducted about 3 billions invested by Germans abroad, leaving a balance of 10 billions. On the other hand, the net import balance for the period 1924—1928 is roughly 9.5 billion marks. It is thus evident that foreign funds have financed the excess imports and cash transfers of the Agent General.

2. Annex VI of the „Experts' Plan of Reparation Payments".

I. Transfer Committee: All payments are to be made to the Bank of Issue to the credit of the Agent General of Reparation Payments. (He can with draw from this deposit in accordance with the Transfer Committee.) This Committee is composed of six members; the Agent General is a member of this Committee and Chairman. The other five members must be qualified to deal with foreign exchange problems and shall be composed of an American member, French, English, Italian, and a Belgian member. Each one of them shall be appointed by the Reparation Commission after the respective foreign member of the General Council of the Reichsbank has been consulted.

II. The Transfer Committee will co-operative with the President and the Commissioner of the Bank.

III. Powers of the Committee:

a) To apply the deposited funds for payments for deliveries in kind and payments under the Reparation Recovery Act, in accordance with a program to be established periodically by the Reparation Commission after consultation with the Transfer Committee.

b) To convert these balances into foreign currencies from time to time and then to remit them in accordance with the instructions of the Reparation Commission.

Both the foregoing powers are to be exercised to that extent to which in the judgment of the Transfer Committee the foreign exchange market will permit without threatening the stability of the German currency.

c) To invest from time to time in bonds or other loans in such amounts as to the Committee may deem wise. The Committee shall proceed to make these investments as soon as the amounts of the credits exceed the sum which the Bank of Issue will keep on deposit. On the other hand, the Committee may sell the bonds which it has axquired, or liquidate the loans which it has granted, whenever, in its opinion, the sum may be converted into foreign exchange or the Bank can accept additional funds.

IV. The goods supplied by Germany to the creditor countries under III (a) s hall be for the sole use of the countries receiving them, except by agreement between the Committee acting unanimously and the German government.

V. In addition to its powers under III, the Committee may on the instruction of the Reparation Commission and on request of the creditor countries transfer marks to private individuals for the purpose of making purchases in Germany.

VI. The German government and the Bank shall undertake to facilitate in every reasonable way within their power, the work of the Committee in making transfers of funds, including such steps as will aid in the control of foreign exchange. When the Transfer Committee is of the opinion that the Bank's discount rate is not in relation to the necessity of making important transfers, it shall inform the President of the Bank.

VII. In the event of concerted financial manoevres whether by the government or by any other group for the purpose of preventing such transfers, the Committee may take such actions as may be necessary to defeat such manoevres, and in such circumstances, it may suspend the operation of article X, may accumulate the funds or employ them in the purchase of any kind of property in Germany.

VIII. The German government shall not tax the deposits or goods purchased for the countries nor investments in bonds or loans.

IX. When the accumulation of funds shall have reached five billion marks: (whether represented by deposits or loans) the payments for the Treaty charges shall be reduced to such an amount as will cover the transfer and payments provided for under the subdivisions without additional accumulation. Such partial suspension shall be operative only during the period that the conditions of transfer necessitate; and the standard of payments shall be resumed at any time when they can be operated without the limits of accumulation being exceeded. The Transfer Committee is authorized to suspend accumulation before reaching five billion marks when two thirds of its members thus resolve.

The elaborate system which the Dawes Committee deemed it necessary to establish in order to transfer the annuities, delonstrate clearly the seriousness with which the Experts approached the problem. They realized very well that there might arise in the future an economic situation which would frustrate any attempt to render available the annuities for the creditor countries without causing disturbances in the stability of the German currency. Doubtless this machinery was set up with the aim of engaging the „good will" of the creditor nations in the transfer of the payments. In the course of the discussion it will become evident that the realization of conditions under which transfers can be effected, depends to a great extent upon whether adequate economic policies of the Allied governments are prevalent.

From the viewpoint of static economic theory, the transfer problem would not afford any difficulty in its practical execution. The process of transferring the anuuities would then be as follows: In the first place the German government would obtain the necessary amount in the nature of taxes imposed upon the various parties as provided in the Dawes Plan. These sums would then be deposited in German currency with the Reichsbank to the credit of the Agent General. The Agent might then avail himself of these funds in two ways. He may either buy goods in Germany and export these to the Allied governments on account of their claims or he may acquire foreign exchange in the market and transfer these receipts to the creditor nations. In the first case the effect of exports of purchased goods would be to lessen the quantity of commodities in the community while the total of money remains the same. As a result the demand in the market would exceed the supply of goods offered for sale and prices would tend to rise. However, the continuous taxation of German industry and commerce by this additional amount of purchasing power would prevent such a rise in the domestic price level. The transfer of the reparation payment by such a process would not occasion any difficulty.

In the second case of the transfer of foreign currencies the situation is fundamentally different. The supply of foreign exchanges in the market represents, normally, the receipts for exported commodities. On the other hand there must be considered the demand of those industries which import goods and need foreign exchange to effect the payments for their commodities. Obviously, the amount which can then be transferred by the Agent

General, without harming importing industries, is limited to the excess of exports over imports.[3]

In view of the necessity of achieving a balance of trade so favorable as to render possible the transfer of the large annuities, certain policies must be pursued by the Agent General to effect this end. His aim is of course to promote a development which will result in increased exports and thus in a greater supply of foreign exchange in the German market. By exchanging his mark-claims for foreign currencies, he is then able to effect the transfer of the annuities to the creditor countries. The process through which such increased exports can be stimulated is a deflation of German prices. As previously pointed out the German government accumulates the amount payable for reparations by taxing the people, and then deposits these sums with the Reichsbank. The effect of the taxation by the Reich is a diminution in the purchasing power of the community. The Agent's task is to prevent a utilization of these deposits for a renewed increase in the purchasing power which would again bring prices to their former level. In order to curb an employment of these deposits for additional credits, the Agent General will „earmark" his claims. The central bank would then be compelled to pursue a credit policy that would permit of these funds being available at any moment for disposal by the Agent.[4]

This would amount to an investment of the sums in papers of short maturity. Such a credit policy on the part of the central institution would soon be reflected in a similar policy on the part of the banks. The effect would be a shortage of funds in the economy and prices would tend to decline. Foreign buyers would be attracted by the lowered price level in Germany and as a

---

3. It is true that for a certain length of time an inflow of foreign capital can render possible a transfer despite an unfavorable balalnce of trade. Due, however, to the fact that Germany is to-day a debtor country, the balance of trade is almost the sole source of its payments.

4. It will be recalled that the Bank Law does not require any reserve for the deposits of the Agent General, while a certain reserve is legally required for other deposits. A transfer of the claims by the Agent General to another party would render necessary an increased reserve against these deposits. In order to maintain its legal reserve ratio the Bank is compelled to pursue a policy which would permit a reduction in the outstanding credits.

consequence, exports would rise and imports fall. Under normal circumstances, large exports cause a greater inflow of money which set in motion a counter-movement viz. higher domestic prices resulting in decreased exports and increased imports. Such tendencies would be neutralized through the continuous purchase of inflowing foreign exchanges by the Agent General. His demands based upon purchasing power originating in a process of production, would suffice to absorb the forthcoming supply of foreign currencies without causing any increase in prices.

Such an automatic transfer as outlined above cannot take place under actual conditions. Our economy is highly dynamic and not static, and consequently there are always frictions and changes in international economic relations which tend to neutralize or to prevent such a deflation of the domestic price level. A drastic example is offered by past experience. During the last five years the reparation payments have not been met with a surplus from exports but with loans contracted abroad. Although such borrowings on the part of Germany cannot go on forever, there are still many other factors tending to frustrate a transfer which deserve careful analysis.

One of the greatest obstacles to a frictionless transfer of reparations is the continuous change in the tariff policy of those countries which are in a position to absorb goods from Germany. It is an utterly complex situation which confronts Germany. Her creditors demand reparations but refuse to acknowledge in their trade policy the undeniable fact that such debts can in the long run only be paid by increased exports from Germany. Would the reparation creditors be willing to accept deliveries in kind for the full amount of the debt, there would be no transfer problem. Germany would then be able to shift a part of her industry to the increased production of such goods as are desired·by the Allies, while the level of prices and wages in Germany would be left undisturbed. It is needless to say that any move of the governments of the creditor countries in this direction would inevitably cause political difficulties for those governments.

The creditor nations will have to face some day the question whether to pursue a tariff policy which will permit an increased export from Germany or whether to suspend the receipts of those payments.

Assuming that the present tariff will not be changed materially in the future the question arises under what conditions these payments can then be effected? The only answer is that this aim can be achieved by a further decrease in the German price level. It is well-known that the existing import duties in the various countries take by their very nature account of the present price structure in Germany. The rates represent the assumed difference in cost of production between Germany and the country in question. In order to increase the exports to those countries beyond the present amount, it is necessary that prices in Germany should decline further. Such a change in the existing rates of international prices may be achieved in three „natural" ways.

In the first place, a decrease in prices may be brought about by an increased production at lowered cost which means lower wages per hour and a lessened profit rate per unit. In this case the laborer and businessman will enjoy the same standard of living but at a higher sacrifice. Considering the low level of wages and the standard of living, it is more than doubtful whether such reductions can be introduced.

Secondly, such excess exports could be achieved, if foreign prices increased while they remain the same in Germany. In this case the laborer and businessman in Germany would enjoy the same standard of living at the same sacrifice and yet contribute to large exports.

The last possibility involves a technical improvement of production in Germany to an extent whereby the industry is able to produce a unit at a lower cost of production without decreasing wages or profits. Needless to say, such a development would be beneficial to the German population and conducive to the payment of the debts.

In the light of actual experience it is very doubtful whether either of the last two alternatives will be realized in the near future. At the present, the technical efficiency of production is in many creditor countries equal and in some nations superior to German industry. One need only analyze the balance of trade in order to verify this statement. The fact that a few German industries are again competing successfully in the world market is deceptive as to the general state of things. Likewise, it is improbable that a decrease in prices can be achieved along the lines of the first alternative.

It is evident that artificial measures must be adopted in order to bring about a lower price level.[5] This effect can be achieved by a rigid deflation policy on the part of the Reichsbank or by a similar policy of the Agent General in disposing of his claims upon the Reichsbank. Considering that even under the Young Plan, the ratification of which is still doubtful,[6] the larger part of the annuities will only be transferable under conditions similar to those provided in the Dawes Plan, it is well to analyze the powers of the Agent General in bringing about a deflation of prices. It is evident that any other body appointed for this task in the future by the creditor nations will also have to pursue the same policies in order to achieve this end.

A deflation of prices can be brought about directly only by the Reichsbank through manipulation of its issue of notes and credit policy to such an extent that prices will be maintained at a level which will stimulate larger exports. Before discussing the potential tendencies which might easily frustrate such a policy, it might not be amiss to analyze the powers of the Agent General in enforcing such a deflation. Under the provisions of the Dawes Plan, Germany is required to deposit the annuities with the Reichsbank to the credit of the Agent General. It is furthermore, provided that „the German government and the Bank shall undertake to facilitate in every reasonable way within their power, the work of the Committee in making transfers", and it is stipulated that "when the Committee is of the opinion that the Bank's discount rate is not in relation to the necessity of making important transfers, it shall inform the President of the Bank".[7] Apparently, these clauses impose the indirect task upon the Reichsbank of pursuing a credit policy which

---

5. The term „artificial" refers to compulsory means which are forced upon the economy.

6. Although the Young Plan has been ratified in the meantim, the following analysis holds still true.

7. Experts Plan of Reparation Payments, Annex VI, 7.

will maintain prices at a level where larger exports are rendered possible and thus sufficient foreign exchange forthcoming.

The Agent General is thus authorized to „inform" the Bank if this situation arises that its discount policy exercises an influence upon the price level which prevents the necessary growth of exports. Not only has the Agent General the right to voice his opinion, but there cannot be any doubt that any indifference on the part of the Reichsbank to such warnings might easily be interpreted as „financial manouvers" to defeat the transfer, in which case the protection of Annex VI section 10 would automatically be removed. It is, of course, impossible to determine beforehand under which circumstances the discount policy of the Bank might rightly be considered as detrimental to the transfer of reparations. Great discretion and a broad viewpoint on the part of the Transfer Committee is required to decide such questions justly.

Of far greater importance, however, is the direct influence which can be exercised by the Agent General. He may „earmark" his claims at the Reichsbank and thus force the institution to a credit policy which will render possible at any moment a reduction of the outstanding credits to such an amount as is in accordance with its legally required reserves. Uncertainty as to the length of time for which these funds will be left with the institution limits their employment. Ultimately the result may be either a transfer of claims from the Agent General to another institution, in which case the Bank will have to provide for these deposits a reserve of at least 40 per cent in domestic bills, or the purchase of the Agent may cause a withdrawal of money in cash from the Reichsbank, which necessitates the provision of adequate gold reserves.

In is obvious that such a cautious credit policy on the part of the central bank will be reflected in a similarly restrained attitude on the part of the other banks. Although the transfer of his claims by the Agent General within Germany will only cause changes in the items, „deposits" or „notes", by a few hundred million marks annually, such fluctuations are in normal periods sufficient to affect the reserve ratio materially. As a consequence, the policy of the Bank will have the same effect as an increased discount rate, i. e. reducing the demand for credit.

As a result of such a deflation policy, prices in Germany will diminish to a level at which exports of goods will rise while imports will decline. The inflowing excess of foreign exchange may then be absorbed by the Agent without setting in motion those tendencies which would again increase the price level to a point where the original ratio between the prices of the various countries would be re-established. The success of such a deflation policy depends, of course, upon the fact that the creditor countries do not adapt their tariff rates to the new price level in Germany. Any such measures would frustrate the attempts to transfer the reparation payments from Germany. On the other hand it requires that pressure be constantly exercised by the Agent General, in order to maintain the German price level below that of other nations.

Apparently, the conclusions which have been reached in regard to the Agent General also hold true if the German government assumes in the future the obligation to effect the annual transfer of a certain part of the annuities. In this case, too, the necessary surplus of foreign exchange must originate in increased exports through a deflated price level.

The premis of unchanged tariff rates abroad must be materialized just as in the case of control by the Agent General.

The question arises whether it is possible to maintain the pressure of a deflation policy upon the price level for such length of time. There are always tendencies among the various countries toward an equilibrium in prices. A reduction of the total credit in circulation through a limitation of credit by the Reichsbank might easily cause an increased velocity of money in circulation and thus neutralize the effect of the deflation policy. Furthermore, the ensuing scarcity of funds in the credit market would tend to increase interest rates in the market and thus attract foreign funds. Never before in monetary history has the attempt been made to execute such a deflation over so long a period. It is very improbable that such a policy can be pursued without seriously affecting the economic standing of Germany in the world market.

Aside from the above mentioned external tendencies to neutralize the effect of a deflation, one must also take into consideration the internal counter-tendencies. In its very nature, a deflation policy causes a more or less pronounced decline in wages. Mention has been made previously of the present low standard of living in Germany due to the low level of wages. It is improbable that any future attempt to decrease wages still further will meet with success. As a consequence, the deflation policy of the Reichsbank viz. a limitation of credit, will force many enterprises to discontinue production. Such a development will in turn diminish the supply of goods and thus partly neutralize the lessened purchasing power in the market.

Furthermore, decreased production results in increased unemployment, thus enhancing the social burden upon productive enterprises and forcing them to add these expenses to their total cost of production. A low standard of living would also promote migration from Germany to countries where a higher level of wages prevails. It is impossible to predict the probable course of the economic development of Germany under the burden of reparation payments. A deflation policy, which is under present conditions, the only way by which exports can be increased, depends for its success upon the willingness of the foreign producer to let the German exporter invade his field. Larger exports tend to diminish the demand for domestic products in the foreign market. Obviously the producers in those countries will not view such a development indifferently but will endeavor to curb the larger inflow of commodities either by lowering their cost of production by lowering wages or by demanding higher protective tariff rates. The latter policy especially has been adopted of late in many countries. Either measure tends to frustrate increased exports.

A deflation policy, furthermore, encounters two other difficulties. In the first place, as Keynes[8] rightly points out, if prices in Germany are reduced by 10% and the volume of export trade is thereby stimulated by 20 per cent the value of exports does not increase by 20 per cent, but only by 8 per cent (1. 20 X 90—108). It must also be emphasized that Germany imports a very substantial part of her raw material. According to the official figures, her

---

8. J. M. Keynes: „The German Transfer Problem" in Economic Journal of March 1929, p. 10.

export trade amounts annually to about 2.5 billion dollars. Of this amount, roughly 2 billions are finished goods, the production of which depends for the greater part upon imported raw material. Considering the annuities of the reparations, amounting to 600 million dollars in standard years, and an estimated amount of about 200 million dollars annual payment for interest and amortization on foreign loans granted to Germany during the past years, her exports must increase by at least 800 million dollars annually or more than 30 per cent. But as she must simultaneously import the raw material necessary for the production of finished goods, the future increase in exports must still be larger than the above assumed 30 per cent increase.[9]

In the second place, it must be remembered that a deflation policy affects the whole community. Although its basic purpose is to decrease the prices of goods for export, it is inevitable that the diminished quantity of purchasing power will also influence the price calculations of industries which do not export. Such a tendency would affect the internal market, and, in turn, would be reflected in the exporting industries.

From the foregoing analysis it becomes evident that the redemption of Germany's obligations is possible only if increased exports are not prevented by the Allies. The good-will of the creditor nations is an indispensable premis if Germany is to meet her obligations. Without such good-will any attempt to obtain the annuities must fail. The shortcomings of a deflation policy in connection with its limitation by economic forces is obvious from

---

9. In connection with Keynes' viewpoint it might not be amiss to mention here an interesting calculation of Dr. Heimann in an article „Das Transfer und die Preishöhe" published in Wirtschaftsdienst 1924, p. 1488. He points out that a rise in exports due to deflated prices increases the purchasing power of the mark above its normal level, i. e. more goods must now be exported to obtain the same amount of money. If the decrease in the price level amounts to 5 per cent, a quantity of goods which formerly was sold for 2631 million marks would just be sufficient to yield 2500 million, or in other words a loss of 131 millions. On the other hand, imports must also be paid for with more domestic goods, a loss which H. estimated at 210 million marks. In this case, Germany would actually pay more reparations than she is supposed to pay.

the above analysis. One cannot but agree with the conclusions reached by Mr. Keynes and other outstanding economists that the burden imposed upon Germany by the reparation payments must some day prove to be beyond her capacity to pay. Such a recognition on part of the creditor nations will then be the last step in the restoration of the world economy and must ultimately lead to a better understanding among the nations of the world.

CHAPTER XII.

THE YOUNG PLAN.

In a previous chapter attention had been called to the fact that the Dawes Plan did not aim to afford a definite solution of the reparation problem. Such a task would have exceeded its competence and would, indeed, have been impossible in the state of confusion which then existed. Accordingly, the Dawes Committee presented a Plan which provided a preliminary settlement for a period sufficient to restore confidence and to reorganize the German economy. It was so framed as to permit a final and comprehensive agreement as soon as the general economic conditions in Germany seemed to warrant such a procedure.

The economic development of Germany during the years 1924 to 1928 has been discussed at length in the preceding chapters. After the economic recovery of Germany in the years 1927—1928, the allied countries and Germany decided to appoint a committee for the purpose of settling definitely the pending questions.[1] On September 16, 1928 the representatives of the governments of Great Britain, France, Germany, Belgium, Italy and Japan reached an agreement at Geneva on „the necessity for a complete and definite settlement of the reparation problem and for the constitution for this purpose of a committee of financial experts to be nominated by the six governments."[2] The negotiations concerning the appointment of a committee were terminated by the middle of December 1928. On December 22, 1928, the six governments made public an announcement on the constitution of the new committee. The mandate of the experts was as follows:[3]

---

1. The favorable report of the Agent General for 1927 was undoubtedly primarily decisive on the part of the creditor nations.

2. Report of the Agent General for Reparation Payments, Dec. 1928, p. 166.

3. Ibid. p. 166—167.

„The German, Belgian, French, British, Italian and Japanese Governments, in pursuance of the decision reached at Geneva on September 16, 1928, whereby it was agreed to set up a committee of independent financial experts, hereby entrust to the committee the task of drawing up proposals for a complete and final settlement of the reparation problem; these proposals shall provide for a settlement of the obligations resulting from the existing Treaties and agreements between Germany and the creditor Powers. The Committee shall address its report to the governments which took part in the Geneva decision and also to the Reparation Commission."

These experts were thus entrusted with the task of completing the work of the Dawes Committee and to submit a proposal for the final settlement of the reparation problem. It is especially noteworthy that Germany was sharing in this conference and was therefore enabled to present her point of view as to the possibilities and limitations of reparation payments. The new committee was composed of 14 members, 12 of whom were chosen among the above nations, each one appointing two representatives, and two experts of the United States of America appointed by the Reparation Commission conjointly with the German government.[4]

The committee of experts met for the first time on February 9th, 1929 in Paris and the oficial conference was opened on February 11th, 1929. Mr. Owen D. Young of the United States was unanimously chosen chairman. For almost seventeen weeks the experts were engaged in the task of drawing up a plan which would be just to the creditor countries and to Germany. The demand of the creditor nations was twofold: — first, Germany should pay an amount sufficient to meet their war damages, and secondly, an additional amount which would cover the Allied debts to the United

---

4. The committee had the following membership: G e r m a n y: Dr. Hjalmar Schacht, Dr. A. Voegler; F r a n c e: M. Emile Moreau, m. Jean Parmentier; E n g l a n d: Sir Josiah Stamp, Lord Revelstoke; B e l g i u m: M. Emile Francqui, M. Camille Gutt; I t a l y: Dr. Alberto Pirelli, M. Fulvio Surich; J a p a n: Kengo Mori, Takashi Aoki; A m e r i c a: Owen D. Young, J. P. Morgan.

States.[5] On the other hand, the German delegates claimed that the annuities fixed by the Dawes Committee were by far in excess of what their country could pay without endangering her currency and economic stability. Besides these two main issues there were many minor points which it is deemed best to discuss in connection with the various provisions of the plan.

On June 8th, 1929, the committee of experts submitted its „Report on Reparations to be paid by Germany" to the Reparations Commission.[6] Doubtless, the Young Plan represents a decided progress in the settlement of the reparation payments as compared with the Dawes Plan. It would be eroneous, however, to assume that the Young Plan had been composed independently of political influences and considerations. Throughout the last decade the people of the various creditor countries have been led to believe that the reparation problem is mostly a political issue. Much has been done by the Dawes Committee and of recent by the Young Committee to introduce economic considerations in the solution of this great international post-war problem.

One cannot overlook, however, that political constellations in the various creditor countries did not permit of a settlement based only upon economic considerations. The complex debt relations of the creditor nations set a certain limit to the concessions which the experts could make to Germany. A deadlock of the negotiations could only be avoided by taking account of these political tendencies. The report states expressively: „that political factors necessarily set certain limits within which a solution had to be found if our proposals were to secure acceptance."[7]

The central feature of the Young Plan is the provision for the creation of a „Bank for International Settlements".[8] By proposing

---

5. In the official report no reference is made to the Allied debts to the United States. Instead, it refers to „Outpayments of the principal creditor powers." It was due to an intervention of the U. S. Government that her delegates obtained the co-operation of their associates in not being too definite officially about the passing of their debt to Germany.

6. The analysis of the Young Plan is based upon the complete reproduction of the report in THE NEW YORK TIMES on June 9, 1929 pp. 28—31.

7. The Experts' Report, part III.

8. In part V, the report states that it „was soon found the amounts were to a considerable extent contingent upon the machinery and form of payment."

this institution the experts went considerably further than the Dawes Committee, attempting to establish the causes which would finally lead up to the situation which the report sought to ameliorate. Repeatedly the experts stress in their report the fact that the establishment of this international bank is expected to facilitate considerably the transfer of the annuities. Furthermore, this institution is also expected to promote such an international situation as will enable Germany to increase her exports to such an extent as is necessary to redeem the annual payments. Before discussing in detail these provisions, it is deemed well to outline first the other provisions in the Young Plan differing from those in the Dawes report.

FOREIGN CONTROL. The plan provides the abolition of all financial and political controls, special liens and securities imposed upon Germany. Instead of the political bodies which formerly exercized control over various German public institutions, the proposed Bank was deemed to justify the provision of a machinery essentially commercial and financial in character.[9] The experts recognized that this institution would be able to command the necessary support and responsibilities that economic engagements imploy. Furthermore, the removal of foreign control over German institutions[10] could only be conducive to the furtherance of gogd-will between the creditor countries and Germany.

ANNUITIES. The Young Committee experienced the greatest difficulties in reaching an agreement about the annual payments to be met by Germany. From the outset it was obvious that an average annuity of 2500 million marks imposed under the Dawes Plan was far in excess of what Germany could pay without endangering her economic structure and currency. The experts differed widely in their opinion as to what Germany could pay. While the delegates of the crediotor countries demanded an average annuity of 2300

---

9. Ibid. part VI.

10. The foreign control provided in the Dawes Plan was exercised by the Commissioner of Note Issue at the Reichsbank, by the Agent General for Reparation Payments, the foreign nationals in the Board of the Reichsbank and by the foreign trustees in the administration of the German Railways.

million marks, the German delegates maintained that 1700 millions were the most their country could pay annually.

A compromis was finally reached. The payments to be met by Germany begin with an annuity of 1707 millions for the first year April 1930 — March 1931, and increase gradually until they reach 2428 millions in the year 1965—1966. The average annuity over this period of 37 years corresponds to 1948 millions exclusive of the service for the Dawes Loan which brings this amount to a total of 2050 millions.

For the second period of 22 years, the annual payments average 1675 million marks. On the basis of an interest rate of 5.25 per cent, as assumed by the experts, the payments for the first 37 years equal a present value of 36 966 millions mark, or, about 8880 million dollars.

Out of the above annuities for the first 37 years, 660 millions mark are unconditional, i. e. payable without any right on the part of Germany to demand postponement due to economic conditions detrimental to the transfer of these sums. This amount of 660 millions is payable in equal monthly instalments in foreign currencies, being thus available for commercialization and mobilization by the creditor countries. The mobilization of the unpostponable part of the annuities for a bond issue is subject to regulations laid down in the report for the purpose to prevent an untimely or overlarge issue in the international market. The flotation of these bonds has to be executed through the International Bank. Of this unconditional part France is to receive 500 million marks annually as a means to reconstruct her destroyed sections. The payment of these 600 millions is gauranteed by the imposition of a special tax on the German Railroads, the latter being the only security directly pledged for the reparation payments under the Young Plan.

The remainder of the annuity is payable in equal monthly instalments in foreign currencies, thus placing the entire burden of transferring the annuities upon Germany. Under the Dawes Plan the Reich had met its obligation by depositing the prescribed annuities with the Reichsbank for the account of the Agent General for Reparation Payments. It had been the latter's task to transfer these sums into foreign currencies without endangering the stability of the German currency or economic life. In the future, Germany will be under the obligation to transfer the annual payments at her own risk. Only in periods of severe depression has Germany the right to demand suspension of the transfer for a maximum period of two years. This protective clause refers only to the postponable part, i. e. after deducting from the annuity the „unpostponable part" of 660 millions. On the sums thus postponed and not utilized by the creditior countries for purchases of commodities in Germany, the Reich has to pay interest at the rate of one per cent above the Reichsbank rate or at 5½ per cent whichever is lower.

MOBILIZATION OF DEBT. The main reason for the consent of the creditor nations to the reduction of the annuities as compared with those imposed under the Dawes Plan was the prospect of being able to mobilize the unconditional part of the annual payments. On the other hand the German delegates were moved to the acceptance of the new average annuity and the provision of an „unpostponable part" by the desire to avoid a new crisis in Germany and also by the desire to obtain in this way an earlier evacuation of the occupied Rhineland.

For the purpose of floating bonds up to the capitalized value of the unconditional payments, the German Government is obliged upon request of a creditor country and approval by the Bank to create issuable bonds. Germany is granted in the plan the optional right to redeem any mobilized part of the unconditional payments on a basis of a 5.25 per cent discount.

SECURITIES FOR PAYMENT. The annuities are to be derived from two sources: the federal budget and the contribution of the German Railroads. It will be recalled that under the Dawes Plan an indebenture of 11 billion marks had been imposed upon the Railway Company which was to yield 5 per cent interest and one per cent amortization, or a total of 660 million marks annually. This contribution from the Railroad was the only source, outside the federal budget, maintained by the Young Plan. However, th Young plan provides that the railway bonds for eleven bill marks, issued and surrendered under the Dawes Plan to Trustes for the German Railroads" shall be abolished togeth the foreign control in the management of that company. the Reich shall impose a tax of 660 million marks ann the railway company, the receipts of which will be guaranteed by the German Government.

DELIVERIES IN KIND. Under the Dawes Plan a certain part of the annuities was to be paid by deliveries in kind. In the Young plan it is provided that this system should be abolished after a transition period of 10 years. It was realized by the experts that an immediate cessation of these deliveries would easily impose difficulties upon Germany's export trade which might be of great harm to her economic capacity to transfer. During the above period of ten years Germany will, therefore, be enabled to make deliveries in kind in a limited and decreasing amount beginning with an equivalent of 750 million marks and diminishing annually by 50 millions but ceasing after the tenth year. These deliveries in kind are to the account of the postponable part of the annuities.

The abolition of deliveries of kind after a transitory period of ten years manifests an optimism on the part of the experts in the future economic development of Germany which does not seem warranted by present conditions. International payments can only be redeemed out of a surplus of exports over imports, i. e. by payments in kind. Attention has previously been called to the recent trend in various countries to impose upon the import of commodities protective tariff rates which in practice amount to a prohibilitno of imports of any apreciable amount. These policies are prompted by industries in those countries which aim to curtail foreign competition in their domestic markets.

Although the report nowhere makes any special reference, there cannot be entertained a doubt that the abolition of deliveries in kind can be traced back to such pressures exercised by industries in the creditor countries which fear increased German competition. In international trade such an attitude serves as an indication that increased exports from Germany are not looked upon favorably by the importing countries. Viewed in this light, an abolition of delveries in kind is apt to impose added difficulties upon Germany's port trade.

As long as the creditor nations were obliged to accept a ntial part of the reparation payments in the form of del- kind, Germany was enabled to pay this part of her debt without bearing pressure upon her industry through a policy of deflating the price level. If the creditor nations really wish to facilitate the transfer of the reparations and thus the reparation payments, one should expect that they would promote increased deliveries in kind. The abolition of these deliveries must therefore create a pessimistic attitude in this direction.

REPARATIONS AND ALLIED DEBTS. It has already been pointed out that the reparation payments under the Young plan bear a direct relation to the war debts of the allied nations to the United States. Although the report never mentions this relation it is a matter of fact that 65 per cent of the annual payments, roughly corresponding to the postponable part, will thus ultimately be transferred to the United States. This percentage represents the amount of the allied debts to America. During the last 22 years the annuities cover only the allied debts to the United States and the total period of 59 years corresponds to the period fixed in the debt settlements between America and her former war associates.

The shifting of the allied debts to Germany is also revealed in the provision that „in the event of modification of those obligations for outpayments by which the creditors benefit, there should be some corresponding mitigations of the German annuities."[11] It is proposed in the plan that if any of the creditor nations receives a reduction in its war-debt during the first 37 years, Germany shall benefit to the extent of two thirds of her obligation thereafter.[12] With regard to the last 22 years the plan provides that any such reduction in war-debts shall be applied to reduce Germany's liability to the full extent of the reduction in her creditor's debt.

If one considers the actual relations, these clauses propose that if America should in the future decide to cancel or reduce her claims against her former warallies, Germany should benefit to the above extent. It must be emphasized, however, that as far as the relations between the United States and the Allies is concerned, the latter alone are liable for the payment of the debt. As long as

---

11. Report of the Young Committee, Annex VIII.

12. The remaining one-third shall be retained by the creditor country receiving the reduction in its debts.

Germany lives up to the agreement the creditor nations will simply transfer their receipts to the United States.

BANK FOR INTERNATIONAL PAYMENTS. An essential feature of the Plan is the proposal for the creation of the Bank for International Payments. The establishment of this institution had been at the basis of all other modifications and provisions of the Young Plan which make the latter differ fundamentally from the Dawes Plan. From the outset on, the experts had come to the conclusion that the Bank was inseparable from the whole plan. Repeatedly, the report stresses the intricate connection between the amount of the annuities and their tranfer as well as the important functions of the International Bank therein. In the relations between the creditor nations and Germany the new institution is to replace the foreign political bodies formerly introduced by the Dawes Committee for the purpose of controlling the execution of the payments.

The experts of the Young Committee realized that the reparation engagements of Germany are rather an economic than a political issue. Accordingly, they wished to remove all those agencies which by their presence were detrimental to the furtherance of good-will between the countries involved. The Bank, therefore, was vested with powers and functions that will put it in a position to replace all political agencies, including the Reparation Commission. Furthermore, the Bank has been vested with such powers as to render it eventually the most powerful instrument in international finance and inter-central banking. But before analyzing the practical possibilities and limitations of such functions on the part of the Bank, it is deemed well to discuss at first its tasks in connection with the reparation payments.

The purpose of the Bank is as its name indicates manifold. In the first place it acts as a trustee for the creditor countries in connection with the annual payments of Germany. It receives and distributes the annuities in accordance with the corresponding provisions of the plan, and it performs the entire work of external administration of the plan. Besides these purely administrative functions it has the very important task to facilitate the transfer of the annuities from Germany. For this purpose it is entrusted with the function „to promote the increase of world-trade by financing projects, particuliarly in undeveloped countries, which might otherwise not be attempted through the ordinary existing channels."[13]

There can be little doubt that this provision of „financing projects in undeveloped countries" has been meant mostly for the German export trade. It is an indirect admission that the creditor nations are under the obligation to facilitate an increased export from Germany from which the latter can meet her annuities. This necessity has been pointed out repeatedly in the preceeding chapter. In the discussion of the transfer problem under the Dawes Plan it had been shown that under existing international conditions Germany was not in a position to increase her exports by an amount sufficient to yield the sums necessary for the transfer of the annual payments into foreign currencies.

Reference had been made there to the recent policy in many countries to protect their industries from increased foreign competition. In many cases this protection is justified from the standpoint of those industries in view of the fact that increased exports from Germany threatened their very existence. The very substantial deliveries in kind from Germany increased the supply of those commodities in the importing countries to such an extent as to cause great reductions in the output of the home industries.

In order to promote larger exports from Germany without creating at the same time increased competetion for their home industries, the Experts deviced the scheme of financing German exports to undeveloped countries. There are many small countries which would welcome increased imports fromGermany but who lack the capital necessary to finance these projects. It is expected that the Bank will be in a position to form the connecting link between Germany and countries desirous of buying commodities from her. The funds which the Bank will dispose of and which in the opinion of the experts will be very considerable from sources to be discussed later on, will enable it to finance extensive projects of construction. In order to achieve this aim the International Bank will then have to re-finance these credits in the money markets of the creditor nations.

---

13. Report of the Experts, part V.

Instead of claims upon Germany the creditor nations will then receive the obligations of these foreign countries. Such a procedure would undoubtedly be apt to benefit both, Germany and the creditor countries. Germany would thus be able to pay her debts by deliveries in kind without being forced to deflate her price level. On the other hand, the creditor nations would by such a process avoid increased competition for their home industries. Although the execution of this new scheme seems to offer an ideal solution of the transfer problem, it seems very doubtful how far such a procedure could be carried on over a period of 37 years without encountering political and economic obstacles. One must bear in mind that the industries of all countries are constantly looking for new markets for their products. Competition in those „undeveloped countries" between the industries of Europe and the Unites States is bound to grow in the future and to assume great dimensions. The cause for such a trend is simply that export is of paramount importance for the maintenance of a stable home-production and thus of a stable price level.

It is impossible to forecast how far German industries will be in a position to conquer those foreign markets and thus contribute to an increased favorable balance of trade for Germany. Above all, however, it must be remembered that these exports must finally be financed by the money and capital markets of the present creditor nations. The financing of German export through the International Bank is merely a preliminary step. The practical limits of this function of the Bank for International Payments must therefore also be left to the future.

The Young Plan contemplates a share capital of the Bank of 100 million dollars, of which 25 per cent shall be paid in upon the issue of the shares. At least 55 per cent of the total capital must be issued in the seven countries participating in the conference. The shares thus issued carry no voting right. But voting rights corresponding to amount of shares originally issued in those countries are to be exercised by the central bank of that country.

The administration of the Bank is entirely in the hands of the board of directors, which is vested with all powers necessary to execute the operations of the institution as provided in the plan. In order that the directors shall be unprejudiced in their decisions it is required that they shall not be affiliated with any political responsibility in their country after being elected to the board. They are nominated in the following manner. The chief executive of the central bank of each of the seven countries, represented in the conference, or his nominee, is a director ex officio. Each of these directors, furthermore, appoints a fellow-national as a director on the board. The Governor of the Bank of France and the President of the German Reichsbank may each appoint one additional director. These fourteen or sixteen directors then elect nine more directors from a list of candidates furnished by the chief executives of the seven central banks, each one submitting four candidates.

Besides these functions as a transfer agent and trustee for the annuities, the Bank for International Payments has been vested with powers and functions independent of those connected with reparation payments. These banking operations to be discussed hereafter, represent the second chief task of the Bank. They are twofold: first, the institution may accept deposits under specified conditions and secondly, it may with the aid of these funds act as a central clearing institution for the various central banks.

As far as the right to receive deposits is concerned, the plan prescribes the sources from which the Bank will derive its funds. The principal sources are the annuities to be paid in by Germany. Besides these amounts the institution may accept funds on currenct account or investment account deposits from central banks Similiarly it may accept funds from central banks for the purpose of establishing and maintaining a fund for the settlement of accounts among the central banks. Furthermore, there will be for the first thrity-seven years a non-interest bearing deposit of the German government equivalent to one half of the average annuity account remaining in the annuity trust account. This deposit will not exceed 100 millions marks. With regard to interest payments the plan permits of such payments on deposits not susceptible of withdrawal until at least one month from the time of deposit.

In relending these funds the Bank may deal first, directly with central banks, secondly with banks, bankers and corporations of any country in performing any authorized function, provided that the central bank of that country does not enter any objection. The institution may thus perform the following functions:

1) It may buy and sell gold coin and bullion, earmark gold for the account of central banks and make advances to central banks on gold as security.

2) It may buy and sell for its account, either wiht or without its endorsement, bills of exchange and other short term obligations of prime liquidity, including checks drawn or endorsed by central banks or for which three obligees are responsible.

3) It may open and maintain deposit accounts with central banks.

4) It may rediscount for central banks bills taken from their portfolio, to make loans to them on the security of such bills or to make adavances to them against the pledge of other securities up to such amounts and for such periods as may be approved by the board of directors.

5) It may buy and sell for its account intermediate or long term securities of a character approved by the board of directors.

The second task is to act as a central clearing institution among the various central banks. For many years past the flow of gold between the countries has been a matter of no little concern to central banks. Besides the costs involved in these shipments, the export of the precious metal has often compelled central banks to increase their discount rate or to limit credits under conditions which would otherwise have warranted a more liberal credit policy.[14]

Doubtless, the International Bank may perform a very useful function in exercising its influence to avoid such gold movements. The very considerable deposits which might ultimately be accumulated will enable it to grant temporarily credit to central banks, which would otherwise be compelled to observe a drainage of their gold reserves without being able to prevent such a development except by raising the discount rate. Such a step puts, however, strong pressure upon the demand for credit and results

---

14. Thus during the first six months of the year 1929, the relatively high rates in foreign markets have caused an outflow of gold from Germany which brought the reserves of the Reichsbank down to the legal limit. The Reichsbank was therefore compelled to pursue a policy of credit restriction, although the demand for credit was not beyond the normal level.

easily in a downward trend in the business cycle. Of recent, central banks resort to the device of „earmarking" their claims in order to aid other central banks. In case of calling off gold from other banks for internal credit purposes the central bank concerned can only prevent such a movement by raising its discount rate. But such gold movements, too, could be avoided with the aid of credit from the International Bank.

But the proponents of the new institution hope for something more. Their aim is to obtain a mechanism that will render unnecessary the large volume of gold transfer caused by fluctuations in the foreign exchange rates. The Young committee seems to have been of the opinion that such shipments could be avoided by a clearing system. Under such a system the claims of central banks would simply be transferred in the accounts of the new institution in the same way as transfer between various banks are operated at present through the central bank of their respective country.

On this phase of the Bank's function, opinion differs widely. Although it seems premature to state at the present time the feasibility of such a mechanism, the viewpoint of the critics of this proposal is of such a nature as to deserve close attention. In an article published in Die Bank,[15] A. Lansburgh voices the opinion that such operations are not only impracticable but moreover, undesirable. Lansburgh points out that movements of gold caused by fluctuations in the exchange rate are but symptons of economic disequilibria. An increase in the rate above the specie point indicates an unfavorable balance of trade, due either to excessive imports or to a relatively low discount rate stimulating the outflow of gold. To prevent the transfer of gold caused by a discrepancy in the various market rates, the new institution would have to be in a position where it could intervene in the policy of the various central banks. Obviously such interference would not be tolerated by the respective countries and is, therefore improbable. So far as gold movements are stimulated by excessive imports any intervention on the part of the Bank could only succeed temporarily. It would not remedy the economic disturbances and must, therefore, fail. Lansburgh also

---

15. Die Reparationsbank, editorial by Alfred Lansburgh published in Die Bank, April 1929.

points out that the function of the Bank as a clearing house between the various central institutions would eliminate the cost of transportation of gold and thus reduce the margin between the two specie points. As a consequence gold transfers would tend to occur more frequently, a fact which might easily accelerate fluctuations in the various national economies.

DISTRIBUTION OF PROFITS: Another outstanding feature of the Young Plan is the clauses concerning the distribution of the bank's earnings. The large annuities and considerable deposits provided for in the Plan together with the institution's capital will vest it with a substantial financial power. Besides its own capital of one hundred million dollars the bank will receive a deposit of about one hundred twenty million dollars from France after the mobilization of the unconditional part of the annual payments. In addition Germany will maintain a special non-interest bearing deposit on the annuity trust account equivalent to about 25 million dollars, while the former allies will deposit at the outset about 50 million dollars. These amounts will give the institution total deposits of about 300 million dollars to start business. Besides these amounts the bank will furthermore receive deposits from the various central banks concerned and other deposits from the various sources analyzed above.

It is evident that the handling of such large funds will yield substantial profits. If the expectations of the Experts are realized the earnings of the bank will suffice to pay Germany's reparation obligations for the last twenty two years. In particular the provisions of the Plan concerning the distribution of the earnings are as follows. Of the total net profits, the bank is required to pay 5% to the legal reserve fund until that fund amounts to 10% of the paid in capital stock of the bank. After making this deduction the shareholders are to obtain a dividend up to 6% of the paid in capital; the dividend is cumulative. Twenty percent of the remaining profits are then paid to the shareholders until a maximum total dividend of 12% is reached. Of the remainder one half is to be paid into the general reserve fund until it equals the paid in capital. Thereafter 40% is paid into the fund until it equals twice the paid-in capital, 30% until it reaches three times the capital, twenty per cent until it equals four times, ten per cent up to five times, and afterward five per cent. This reserve fund is to be built up for the purpose of meeting any losses incurred by the bank. Upon liquidation of the bank the fund will be divided among the shareholders.

The remainder of the annual earnings after the above deductions are made is to be paid into special funds. Seventy five per cent shall be paid to the government or the Central Banks of the seven countries which maintain with the institution time deposits of an amount to be determined by the administration of the bank. The remaining twenty five per cent is to be used to aid Germany in paying the last twenty two annuities.

In addition to the above analyzed provisions the plan contains clauses concerning the formation of an organization committee and various other minor issues related to the formation of the bank. In its general scheme the Young Plan offers very material advantages over the Dawes Plan to both the creditor nations and Germany.

However, the great practical limitations and obstacles as analyzed above cannot be overemphasized. The total burden of the war costs has been imposed upon Germany. From a purely economic standpoint it is very doubtful whether Germany will be able to pay the annuities even over the greater part of the provided period of 59 years. This fact must be faced by all participants in the Young agreement. One must bear in mind that these payments equal almost the normal rate of progress of Germany during the last 50 years. Thus, Germany would be unable to accumulate and increase her capital stock, while at the same time the creditor nations would enjoy the benefit of these annuities together with the normal increase in their capital fund. Such a development is econonmically untenable for the length of time provided in the Young Plan.

In the report of the experts this pessimistic view about the execution of the plan over such a long period is revealed in the conclusion of the experts that „it requires the co-operation of all parties. If their attitude should be tinged with antagonism, even with suspicion or a desire to create or continue one sided economic discriminations, a settlement perfectly feasible with good will would sooner or later encounter difficulties, so that the long low patient task of reconstruction in Europe would definitely be retarded. For without good faith and mutual confidence all agreements, all guarantees are unavailing."

CONCLUSION.

RECENT ECONOMIC DEVELOPMENT IN GERMANY AND FUTURE PROBLEMS.

At the end of 1928, Germany appeared to have attained an economic stability which she had not enjoyed since pre-war periods. Her currency was based upon a gold standard and the stock of gold in the vaults of the Reichsbank rendered the German currency as stable as any other currency. Unemployment and business failures were not much in excess of the corresponding pre-war figures and at the same time far below those of any period after 1924. In spite of these favorable signs, there still prevailed certain shortcomings in the economic structure of Germany which did not become evident until the year 1929. It is, therefore, deemed well to analyze those events for the purpose of understanding the present and future problems of the German economy.

It was particuliarly during the first half of the year 1929 that the economic stability of Germany was severely taxed. External and internal influences combined exercised a very strong pressure upon the entire economic structure. The most important external influence was a recession in the inflow of foreign funds into Germany. Only 289 million marks loans were obtained abroad through the issues of bonds during the first six months of 1929 as compared with 1128 millions in the corresponding part of 1928.[1] This decrease in the absorption of bonds by foreign markets was due to two factors: the conditions in the New York stock market and secondly, the reparation conference in the spring of 1929.   [1]

---

1. Report of the Agent General for Reparation Payments, June 1929 p. 108.

As far as the stock market in New York was concerned, the high money rates prevailing therein and a strong speculative movement attracted funds which otherwise would have been diverted into the bond market.[2] The rates in the German money and capital market were not sufficiently high to overcome the influence of the New York stock market. Moreover, the conditions in the latter market also intensified a tense money situation in other international money and capital markets.

In spite of this international tension indicating an approaching growth in the demand for credit, the Reichsbank lowered its discount rate on January 29th, 1929, from seven per cent to six and one half per cent. It was partly prompted in this policy by the very considerable supply of gold and foreign exchange which it had accumulated during the preceeding years. At the end of the year 1928, the legal cover for the notes in circulation amounted to about 65 per cent and the stability of the German currency was most satisfactory.

Although the Bank of England and the Bank of the Netherlands had raised their discount rates in February, the Reichsbank maintained its rate unchanged until April 25th, when it was increased to seven and one half per cent. The causes for the adherence to such a relatively low rate will be discussed in connection with the other external event affecting the economic trend in Germany, i. e. the Reparation Conference in Paris.

As mentioned already in the previous chapter, the Reparation Conference, which later on formulated the Young Plan, lasted for almost 13 weeks from February to June 1929. The frequent deadlocks in the negotiations provoked an international uncertainty as to the possibility of a final settlement. A growing disinclination on the part of foreign banks and investors to buy German bills and bonds ensued. Later on, foreign banks became even disposed to withdraw a part of their demand deposits. The result was an increased demand for foreign exchange in the market and a scarcity of funds at the disposal of banks.

---

2. The rates for call money in the New York stock market during this period were as follows: February: 6—10 per cent, March 6—20 per cent, April 6—16 per cent, May 6—15 per cent. See 'Report of the Agent General for Reparation Payments' June 1929 p. 103.

Especially French banks which had previously been a considerable investor of funds with Germany withdrew their support and called off a substantial part of their short term loans. Within Germany similiar evidences of distrust became manifest and increased the demand for foreign exchange and in turn caused a shrinkage in the supply of funds. The Reichsbank nourishing the hope of an immediate settlement of the pending reparation conference hesitated to raise its rate. It assumed that a favorable settlement would render superfluous such a measure and would cause the inflow of larger funds and strengthen international confidence. These expectations did not come true until considerable time had elapsed and a substantial part of its supply of gold and foreign exchange had been exported.

In addition to the external events mentioned above various seasonal and political events in Germany exercised a similiar unfavorable influence upon the economic conditions. The cash position of the Reich Treasury during the first few months of the year was tense and the banks were called upon to supply a substantial amount of credit for the Reich. Strikes and lockouts in the coal industry and disputes over wage scales between employers and labor-unions also aggravated the situation.

Of great influence upon the economy was the extraordinary severe winter of 1928/1929 which interfered considerably with transportation and the building industries as well as with many kinds of outdoor work. Moreover, the extensive period during which the .abnormally low temperatures prevailed, seriously handicapped an uninterrupted indoor production which depended upon a steady flow of material. The rapid increase in the official figures of those receiving unemployment relief reflects the general recession in the business trend. While in November 1928, the total of unemployed amounted to 1 030 000 this figure had increased to 1 702 000 in December and to 2 246 000 in January 1929. In February the total reached the unprecedented height of 2 461 000 receiving unemployment relief. Althought unemployment was much intensified by adverse weather conditions the influence of the other factors mentioned above should not be overlooked.

The growing demand for foreign exchange resulting from these unfavorable conditions was further enhanced by a growing unfavorable balance of trade and by tranfers of reparation funds by the Agent General during the first few months. During the five months January — May the Reichsbank's supply of gold and foreign exchange diminished by about one billion marks amounting to only 1765 millions at the end of May as compared with 2729 millions in January. It was especially in the month of April that the international distrust in the possibility of a settlement of the reparation question resulted in a loss of 700 million marks in gold by the Reichsbank.

On the other hand the demand for credit shows a somewhat different trend. From January to March the total of bills and cheques discounted by the Reichsbank diminished substantially, owing to lessened production. At the end of January the Reichsbank portfolio contained bills and cheques for only 1783 millions as compared with 2679 in December 1928. In February this total increased slightly to 1889 millions. In March an expanded business activity was again resumed and the demand for credit increased consequently. Besides increased business activity the above mentioned factors caused also a larger demand for funds. The Reichsbank was called upon to supply the necessary funds and in May its portfolio showed a total of discounted bills and cheques exceeding three billion marks. During the months April and May when the gold supply of the Bank had diminished by about 800 millions its short term credits rose by about 1300 millions. Although the institution increased its discount rate on April 25th to 7½ per cent the demand for credit was not materially checked. The situation became critical in view of the rapidly declining cover for the notes in circulation which at the end of May was only 40.95 per cent or barely a fraction above the legal minimum.

Such a development called for immediate measures on the part of the Reichsbank. The latter could have further increased its discount rate in order to arrest a growth in the demand for credit. Instead, the Bank resorted early in May to the resumption of a policy of credit restriction. The high discount rate and the rationing of credit effected an immediate decline in the discounts at the Reichsbank. At the end of June the total of credits had decreased to 2843 millions and further diminished to 2621 millions in July.

The drastic measure adopted by the Reichsbank helped to restore confidence abroad in the stability of the German currency. Foreign investors were again attracted by the high rates in the German money market. The final settlement of the Reparation problem in Paris in June strengthened this tendency.

The inflowing funds eased the tension in the German market and brought forth a larger supply of foreign exchange. On May 25th, the rate for the dollar and the pound sterling was quoted below par; the rate of the latter even decreased to the gold import point. This facts the more noteworthy if one contrasts this situation with conditions in April when the general distrust in the stability of the mark drove the foreign exchange rate of the dollar and the pound above the gold export point.[3]

During the second half of the year 1929, the economic development in Germany was no longer subject to severe fluctuations and normal forces asserted themselves again. The gold supply of the Reichsbank rose to 2240 million marks in November 1929 and the total of foreign exchange eligible for legal cover was about 400 million marks. The total of bills and cheques discounted by the Reichsbank approximated 2350 million, which low figure was due to seasonal influences. Unemployment, which numbered about 700 000 in August, had increased to 1 200 000 in November, also due to seasonal factors.

It is particuliarly the economic development during the first part of 1929 which offers valuable conclusions as to the present state of the German economy.

In various industries Germany has succeeded not only in becoming again a strong competitor in the world market but some of these industries also achieved a supremacy in their fields which assured them a substantial control of the demand. The outstanding examples are the German Dye Trust, the electric concerns, and the German merchant marine.[4] The German potash industry, and the

3. On April 26th, the dollar rate was quoted 4.235 marks per dollar after the close of the Bourse, a rate which was in excess of the rate for cable transfers. See Julius Landmann „Kurzfristige Auslandsverschuldung" Archiv für Sozialwissenschaft und Sozialpolitik, Heft 1, 1930, p. 8.

4. The German merchant fleet has been considerably strengthened in its power through the creation of a working partnership for fifty years entered

chemical industry are also strong competitors in the world market. Furthermore, the German Air Trust and the Zeppelin Corporation, although still subsidized by the Reich, are strong potentialities for the future.

On the other hand, a number of industries in Germany has failed in their effort to adopt American standards of rationalization. An unwillingness to reorganize radically regardless of the immediate losses coupled with a lack of funds and a sufficiently broad domestic market to warrant such a programm are the outstanding causes for this failure. In addition the tax burden and the limited capital market also form serious obstacles at the present. It is still an open question whether German industry will fare better by adhering to its pre-war principle of producing high grade products or by manufacturing large quantities of standard goods.

The scarcity of capital funds is well revealed in the considerable proportion of foreign funds deposited with German credit banks. Although exact figures are not published, reliable estimates assume that from forty to fifty per cent of the deposits with the German Great Banks are of foreign origin.[5] Their total is approximately six and one half billion marks. In addition to this amount there are the short term obligations of other private credit institutions estimated at two billion marks. Although foreign deposits with German banks were already considerable before the Great War, it is the change in the nature of these deposits which renders them partly of disadvantage to the German economy. Prior to 1914, foreign credits were to an overwhelming extent the result of purchases of German bills of exchange ensuing from international transactions. At present these credits represent mostly demand deposits attract ed by the high rates in Germany.

---

into by the North German Lloyd and the Hamburg America Line on March 25th, 1930. see NEW YORK TIMES March 26th, 1930. International working agreements have also been completed between the General Electric Concern of America and the German General Concern. Similiar cooperation exists between the General Electric Concern of America and the Siemens Corporation in Germany furthermore, the German Dye Trust has completed working agreements with American Concerns and owns a minority stock in the German Ford concern.

5. Landmann, Kurzfristige Auslandsverschuldung, ibid. p. 16.

A serious problem for Germany is, therefore, the upbuilding of sufficient capital reserves to provide the funds for industry and commerce. The savings of a community are the main resource for its capital requirements. At the end of 1929, the total of savings deposited with German savings banks and credit institutions exceeded seven and one half billion marks. However, the steady growth of savings was partly neutralized by a similiar increase in the foreign indebtedness of Germany. To achieve a real surplus the savings of a country must be larger than the rate of interest paid on foreign loans plus a reasonable rate of amortization for these debts. Here, the future task for the German economy consists of availing itself of foreign funds in such a way as to produce values in excess of the debt plus the annual outpayments for reparation payments. It must be remembered that these reparation payments mean economically an annual loss of a part of the national income.

The burden imposed upon Germany by the reparation payments has been amply discussed in previous chapters. Their effect cannot be overemphasized. The annuities imposed under the Young Plan, altho far less than those provided for in the preceeding Dawes Plan, amount to 2.6 per cent of the national income of Germany in 1928. Compared with the interest bearing debt of the United States, after taking into consideration the relative standards of living and income, reparations represent a burden two and a half times as heavy.[6]

The real problem of reparations and their effect has been most adequately expressed by Owen D. Young in a recent speech in California, in which he emphatically points out that any national policy which is actuated by political ambitions rather then economic considerations must prove disastrous. „Politics and economics, servants of civilization, must move together, not in one country alone, but everywhere. That way only can civilization be enlarged — that way only can peace come."[7]

---

6. Professor J. W. Angell, The economic recovery of Germany. 1929 p. 341.

7. This adress was reproduced in the New York Times on March 25, 1930. The problem of reparations has also been very adequately dealt with in an article by Professor H. L. Lutz „Debts, Reparations, and National Policy" published in the Journal of Political Economy, Chicago February 1, 1930.

BIBLIOGRAPHY.

I. Official Publications.

Deutsche Reichsbank, Verwaltungsberichte der Reichsbank 1876 to 1928 published annually by Reichsdruckerei, Berlin.

Deutsche Reichsbank, Die Deutsche Reichsbank 1876—1900. Berlin: Gustav Fischer, 1913.

Deutsche Reichsbank, Die Deutsche Reichsbank 1876—1910. Berlin: Gustav Fischer, 1912.

Deutsche Reichsbank, Die Deutsche Reichsbank 1901—1925. Berlin: Druckerei der Reichsbank, 1925.

Deutsche Bank, Geschäftsberichte der Deutschen Bank 1924—1927. Published annually by the Deutsche Bank, Berlin.

Statistisches Reichsamt, Statistisches Jahrbuch für das Deutsche Reich. Published annually by Reichsdruckerei.

Reparation Commission, The Experts' Plan for Reparation Payments (Dawes Plan), published 1924.

Reparation Commission, Report of the Commissioner of the Reichsbank. 1924—1928. Published annually, Berlin.

Reparation Commission, Report of the Agent General for Reparation Payments 1925—1928, published semi-annually, Berlin.

The Report of the Experts on the Reparation Payments (Young Committee) reproduced in the New York Times, June 9th, 1929.

II. Legislative Acts.

Das Bankgesetz vom 14. März 1875. Published in the Reichsgesetzblatt, March 18th, 1875.

Verordnung über die Errichtung der Deutschen Rentenbank vom 15. Oktober 1923, published in Reichsgesetzblatt 1923, I. p. 963.

Gesetz über die Errichtung der Deutschen Golddiskontbank vom 19. März 1924, published in Reichsgesetzblatt 1924 II p. 71.

Das Bankgesetz vom 30. August 1924, published in Reichsgesetzblatt 1924 II p. 383.

III. Literature.

Angell, J. W.: The Economic Recovery of Germany. New York 1929.

Beckerath, Herbert von: Die Gefahren übermäßiger Auslandskredite für Währung und Wirtschaft. Published in Kölner Vorträge, Bd. III, 1927.

— Reparationsagent und deutsche Wirtschaftspolitik. Bonn: Schröder, 1926.

Bergmann, Karl: The History of Reparations. Boston: Houghton Mifflin & Co. 1927.

Bernhard, Georg: Politik der Reichsbank im Kriege. Published in the Archiv für Sozialwissenschaft und Sozialpolitik, v. 40 p. 43—87, Tübingen, 1914.

Bosch, Werner: Die Kreditrestriktionspolitik der deutschen Reichsbank 1924/1926. Hamburg, 1927.

Cassel, Gustav: Money and Foreign Exchange after 1914. New York 1924.

Dalberg, Rudolph: Die neue deutsche Währung nach dem Dawes-Plan. Berlin: C. Haymann, 1924.

— Deutsche Währungs- und Kreditpolitik 1923/1926. Berlin: R. Hobing, 1926.

Dawes, Rufus C.: The Dawes Plan in the making. Indianapolis: The Bobbs-Merril Company, 1925.

Dierschke, Kurt & F. Müller: Die Notenbanken der Welt. Berlin: Verlag für bargeldlosen Zahlungsverkehr, 1926.

Eynern, Gert von: Die Reichsbank. Jena: G. Fischer 1928.

Fürstenberg, Hans: Ein Land ohne Betriebsmittel. Berlin: Liebheit & Thiessen. 1925.

— Drei Jahre Goldwährung. Berlin: J. Springer, 1927.

— Germany four years after stabilization. New York 1927.

Harms, Bernhard: Strukturwandlungen in der deutschen Volkswirtschaft. Berlin: R. Hobing, 1928.

Hänlein, Albrecht: Die deutsche Rentenbank-Kreditanstalt. Published in the Jahrbuch für Nationalökonomie und Statistik v. 69, 1926.

Hahn, Albert: Goldvorteil und Goldvorurteil. Frankfurt: Frankfurter Societätsdruckerei, 1924.

Hartmannsgruber, Franz: Die Kreditrestriktion der Reichsbank und ihr Einfluß auf die Volkswirtschaft. Wolfsrathhausen, 1926.

Helfferich, Karl: Beiträge zur Geschichte der deutschen Geldreform. Berlin 1897.

— Die Entwicklung des deutschen Notenwesens unter dem Bankgesetz von 1875. Published in Schmoller's Jahrbuch. Leipzig 1899.

— Der deutsche Geldmarkt 1895—1902. Published in the Schriften des Vereins für Sozialpolitik, v. 110, 1903.

Heichen, Arthur: Reichsbank und Währungspolitik 1924—1926. Published in Weltwirtschaftliches Archiv v. 23, 1926.

Hirsch, Julius: Die deutsche Währungsfrage. Jena: G. Fischer, 1924.

Keynes, Maynard J.: Monetary Reform. New York: Hartcourt, Brace & Co. 1924.

— The German Transfer Problem. Published in the Economic Journal, March 1929. London.

Landmann, Julius: Kurzfristige Auslandsverschuldung. Published in Archiv für Sozialwissenschaft und Sozialpolitik, Heft 1, 1930, p. 1—43.

Lansburgh, Alfred: Die Maßnahmen der Reichsbank zur Erhöhung der Liquidität der deutschen Kreditwirtschaft. Stuttgart: F. Enke, 1914.

— Die Politik der Reichsbank und die Reichsschatzanweisungen nach dem Kriege. Leipzig: Duncker & Humblot, 1924.

Lotz, Walter: Geschichte und Kritik des deutschen Bankgesetzes vom 14. März 1875. Leipzig: Duncker & Humblot, 1888.

— Valutafragen und öffentliche Finanzen. München: Duncker & Humblot, 1923.

Lutz, H. L.: Debts, Reparations and National Policy. Journal of Political Economy. Chicago University Press. Februar 1930.

Naphtali, Fritz: Währungsgesundung und Wirtschaftssanierung. Frankfurt a. M.: Societätsdruckerei, 1925.

Prion, Wilhelm: Die deutsche Kreditpolitik 1919—1922. Schmoller's Jahrbuch, 1923.

— Kreditpolitik. Berlin, 1926.

— Geldmarktlage und Reichsbankpolitik. Leipzig: Duncker & Humblot, 1927.

Schacht, Hjalmar: Die Stabilisierung der Mark. Stuttgart: Deutsche Verlagsanstalt, 1927.

Schönthal, Justus: Deutsche Währungs- und Kreditpolitik seit der Währungsfestigung. Berlin: Volkswirtschaftliche Verlagsgesellschaft, 1926.

Spohr, Werner: Die Neugestaltung der Reichsbank. Stuttgart, 1925.

Sombart, Werner: Die deutsche Volkswirtschaft im 19. Jahrhundert. Berlin: G. Bondi, 1913.

— Der moderne Kapitalismus, part III v. 1 & 2. München: Duncker & Humblot, 1927.

Terhalle, Fritz: Die Reparationskontrolle. Jena: G. Fischer, 1925.

Taussig, F. W.: Deutschlands internationaler Handel und das Reparationsproblem. Archiv für Sozialwissenschaft v. 60, 1929.

Wilmersdorfer, Ernst: Das neue Reichsbankgesetz. München: Duncker & Bumblot, 1925.

IV. Periodicals.

BANK ARCHIV, published weekly by Riessner, Berlin.

DIE BANK, published monthly by Alfred Lansburgh, Berlin.

DER DEUTSCHE VOLKSWIRT, published weekly Berlin.

DIE WIRTSCHAFTSKURVE, published quarterly by Die Frankfurter Zeitung, Frankfurt a. M.

DER WIRTSCHAFTSDIENST, published weekly by Kurt Singer, Hamburg.

VIERTELJAHRESHEFTE ZUR KONJUNKTURFORSCHUNG, published quarterly by the Institut für Konjunkturforschung, Berlin.

V. Newspapers.

BERLINER TAGEBLATT .

DIE FRANKFURTER ZEITUNG.

THE JOURNAL OF COMMERCE.

THE NEW YORK TIMES.

INDEX.